Save Your Company
Don't Feed the Beast

The Employer Healthcare Success Formula

Written by Matt Ohrt

Published By River Bluff Publishing Company LLC

Written by Matt Ohrt

Cover Design by Mikey Hubacek

Interior Design by Elizabeth Krogwold

© Copyright 2023. River Bluff Publishing Company LLC

All rights reserved.

Matt Ohrt

His diligence and gritty leadership have sparked and supported a healthcare improvement movement in Wisconsin.

Matt and his 4 year old adopted son, Noah

About The Author

As the VP of Human Resources at Merrill Steel, Matt embarked on a healthcare journey that took him places he never would have imagined, ultimately discovering a repeatable path for employers to fix their healthcare.

Matt cofounded Self Fund Health and is a Co-Chapter Leader for the Free Market Medical Association (FMMA). His diligence and gritty leadership have sparked and supported a healthcare improvement movement in Wisconsin.

Matt is the recipient of the 2019 CWSHRM HR Professional of the Year, the Alliance 2020 Healthcare Transformation Award, the 2020 National Employer/Purchaser Healthcare Excellence Award (previously won by Disney, Boeing, and Walmart) and the 2022 Free Market Medical Association's (FMMA) Be the Beacon Award.

Matt and his wife Denise have been married 27 years and live in central Wisconsin. They have five children —one adopted—and serve as champion foster parents for Marathon County. In 2018, Matt and Denise founded NOAH, a nonprofit supply closet. In 2020, they were given the Governor's Foster Parents of the Year Award for Wisconsin.

Table of Contents

About the Author 3
Dedication 6
Acknowledgment 7
Foreword 8
Introduction 10

My Trip to the Emergency Room

- Who Says That?
- The River Bluff
- And then...
- Coming to Grips with Reality
- How Badly am I Hurt?
- First, Complete this Paperwork!
- Stay the Night
- Charges for Services Not Received
- Home to Heal
- Back to Work
- Reflection

1 The Bad News and Good News 22

- Let's Learn Together
- The Bad News
- The Good News
- Status Quo'ers and Disruptors

2 The Employer Healthcare Success Formula ... 30

- You Are Not Alone
- Healthcare or Sickcare?
- A Time for Decision
- A Step Forward
- New Beginnings
- Others Take Notice
- The Employer Healthcare Success Formula Diagram
- The Employer Healthcare Success Formula Overview

3 Understand Your Current Situation .. 42

- A Low Value Proposition
- Healthcare Is Unintentionally Broken
- Healthcare Is Intentionally Broken
- The Core Problem
- All Aboard the Healthcare Gravy Train Express!
- Our Human Nature
- Who Is the Beast?
- Hospital Systems and Monopolies: It's No Game
- Insurance Carriers: This Boat Always Floats
- Pharmacy Benefit Managers: The Kickbacks Have Kickbacks
- Healthcare Brokers: Buyers Beware
- Broker Behaviors
- Employers, Suit Up and Get in the Game
- A Raging Capitalist and a Bleeding Heart
- To Regulate or Not Regulate: That Is a Fair Question
- A Seat at the Table
- Important Concepts to Understand in Employer Healthcare
- Types of Healthcare Insurance
- Pricing Models
- Utilization Management/Utilization Review
- Healthcare Cost Assessment

4 Develop Your Free Market Healthcare Strategy 100

- Free the Free Market!
- Who Has the Power?
- Buying a Vacuum
- BATNA - One Thing You Must Know About Purchasing
- Lessons from the Big 3
- Overview of the Proven Strategy
- The Chicken and the Egg Dilemma
- Craft Your Free-Market Healthcare Strategy
- Your Financial Strategy
- Your Medical Strategy

5 Choose Trustworthy Partners 142

- An Early Morning Revelation
- Trust as the Foundation
- Trust Building Behaviors
- Choose Trustworthy Partners
- Choose a Trustworthy Broker
- Choose a Trustworthy Direct Primary Care (DPC) Clinic
- Choose a Trustworthy Third Party Administrator (TPA)
- Choose a Trustworthy Pharmacy Benefit Manager (PBM)
- Choose Trustworthy Independent Network(s)
- Choose Trustworthy Independent Specialty Providers
- Breaking Up Is Hard to Do
- How to "Select" Trustworthy Partners
- Support and Education for Medical Professionals Who Go Independent

6 Lead the Change from Here to There 170

- Change Management
- That's the Way We've Always Done It
- How Are Your Enrollment Meetings Going?
- Transformational Leaders
- Flavor of the Month
- People Are Messy
- Set the Tone for Change
- What's Your Word?
- Involve the Experts
- Change Management Models
- What's Your WIFM?
- We Are All Wired Differently
- Let's Embark on the Change Management Journey
- You are HERE
- New Beginnings
- The Desert Middle
- The Home Stretch
- There – Mission Accomplished
- The Winner's Circle
- Difficult People

A patient cured is a customer lost

Employers across the nation share the desire to offer access to high-quality, affordable healthcare for employees and their families. They also share many challenges.

7 4P Alignment 208

- 4P Alignment
- With Orchestral Brilliance
- We Must Build It So They Can Go
- Obedience to Authority: The Stanley Milgram Experiments
- Do Americans Care About Their Own Health?
- Health or Wealth: Which Is More Valuable?

8 Win-Win Positive-Sum Outcomes 216

- Cutting Edge
- How to Get Where You Are Going
- Dare to Dream
- The Future of American Healthcare

Dedication

This book is dedicated to my dad, who has been my biggest fan throughout my life. He passed away before final publishing, after an 11-year bout with cancer. He was very excited for me and was always there to give me a word of encouragement. My wife Denise and my children, Cassidy, Hannah, Lincoln, Gracelyn, and Noah, all supported me through this process. They sacrificed many hours of "dad time" to allow this to happen.

Acknowledgments

Mikey Hubacek, a former coworker and friend illustrated the cover. Ann Klefstad was instrumental in helping to edit the book into final manuscript form. The final polishing and graphic design was done by Beth Krogwold.

Many people have contributed ideas, content, or are working tirelessly to drive the movement forward. These gracious individuals include Karen Rajek, Roger Hinner, Rick Hinner, Mike Klussendorf, Fred Schwalbach, Jake Bandura, Greg Rajek, Katie, Franzen, Jill Fry, Stacie Hinner-Gruna, Tim Hinner, Brooke Hubacek, Jesse Hinner, Mary Godsey, Voigt Smith, Alex Sommers, Jennifer Stengle, Lisa Sommers, Justin Sladky, Laura Strek, Chris Gustafson, Matt Young, Stacey Robertson, Jon Baran, Ben John, John Torinus, Brian Dominick, Ken Strmiska, Sabina Singh, Brian Erdmann, Drew Leatherberry, Keith Smith, Steve Lantier, Jay Kempton, Kelly Kempton LynAnn Henderson, Todd Rogers, Mark Bakken, Tom Conti, Marty Makary, John Nelson, Jacob Fast, Andy Niemi, Tim Murray, Chris Habig, Dave Chase, Marty Makary, Ross Bjella, Ryan Barbieri, John Preuss, Tim Schierl, Candace Meronk, Marshall Allen, George Hess, Lou Holtz, Mick Price, Carl Schuessler, Michael Hoseus, Sandy Fragale, Darrin Schumacher, Bob Pfeiffer, Sara Hames, Chris Deacon, Cori Zavada, Jon Wilkerson, Jeff Williams, Eric Inman, Ron Piniecki, Jason Sansone, Cheryl DeMars, Melina Kambitsi, Mike Roche, Kyle Monroe, David Foucachon, Will Walker, Pat Gelhaus, Pat Blackaller, Michelle Golden, Jake Nolin, Chris VanderHeyden, Brian Adesso, Ellen Ask, Al Lewis, Curt Kubiak, Matt Knight, David Usher, Diane Peterson, Nicole Hemkes, Mary Yun, Lynn Sweet, Brian Woodridge, Paul McGraw, Shawn Needham, Leo Dunlavy, David Lange, Clint Flanagan, Noel Tupp, Lori Kisting, Joshua Rodgers, Rodney Hahn, Wendy Molaska, Amanda Preimesberger, Heng Chin, Mark Bouwer, Rob Worth, Tim Thorsen, Saylee Crawford, Peter Grimes, Jeff Utoft, Mark Mousty, Josh Golden, Troy Reichert, Brian Woodbridge, Pete Dewar, Tom Madden, Shay Sherfinski, Michelle Froehlke, Jason Nordby, Kelsey Stacks, Traci Licari, Jennifer Meinholz, Matt Malkin, Harlon Pickett, Corey Koskie, Megan Zimmerman, AJ Washington, Patrick Moore, Rich Zenisek, Luke Grundman, Scott Sherman, PJ Anast, Taylor Orton, Gavin Celia, Josh Bergman, Mike Johnson, Dan Nolde, Chris Dubos, TJ Morice, Jay Scott, Rae Ann Beaudry, Melissa Duffy, Steve Nevrla, David Cameron, Michael Havig, Karen Simonton, Kate Grohall, Eric Miller, Rebecca Gilbertson, Jake Brehm, Erin Duffy, Leo Wisniewski, Jocelyn Labombarde, Spencer Smith, Stacey Richter, Gayle Marshall, Matt Hobler, Zach Zeller, Felica Wilhelm, Michou Dorfer, Jane Sanford, Jeff Rosengarten, Larry Rosengarten, Eric Haberichter, Darren Fogarty, and many many others.

Foreword

By Keith Smith, MD

Medical services in the United States are expensive and becoming even more so, on an unsustainable path, primarily due to the crony favoritism on regular display at Uncle Sam's auction house. It could be worse. More socialized countries have taken a brutal and deadly approach, targeting the total amount spent, an approach that relies heavily on delays (years) or denial of care. The many Canadians receiving surgical care in the United States and at the Surgery Center of Oklahoma (thereby avoiding 3-5 year waits for a hysterectomy or a simple orthopedic procedure) are a manifestation of the unavailability of care resulting from the more socialized approach. Euthanasia is now the 6th leading cause of death in Canada, the only escape many can see, unfortunately.

We can do better and my friend, Matt Ohrt, has shown how in this important and unique book. Matt agrees with me that the reason prices are high and quality is sporadic in this country stems from an

> Thanks to Matt's book, the shysters and the conflicted HR executives now have no place to hide.

absence of the discipline of the free market, a harsh discipline inflicted every day on non-medical businesses that forget to pay the respect due their consumer. Currently, third party buyers of medical services are the consumer that medical businesses and physicians fear, not patients. Therein lies the problem-and the solution.

While no individual patient purchasing the removal of their gallbladder will change the marketplace, there is what my friend Marty Makary calls the "proxy buyer," the self-funded buyer (spending dollars held in trust for the benefit of individual employees) which represents a large enough force to change the marketplace dramatically. Why haven't they flexed their buying "muscle?"

Most self-funded buyers (typically companies with 50 or more employees) are asleep, having drunk the rufie-filled Kool-Aide served to them by unscrupulous broker-consultants and intermediaries. They've been hoodwinked by these grifters and in the following pages Matt shows exactly how the scam works. Until this book, the purposefully over-complex scam foisted on employers has been a mystery, a webbed quagmire that was impenetrable by all but the select few. Many human resource executives are either unaware of what Matt's book reveals or have conflicts of interest involving the shysters who've hoodwinked their company. The vast majority of HR executives simply lack the empowerment this book provides.

Thanks to Matt's book, the shysters and the conflicted HR executives now have no place to hide. Company CEO's, CFO's and empowered HR teams now have a plain-spoken guide to how the scam works and, more importantly, a way out. When the self-funded buyer awakens, all who provide medical services will bow to market discipline, or be crushed by it, as this buyer represents half the money spent in the industry (an amount too large for any who sell medical services to ignore). Prices will fall and quality will soar, as happens in any industry where competition is allowed to flourish. This process will benefit everyone in this country, as a medical marketplace with visible pricing continues to develop. This is the fuse that can only be lit by the self-funded buyer, as Matt shows.

Matt has drawn on his extensive and real-world experience in human resources to help deliver us from this nightmare. His passion for a medical marketplace characterized by mutually beneficial exchange is obvious to any who have had the good fortune to meet him. You will learn much and without meeting him, know Matt, after reading why we shouldn't feed the beast.

INTRODUCTION

My Trip to the Emergency Room

Life comes at us pretty fast sometimes and things can happen when we least expect it. Several years ago, on a warm summer day in Wisconsin, life happened to me. Or maybe I should say, death *almost* happened to me. My day started out like any other, and it went from normal to life-threatening emergency in the blink of an eye. It was an experience I wish I could forget, but never will.

Who Says That?

At the end of the day, lying battered and broken in a hospital bed, I would reflect on my day and utter the phrase, "Today, I was run over by a 4,000-pound tractor." I don't suppose too many people say that out loud. I mean really, *who says that?* At least, no one who's alive says that. Somehow, I was alive.

It was my cherished work tractor—a 1959 Ford Workmaster 641—that rolled backward, directly over my body, down the bluff slope and into the mighty Wisconsin River. I still don't understand why or how my life was spared. Most likely, I shouldn't be sitting here right now, typing the pages of this book. My name, *Matthew Royce Ohrt,* should be carved on a slab of granite in the local cemetery and I should be six feet under. I have replayed the story over and over in my head and it seems my survival was a 1-in-100 chance. Yet not only did I live, I was not paralyzed or maimed in a way that would leave significant, permanent damage. It is only by the grace of God that I live to tell my story.

I've talked with a few people that have been through traumatic life-and-death experiences. A few have shared that they saw angels. I was a person of strong faith before the incident, and I remain a person of strong faith today, but I didn't see any angels, nor did I see anything in the spiritual realm, other than watching an engaged parking brake mysteriously pop loose on a fully functioning, restored tractor. I don't know how and why that parking brake released on its own, but it did, and it was the spark for an event that forever changed my life.

Who would have guessed that enduring this traumatic experience, followed by an equally traumatic healthcare experience, would motivate me to try to fix something that most agreed was unfixable? I would use that trauma as fuel for my fire, to muster every ounce of energy and to hone my abilities to attempt to fix the most complex problem I had ever encountered—employer-sponsored healthcare.

The River Bluff

It was a Saturday morning in late June, just before noon. My wife was away on a two-hour road trip to buy some laying hens for a couple of chicken coops we'd just built. My twenty-year-old daughter, Hannah, was home – as was my fifteen-year-old son, Lincoln. Both were busy in the house doing their own thing. I was outside, working in our backyard along the river bluff edge. The bluff was very steep, far above the water level. It was 42 feet down to the intimidating 300-foot-wide Wisconsin River that flows through its valley to join the great Mississippi in northeast Iowa. The rocky bluff was too steep to walk, at least not without clinging to the bushes that grew out of it sideways. I was using "Old Red," my utility tractor, to hook up to fallen trees. I pulled them up the slope and onto the flat ground, planning to bring in a backhoe the following week to dig out the rest of the riverbank. Eventually I wanted to put in a boat dock.

I'd pulled up several trees that morning and only one remained. I was using a heavy log chain. I'd wrap it around the stump of a downed tree and attach the other end of the chain to the tractor drawbar. Once hooked, I would drive forward with the tractor to pull it up the bank. I was making good time and had other things planned that day. I would pull the last remaining tree up the bank and I'd be done with this job.

And then . . .

> "My body is being destroyed right now. I am being torn to pieces and there will be nothing left of me."

I was standing on the steep slope, leaning forward, attempting to wrap the heavy chain around the trunk of the last remaining tree. Suddenly, I heard a pop and saw that the parking brake had released on the tractor. It didn't make sense. No amount of force on the chain should have caused the parking brake to disengage. In fact, pressure should have strengthened its engagement. But it didn't care about my logic. I saw that the tractor was beginning to roll backward slowly. I crawled up the bank on all fours like a man half my age.

I remembered a trick I learned growing up on a farm in central Iowa. Being careful not to get in the path of the tractor, I positioned myself alongside its left rear and began to push on the top of the large rear wheel. Typically, even large tractors can be moved by pushing on the rear wheel, because it offers great leverage. But just as I put my hands on the tire, the tractor hit a small dip in the ground and jolted backward abruptly, pinning the toe of my left boot underneath it. I was wearing steel-toed boots, which protected my foot from being crushed, but I would now be caught in a sequence of traumatic events I had no power to stop.

Immediately, I was thrown to the ground, directly behind and then under the rolling tractor. I cannot express how fast this happened— almost instantly. As a farm boy from Iowa and a former college athlete, physical activity is something I am used to. None of that mattered here. I was now directly in harm's way.

The big left rear wheel of the tractor rolled directly over my chest. The rear wheels of the tractor were fluid-filled, which is commonly done for added weight and traction. This added an additional 200 pounds to each wheel. In my fall, I was not caught or struck by the rear drawbar—a thick piece of heavy steel that is used for hooking up wagons. It protruded out of the rear of the tractor a couple feet, like a dull spear. Somehow I was thrown under the rear of the tractor so quickly that the rear axle housing of the tractor mysteriously cleared my body. On flat ground, the bottom of the rear axle housing abides about ten inches off the ground. I am a big guy and would not have fit in such a space. The reason I was not crushed by the housing is because the left rear wheel rolled over my chest, raising the whole tractor just enough to clear my body. A couple days later the bruises, in a pattern of ribbed tire marks across my chest, would make the exact path of the tractor obvious. I would have five very painful broken ribs to serve as a reminder.

I would have to put the pieces of the accident together afterward. The big grease spot on my right shoulder and arm indicated where I'd rubbed across the bottom of the tractor's oil pan. The gashes and cuts on my back were from small trees, rocks, and raspberry bushes sprouting out of the bluff. I had taken my shirt off that morning to get some sun. After the chaos, my back looked like I had taken 50 lashes.

The best I can describe this incident, from the time my foot was caught under the rear wheel, to being pulled under the tractor, to being run over, is VIOLENT—violent thrashing down a steep, rocky, thorn-ridden river bluff slope. I don't specifically recall the left rear wheel running over my chest, and I don't specifically recall the left front wheel rolling over my legs. But my bruising indicated they surely did. Although it was mid-day and the sun was shining, in my world it was dark, very loud, and during those few seconds of pure raging violence, there was only one thought that passed through my mind: *"My body is being destroyed right now. I am being torn to pieces and there will be nothing left of me."*

I was never unconscious, but it almost seemed as if I was – as I opened my eyes and came back to reality at the bottom of the bluff on the rocky shoreline, facing the deep river. I remember being severely winded; so much so that I struggled to get a single, satisfying breath. I was terrified to lower my eyes downward and examine my body, but I knew that I must force myself to look. I expected graphic morbidity. Surprisingly, that was not the case. I quickly scanned my body in a panic, up and down my arms, over my abdomen, and then up and down my legs. I was not gashed, stabbed, noticeably crushed, or ripped apart. I did not see any major slashes or pools of blood. I lifted my right hand from my side, palm up, and saw that I had two dislocated fingers pointed in the wrong direction. I suspect this was from when I put my hands on the rear tire and the tractor jumped abruptly, but I'm not sure. As I stared at the palm of my right hand, my middle finger was pointed 90 degrees sideways to my left, starting at the middle joint, and my thumb was awkwardly bent downward, sitting in the palm of my hand. It made my stomach turn. With my other hand, I instinctively moved them into their normal place, thinking they were destroyed. However, to my surprise, they stayed in place. This gave me a little hope.

Coming to Grips with Reality

I laid back and rested my head against the rocky, thorn-ridden bluff. I felt completely alone on that shore. There were no passing boats or paddling canoers. I began talking to myself: *"This actually happened, this actually happened."* It seemed to be my way of coping, beginning to accept the shocking reality of my new situation. My mind raced. How stupid of me, I thought. Not only did I lose my beautifully restored tractor, I got in its way and it almost crushed me. I knew I was hurt badly. I can't explain how strongly I desired to go back in time. I wanted that split second back. I wanted a redo. I would do it differently this time; I would do it better. But that was not going to happen. This was real, and my injuries were inescapable.

I was lying on my back, nearly upright on the steep shore. I remember watching the tractor, which somehow did not flip over, roll backward on all four wheels and fade away— slowly, deeper and deeper into the water. It was still running, and eventually the consuming water would engulf the engine and starve it of air. The water covered the tractor and it sputtered for a few seconds and stalled. The tractor disappeared. Now it was completely quiet. I was panting heavily, struggling to catch my breath. I began reflecting. My outside was battered, bruised, scraped and cut, but what about my internal organs? They could be crushed, or I could be bleeding internally and not feel it yet.

It would take about 20 minutes for the pain to really set in. My chest and ribs began to hurt intensely. I lay there for another minute, breathing

1959 Ford Workmaster641

heavily—gasping for the next breath, searching for comfort that I never found. I knew no one would see me at the bottom of the river bluff and if I didn't act quickly, I could die in that place. I searched my pocket for my phone and realized it was in the building, at the top of the bluff, about 500 feet away. I arose, turned my body toward the slope, and began to climb. Each unsatisfying breath brought stabbing pain, but I had to try. Instinctively, I grabbed a small tree with my right hand to pull myself forward, causing my finger and thumb to dislocate to their previously dislocated place again. Using my left hand, I put them back in alignment again, and rested my right arm to my side. I couldn't use it. In pain and exasperation, I somehow made it up the bank to flat ground and staggered past the house to the building to get my phone. Immediately, I tried calling my wife. There was no answer. I hung up as the voicemail message started to play. I immediately texted my dad, who lives 400 miles away Iowa. In a jumbled message, I typed, *"Pray for me, I have been run ovet by a tractir."* I learned later this message created a bit of panic with my family in Iowa.

How Badly am I Hurt?

I stumbled back to the house, still contemplating in my mind whether I should call 911 for an ambulance. Having worked in HR my whole career, my knowledge of extreme medical bills and bankruptcies made me hesitate and dissuaded me from calling right away. I realize this wasn't the best decision. Every minute mattered. I wasn't thinking clearly and was still in shock from the trauma I'd experienced. Hannah found me and in true shock-filled form, I had her take some quick pictures of me. I winced as I posed. I could barely stand at this point.

My two children did not realize, at first, how dire the situation was. After all, I was walking around. They asked me what happened and I told them the tractor rolled over me and into the river. They have seen me get into all sorts of mischief and it wasn't all that uncommon that I would strain a muscle or injure myself in some way, but this one was different. This was serious. I said it again: "I was run over by the tractor." Lincoln said, "The big Ford tractor?" I confirmed with a quiet gasp: "Yes." They began to understand the gravity of the situation and each began to cry. Hannah showed good composure and called her mother from her phone.

Not yet thinking clearly, I looked down and saw my chest and what looked like lashings. Still short of breath, I said quietly to them with all the voice I could muster, "It will be painful if all this sand dries in my wounds. I am going to rinse off in the shower." And that's what I did. I grimaced as I stepped into the shower for a quick rinse. I dried myself off, put on a pair of athletic shorts and laid down in my bed. I was now in a resting position, and although I felt better about my surface wounds, the internal pain was really beginning to set in. I could barely move. I lay there thinking, wondering, if I would die right there in my bed.

At that moment, my phone rang. It was my wife. Hannah had reached her. Everyone now understood the gravity of the situation and Hannah cried as she shared the news. My wife Denise knew how I felt about the hospital and medical bills and she got very direct with me. She adamantly gave me two choices. She said, "You can let Hannah take you to the hospital or I will call for an ambulance to come get you." We had just celebrated our 25th wedding anniversary and she has always been good at keeping me grounded. I gave in and suffered a painful ride in the tiny passenger seat of my daughter's Kia Sorento. It took a long 20 minutes to reach the ER. I felt every bump in the road.

> They asked me what happened and I told them the tractor rolled over me and into the river.

First, Complete this Paperwork!

We arrived and my view of the healthcare industry was further dampened. I somehow made it out of the passenger seat and Hannah, who was studying to be a nurse, promptly grabbed a wheelchair by the door and pushed my broken body up to the counter. The receptionist was typing and didn't look up for what seemed like an eternity. She casually finished, looked up at me, and asked what happened. I said, with a bit of aggravation, "I have just been run over by a 4,000 pound tractor. I need to see a doctor right away." Without urgency, she handed me a piece of paper on a clipboard and asked me to complete it.

During the long wait to get the receptionist's attention, I had pulled a card out of my wallet that I had made just for this kind of situation, and handed it to her. The card had a specifically worded paragraph of 29 words that I learned from Al Lewis, a Harvard-trained attorney who helps patients prevent exorbitant ER bills. It stated that I would only pay 2x Medicare rate. She refused to accept the card or make a copy and seemed annoyed that I gave it to her. She handed it back to me and said, "You can deal with that later." Of course, that opportunity never came. I was getting increasingly upset, but I didn't have time to argue. I needed medical help.

As each minute passed, the pain grew. I could barely move an inch at this point. They laid me on a very hard table and lit me up with CT's. I learned that one CT has the radiation of something like 100 x-rays. I am probably still glowing. Nonetheless, it was necessary. My life was at risk. They needed to know what was happening on the inside. After an hour or so of lying on my back on the table, my pastor arrived. My wife had called him. He was also my friend. He prayed with me and I shared the violent experience I had just endured. After a couple hours, the doctor approached me. The diagnosis included a temporarily dislocated left shoulder (apparently it went back in place on its own), 5 broken ribs on my right side, skin lacerations throughout my body, a severely bruised left calf, a badly bruised right heel, and 2 severely dislocated fingers.

It was nothing short of a miracle. No immediate procedures or surgeries were needed. My hopes of no internal injuries were confirmed. Now, I wanted to go home. I had seen far too many hospital bills in the tens of thousands of dollars for much lesser medical issues than this. I could hear the cash register "cha-chinging" in my mind: How much was this going to cost?

There are many things I can't explain about this story. One of them is an almost miraculous timing of things. Just a week prior, I had visited a furniture store an hour away that was having a closing sale, and although I made the trip there to buy each of my daughters a new bed, I chose also to buy my wife and I a new bed, which was equipped with a power incline. The price was too good to pass up and I justified the purchase, telling myself that it would be good for bedtime reading. I would soon learn that without this device, I literally would not have been able to get in or out of bed.

Stay the Night

While was still on the emergency room table, the doctor approached me and recommended I be admitted and stay overnight for medical observation. From a medical standpoint, this was the right thing to do. From a cost standpoint, I was fearful. I had seen bills for as much as $20,000 for an overnight stay. I wanted to go home. I stood up and tried two separate times to shuffle out of the ER. I hadn't even changed out of my gown. Both times I became nauseated and dizzy and had to sit back down. After the second unsuccessful try, I conceded. I would stay the night.

I spent the night in a hospital room, refusing the suggestions to take fentanyl. Instead, I chose over-the-counter pain medications.

It wasn't until about 11 a.m. the next day that I would try to walk again. I went for a short, excruciatingly painful stroll down the hallway. Each step hurt something awful, but the good news was that I did not become nauseated. Upon returning from my walk, I sat on the edge of the bed. A physical therapist stopped in and began talking with me. I told him, "I have access to a doctor-level PT through work who can help me at no cost." I told him clearly that I did not need his services. He said the hospital required that he stop by, and that he was required to ask me a few questions. He was with me less than five minutes and I received no care or benefit from him. He asked several times if I wanted to schedule physical therapy appointments. Each time I told him no.

> He was with me less than five minutes and I received no care or benefit from him.

Charges for Services Not Received

A few weeks later, when I received the bill for physical therapy, totaling $388, I was upset. "I knew this would happen!" I said emphatically. That was just a part of it. Several other charges were in question. I called the hospital billing department to inquire about these charges and to request an itemized summary. It took me several days of trying, waiting over 45 minutes on hold each time. I finally was able to reach someone. I raised the questions about services not received and the billing specialist made me feel like I was out of line for asking. She reminded me that it would go to collections if I delayed too long to pay the bill and asked if I wanted to make an immediate payment. I explained that I would have to drain my HSA account and my savings account, and I wanted to see an accurate bill first.

Overall, an hour on the ER table, several CT scans, and a night in the hospital resulted in a total bill of over $19,227.39 from the hospital. That turned out to be one expensive overnight stay. It ended up costing me my maximum out of pocket, which was much larger before we had improved our benefit plan. Not knowing what I know today about how to push back against fraudulent bills, to avoid collection notices and my wages being garnished, I paid the full amount, without formal dispute. I was still hurting and I didn't have the time or energy to fight it. This was a mistake. I should have and could have fought to pay a fair, accurate amount. From that day forward, this experience would motivate me to try to protect others from these traumatic and financially threatening experiences.

Home to Heal

I returned home and spent the rest of that day and most of the next week bedridden. I had a lot of healing to do. It hurt to move, even an inch. After about four days down, on Wednesday I was able to force myself to get out of bed. Although it hurt more than words can describe, over the course of the next few days I would experience what turned out to be a reasonably expedient recovery. Those around me called it a miracle, although from my perspective, I didn't think miracles should hurt so much. I ended up missing only one week of work. I had to sleep on my back for six weeks due to the broken ribs, which was no fun for me, being I am a side sleeper.

Back to Work

The following week, I got back into my work-life routine. Getting in and out of the car to travel to work was the hardest part of the day. In everything I did, I moved gingerly, in slow motion. Coworkers and friends would talk with me as if I was feeling normal. They had no idea how much pain I was in. It was about four months until my leg, calf, and foot were healed. My calf was numb for about a month and then, out of nowhere, it began sending electrical shocks through my body when I put my foot wrong. This carried on for a couple more months. It was unpleasant and memorable. To this day, I still step with caution on that side.

My finger had what is called a boutonniere, which meant the endmost finger joint was locked upward instead of bending downward - the way it is supposed to bend. Concerned that I may have damaged tendons, I acted quickly to see if surgery would be required. My first call was to Keith Smith at the Surgery Center of Oklahoma. One of their surgeons called me within a few hours. He cautioned against immediate surgery and recommended a hand specialist and a brace for my finger. As Keith likes to say, "My favorite ones are the ones in which my team proclaims—no surgery is needed." I ordered a brace online for $23 and wore it for about 3 months. The brace healed my finger. Other than a swollen middle knuckle due to a slipped tendon, I made it through this experience without lasting ailments. No surgery was needed. I can't help but wonder what other surgeons might have recommended, had I called them.

Reflection

I am still not sure how or why my life was spared. I am so grateful that I can talk, walk, and do everything I could before the incident. I am especially glad I did not orphan my four biological children or my foster son, whom we had adopted just one month prior. I am also glad I did not widow my wife— on a day that started just like every other day, until that split second when everything changed so quickly.

Although I have been around safety precautions my whole career, sometimes the personal experiences are the best teachers. A lasting takeaway for me is that safety is worth the time to take that extra step, because there are no mulligans or redos. I should have taken more precautions. I should have shut off the tractor and I should have placed a log behind the wheels.

If you are wondering about my 1959 Ford Workmaster 641 tractor, my son Lincoln found a wrecker service that was willing to come and pull the tractor out of the river, up the steep bluff. They had it out of the water and on dry ground that afternoon, with a bill of something like $300. That would be the fairest bill I would have through this whole experience. Further, I had a mechanic friend who graciously stepped in, changed all the fluids in the tractor, and it started right up. It barely had a scratch. I did not expect to recover the tractor after it had been sitting at the bottom of the Wisconsin River. People today ask me if I still have a passion for tractors. My regular response is, "Yes, but I prefer to be on them instead of under them."

I share my story, mostly because so many people said I should. It's kind of personal, yet it brings out some of the thoughts and worries that many people have related to getting proper medical care. In my opinion, a person should never have to avoid necessary medical care for fear of being gouged or driven into bankruptcy. Maybe you or someone you love has had these thoughts when they were in need of important medical care. I am thankful to be here and to continue writing my story and I am now motivated more than ever to fight the good fight, in order to make healthcare a positive topic again in our great country. Won't you join me in this healthcare movement?

CHAPTER ONE
The Bad News & Good News

I am a lifelong learner, and perhaps you are as well. You may have questions about the material this book covers. Asking questions is a great place to start, and a great ongoing approach. The person who has passion, curiosity, and humility will always do well, because no matter how much he or she may know about a given topic, there is always something more to learn.

Let's Learn Together

For the better part of the last decade, I have been asking questions, conducting case studies, and searching for answers on the topic of employer-sponsored healthcare. I like to think of this question-and-answer process in the context of *best practices*. By studying best practices, we can find practical and proven examples of how others have succeeded. There is no need to reinvent the wheel. As we implement more and more of these good ideas, we can begin to put the pieces together to form an overall strategy. This is the approach I have taken.

In 2018 I started a local "Healthcare Best Practice Group" with a colleague in central Wisconsin. Participation was informal and for several years, I could count the participating employers on one hand. My colleague took another role, and she posed the question to me of whether I would like to keep the group going or to dissolve it. I decided to keep it going. Then Covid hit and everything shut down. As business revived, I continued to educate and equip local employers. Today, through much hard work and persistence, this group has grown to about 300 employers and about 1,200 total individuals who support free-market healthcare practices.

> This publication is geared toward employer healthcare, and is written for all who swim in that pond.

In the spring of 2022, I began facilitating one-day conference events throughout the state, inviting employers to share their stories and the best practices they have implemented. There has been much ongoing interest from both private and public employers and the group continues to grow. Through my experiences in leading this group, collaborating with other companies who have been successful with healthcare while also implementing best practices first-hand, I have developed a comprehensive solution that I believe will interest you. I call it the *Employer Healthcare Success Formula* and I am excited to share the concept with you in this book.

This publication is geared toward employer healthcare, and is written for all who swim in that pond. This includes employers, and all those who support employer healthcare, such as brokers, providers, administrators, and independent networks. A few conventional hospital and insurance carriers have attended our best practice events. When people ask me why, I can't give an answer. Maybe they were curious about this movement; maybe they had genuine interest in learning; maybe they were spying so they could counter with strategy; or maybe they wanted to take a picture of me, so they could put it on their dartboard. While I hope it's not the latter, it doesn't worry me. I will continue to openly facilitate the sharing of wisdom, knowledge, and best practices. We ALL have something to gain from this movement.

The topic of healthcare has become the elephant in the room. Most people are aware of the issues and have lived through their share of bad experiences, but they are quieted by an underlying impression of powerlessness, maybe even intimidation. I have always believed in the philosophy, "If there is an elephant in the room, introduce it!"

As I travel around Wisconsin communities, I regularly spark conversations with people I meet— the person standing in line next to me at the bank, a waitress in a restaurant, or a fellow Little League parent in the bleachers at a baseball game. I can tell you this: in Wisconsin, it is not difficult to stumble across someone carrying frustration or debt as a result of a healthcare experience. It is commonplace. The stories are replete with examples of rushed or disjointed care, endless referrals, charges for services not received, and missed time from work—followed by a piecemeal of grossly overpriced and difficult-to-understand bills. The stories all seem to follow the same pattern. They are like a broken record, playing the sounds of the suffering of hard-working Americans. The $100 aspirin, the $87 blanket, or the $359 ice pack are not fallacies, but real examples of how ridiculous healthcare billing has become. And these are just the small things. I saw a bill recently in which the hospital charged $39.35 for brief "skin to skin" contact after the mother had given birth. I had to read it twice. They actually had a line-item charge on the bill for what they viewed as "medical care"—holding and hugging a newborn baby! My wife and I are foster parents and we love babies. The thought of charging a fee to hug a baby is inconceivable to me.

It is not uncommon for all of this hullabaloo to result in a family needing to file for bankruptcy, because as a consumer of healthcare, the patient is at the mercy of the merciless. Imagine having your wages garnished, a lien placed on your home, and losing your life's work through a bankruptcy, not because you made bad decisions, but because you had something unexpected happen and needed higher-level healthcare.

I live in Wisconsin, which happens to be one of the worst states in the nation for healthcare cost, but this issue of exorbitant cost is not unique to Wisconsin. It is a national issue and even the states with the lowest cost, aren't that low.

Candidly, when we talk about employer healthcare today, we talk mostly of bad news. Has someone ever said to you, "I have good news and bad news—which do you want to hear?" I'm not sure about you, but I always choose to hear the bad news first. With healthcare today in America, the buyers of healthcare, employers and employees, are faced with a continual barrage of bad news.

The Bad News

For the past twenty-plus years, healthcare costs have been rising at an unsustainable pace. For group health plans, it is not uncommon to hear of single-year increases of 20%, 30%, or 50% or more. Employers of all sizes are feeling the pain. Unable to find solutions, a concerning number of smaller employers have thrown in the towel, unable to afford the premiums. Larger employers have been able to absorb the blows a little better. Notwithstanding a couple of black eyes, they are still on their feet, but their knees are getting wobbly and the room is starting to spin. No matter how big or strong, the repeated blows eventually take their toll.

We see this effect with employer health plans, which have steadily degraded, year over year, to the point in which most are now only catastrophic in nature, leaving members "functionally uninsured." This is to say they have an official-looking insurance card in their wallet but the coverage is inadequate to protect their families from financial harm. A few concerning statistics tell this story:

- Two-thirds of family bankruptcies in America are related to healthcare and three out of four of those families had health insurance. *(American Journal of Public Health)*
- About 100 million, or 41% of American adults, have medical debt, with a quarter of them currently owing over $5,000. *(Kaiser Family Foundation)*

- In 2013, the projected annual medical cost for a family of four was 22,030 U.S. dollars whereas this cost increased to 30,260 U.S. dollars in 2022 for employees on employer sponsored healthcare plans. *(Milliman Medical Index)*

> **By 2030, the average American healthcare spend for a family of four is expected to be over 50% of annual household income.**

Employers and employees are losing trust in the American healthcare system, which has unfortunately become more about profit than patients. The depreciating effect these issues are having on employers, families, and communities is unsettling. We are talking about the health of an entire nation. Americans need real solutions, not more rhetoric and bureaucracy.

The Good News

Thankfully, there is some good news. It starts with employers recognizing the problem, and realizing that as the buyers, they have the power. If you have been searching for solutions and you would like to make healthcare a positive topic in your company again, you are holding the answers in your hands. The Employer Healthcare Success Formula has been empirically developed over a period of years, with information taken from real-life employer case studies. It is tried and tested, and has been proven to work in a variety of environments, in both rural or urban areas, with small or large employers, and with privately owned, publicly traded, or government entities. It's a sustainable option for employers and employees alike, and it strengthens with time.

Status Quo'ers and Disruptors

Thus far, there have been a few fearless leaders across the country who have taken on the challenge to redesign and rebuild their health plans. While they have been more the exception than the norm, more and more employers are beginning to engage. Candidly, most people are not interested in trudging through the wilderness when the trail has not yet been cut. However, once someone "goes in," it seems more are willing to go second, a few more are willing to go third, and so on. Many prefer at least a gravel trail if not a smoothly paved road. Jim Hightower said it well: "The opposite of courage is not cowardice, it is conformity. Even a dead fish can go with the flow." He makes a good point. It is always easier to go with the flow, which is the current road—the easy road—even if the topography has changed so that it now leads nowhere.

The healthcare industry often refers to these trailblazer folks as *disruptors*—individuals who have become conscious of alternatives, those who do not unconsciously, automatically go with the flow; those who are willing to be risk takers and to change the status quo path.

I can say that many people have called me a disruptor. Candidly, I have never liked the sound of that word. It seems to give the impression that I have incendiary intent—that I wake up, kick my feet over the edge of the bed, and say, "What trouble can I stir up today?" One respected colleague told me that he views the word *disruptor* as a compliment. Maybe, but I still struggle with that.

The inherent nature of the word *disruptor* seems to take the perspective of the one who is being negatively affected by the disruption. Yet, from the disruptor's perspective, a more appropriate word might be *transformational* leader—a type of person who acknowledges a problem and sees an opportunity to help—one who views problems as opportunities in disguise. This type of person can lead a group of people through a change, from "here" to "there"—guiding, teaching, and even sometimes strategically nudging people out of their comfort zones, to a new normal.

The theory of disruptive innovation, first developed in the 1970s, asserts that companies can differentiate themselves from competitors with a business model that offers completely new products or services to fill the same current needs. In doing so, they can effectively make a big splash in an industry by changing the status quo. As young pupils in elementary school, most of us were not encouraged to be innovative. Rather, we were taught to follow the status quo and to conform. Learning was more or less synonymous with memorization, and there was little opportunity or encouragement for critical thinking. We were instructed to stand in a single-file line with no talking allowed.

When it came to classroom etiquette, I was a good little student. I conformed to the rules, I earned good grades, and I was somewhat quiet and reserved (if you know me, you might find that hard to imagine). However, I remember one particular day in which I was overly talkative in class—I was disruptive. The teacher wrote my name on the board, which was followed by her underlining my name, and finally, circling my name. Three strikes and I was asked to stand outside of the classroom. I was not listening, and I was guided back to conformity.

We can presuppose that as long as authority figures are ethical and responsible, conformity is a good thing. It is important we live and work together well to form a civil society. Yet, as adults, what are we to do when authority figures lose their way, and by reasons such as power and greed, begin to oppress and harm the communities they are tasked to serve? In such instances, I hope you would agree that speaking up and leading others away from the status quo in search of a better way is the right thing to do. In my opinion, all of us have a responsibility to do this. Interestingly, through the courage and struggle of common people like you and me is how the United States of America came to exist. Having a taste of freedom, early settlers, who eventually became Americans, were not easy to control.

Similarly, when it comes to employer healthcare, I believe our motivation should be to right a wrong— to seek justice— to choose not to stick our head in the sand and wait for someone else to solve the problem; to stand up for people who are burdened by the current healthcare system and are forced to deal with the unfavorable outcomes it produces.

Some temerity and nonconformist thinking will be required to solve these complex social problems. We must be willing to think outside the box and veer off the beaten path. This new path may be dimly lit and a bit rugged at first. Yet we know that the experience of blazing this new trail will make a way for others to follow. It is on these uncharted, unconventional paths that the real solutions are usually found.

Dr. Keith Smith and Dr. Steve Lantier, cofounders of the Surgery Center of Oklahoma and pioneers of the free-market healthcare model, are a great example of this. In 2009 they began offering transparent, bundled pricing on their website. Today, hundreds of people fly in from all over the world each month for surgeries. This has come to be known as "medical tourism." People are willing to travel because they cannot find high-quality, affordable surgeries in their home state or country. Dr. Smith is passionate about the health of American healthcare. He shares his insight on the Hippocratic oath physicians take in medical school. It is an oath we are all familiar with: "First, do no harm." He states, "For a physician to do no harm, one must care for a patient's physical needs at a fair cost. For what good does it do if we heal a patient physically, while bankrupting him or her financially?"

Having worked my entire 25-year career for employers, I see the world through an employer lens. Employer-sponsored health plans account for the purchase of approximately 58% of healthcare, with the government paying for the remainder. In Wisconsin, employer plans account for 68% of healthcare coverage. As the payers, employers have the most influence. Therefore, they have the most responsibility for fixing our country's collective healthcare issues. A majority of employers are not educated on this topic, and as a result they are not yet acting as true fiduciaries of their plan. A fiduciary is a person who has the legal or ethical responsibility of trust with one or more parties. Employer healthcare transformation is still an ambiguous topic, but it doesn't have to be! Employers must own these problems and should no longer delegate the management of their benefits, including important decisions, to a traditional broker, whose interests are often financially conflicted.

This book was written with two primary goals: education and practice. Both are critical to success. A person can know everything there is to know about a topic, but if this knowledge is not put into practice, the information is useless. Similarly, if someone is active, but does not have a sound strategy or make good decisions, the effort will be fruitless. A sound strategy, mixed with good decisions and a willingness to act, is where the rubber meets the road.

Having led one of the rare employer healthcare success stories in Wisconsin, I have something to say on this topic. Fueled by an intrinsic motivation, I have dedicated the rest of my career to help all employers do the same. It is my hope that in taking the time to read this book, you will feel equipped to lead your company on a successful healthcare journey. As the great coach Lou Holtz said, "Remember. Every day, some ordinary person does something extraordinary. Today, it's your turn."

If you are ready to join me, buckle up and hang on. It's going to be a life-changing experience.

CHAPTER TWO
The Employer Healthcare Success Formula

Employers across the nation share the desire to offer access to high-quality, affordable healthcare for employees and their families. They also share many challenges.

You Are Not Alone

We might say that employers are collectively in the same boat, peering over the edge of the bow. The problem is that the boat is the Titanic and it is sinking deeper and deeper into the ocean with each passing year of status-quo thinking. This is not to say that some employers haven't tried a few things, listening to the advice of their traditional brokers. But it has become apparent that these suggestions have had little effect on healthcare plan outcomes. Ultimately, they have amounted to mere conjecture: ineffectual efforts to rearrange the deck chairs on the Titanic. With good intent, employers have avoided conflict, hoping that someone else would fix the problems. This collective acquiescence has caught up with them. The time has come that employers can no longer tarry—they must find and implement real solutions.

Healthcare or Sickcare?

Slowly and steadily, over the past few decades, healthcare has become big business. Some go as far as to say *healthcare* is no longer an appropriate term, because the industry focus has shifted to become all about money—profits over patients. Their impression is that *sickcare* would be a better description for the type of care being provided today, because the industry does not profit when its customers are healthy.

> A patient cured is a customer lost

This view questions the very core of the methods and motives of the current healthcare system, Is the first priority to heal the patient? It's no secret that more money is made if an illness is treated regularly and repeatedly, yet not resolved, prolonged for years, or even a lifetime. This might explain the apparent trend of less and less effort to find the root cause of maladies and more and more effort to provide nominal care, such as addressing symptoms with expensive recurring medications. The pharmacy industry has grown exponentially. Twenty years ago, pharmacy costs typically made up less than 5% of a health plan's total cost and today this number is closer to 25%.

A Time for Decision

The time has come for employers to stop sailing this sea of dysfunction and to think differently. Albert Einstein said, "We cannot solve our problems with the same thinking we used when we created them."

This pending decision rests on the shoulders of employers like an itchy sweater. What will you do? Every journey must begin with a first step, and sometimes that first step can be the scariest one to take. If you have some fears about change, it is important to remember that you are not alone. Fear is a normal emotion, experienced by even the greatest leaders. To deny fear is to deny being human.

Inevitably, you are faced with a choice. You could change nothing—which is a choice: to stay in a place that is known but rapidly deteriorating. Alternatively, you could choose to join this nascent movement and choose to "move"—to be a person of action—to be a victor and not a victim. As Spencer Johnson put it so simply in his book, Who Moved My Cheese, someone has moved your cheese and you will ultimately decide if you will take the first step to find some new cheese.

I can empathize with this dilemma. I have been there, and done that, and I have the T-shirt. I have walked in those shoes. I know exactly how it feels. All kinds of questions run through your mind. What if things don't go as planned? What if the changes you make cause things to become even worse than they are today? What if things go so badly you lose your job? All of these things could realistically happen. What if….

However, what if things do go as planned? What if the changes you make help families put food on their table, have access to affordable healthcare, and stay out of bankruptcy? What if things go so well that you get promoted, are asked to speak at conferences to tell your story, or are recognized with an award? All of these things could realistically happen as well. What if….

Which emotion will win in your heart—fear or courage? By picking up this book, you have already shown courage.

A Step Forward

In 2016, I took a first step of courage into the unknown. I had just relocated my family to take on a new role: leading Human Resources for Merrill Steel, headquartered in Schofield, Wisconsin. Merrill Steel is the largest steel fabricator in the Midwest, a family-owned company with about 450 employees and 1,000 health-plan member lives in Wisconsin and Missouri.

Before my arrival, for the previous five years, the company had averaged 9% annual increases in total healthcare spend. We were already self-funded but we needed a medical strategy. Something had to be done. We didn't really know what to do. We recognized that the healthcare industry had a strong grasp on us. As an employer, we were in a jail cell and the door had been slammed shut. If I heard the question, "Are you in-network?" one more time, I might have lost it. It was a bit overwhelming.

Then came a revelation. We began to realize a simple notion: the payer is the one with the power. We realized we were the ones who were holding the key to the jail cell door! We could take the first step, and stumble in the dark toward the lock. We could twist our body and maneuver our handcuffed arms from behind our back to insert the key into the lock and turn….. Click! the cell door opened. We were on our way out of bondage. We were poised to march to freedom, to the promised land.

Insurance plays an interesting role as the intermediary. They pose as the payer, while in reality they are the only the reimburser. The real payer is the employer! This realization would help us begin to utilize our "payer power", and it was the spark that ignited my internal fire. I began to learn and study everything I could on the topic of employer healthcare strategy. I learned about the scope and severity of the problems, and how they were affecting my company. I had discussions with a variety of local healthcare experts. I took copious notes and began to put the puzzle pieces together in my mind. I searched the internet for articles and I read every book I could find on how to fix employer healthcare.

I realized there were many things outside my control; I realized too that the prominent and powerful healthcare industry players were doing very well with the status quo. They openly resisted any requests or attempts to change. I came to the conclusion that there is no way to win with them, which meant I would need to find a way to win without them . . . or at least to utilize them less. My goal would be to avoid the hospital and insurance games as much as possible and create better alternatives that enabled shared-win relationships between the buyers and sellers of healthcare services. I realized that I must change my perspective. My focus must be to "purchase healthcare services," instead of the common traditional view, to "purchase insurance."

New Beginnings

During the first few months in my new role at Merrill Steel I got to know Karen Rajek, a second-generation owner, who had many ideas and a great passion to help employees and their families. She enabled and supported our healthcare efforts from the beginning and without her, the Merrill Steel success story would not have been possible.

We started by remodeling an 1,800-square-foot space on the second floor of our office building, accessible by stairs from the main lobby entrance, which would become the Merrill Steel Family Clinic. An elevator was available through a back entrance for patients who were physically unable to climb stairs. This clinic would be operated by an independent direct primary care (DPC) provider called Astia Health, founded by Dr. Alex Sommers. It would be available to all employees and their families at zero net cost and although we didn't realize it at the time, the DPC would become the heartbeat of our medical strategy.

> We certainly had hoped for cost savings, but we did not expect them so quickly.

The total investment for construction and clinic furnishings totaled $250 thousand: not a small number by any means. Yet, with an annual healthcare spend of just under $5 million, which was rising at an unsustainable pace, the owners were willing to experiment. I reminded the owners regularly that when we were talking healthcare, we were not talking in one-thousand or ten-thousand-dollar increments—we were generally talking in one-hundred-thousand-dollar increments. Big investments could reap even bigger savings.

They realized that they could no longer continue to carry the heavy burden of the healthcare cost increases, and they were adamant about not doing what most employers had done the past 20 years, which was to pass a big share of the cost on to employees and their families. At Merrill Steel, the family owners did not view the employment relationship as just relating to the employee. When they hired someone, they viewed it as hiring the person's whole family, and providing exceptional healthcare is a great way to live out that philosophy.

We kicked off the grand opening of the Merrill Steel Family Clinic with a formal ceremony, covered by local news channels and attended by various community leaders. I spoke for a few minutes to explain the completed construction. I explained why an employer would have a need for an independent primary care clinic, and I expressed gratitude to the owners for supporting the initiative. The president and second-generation owner,

Roger Hinner Jr., used a cutting torch to cut a long piece of rebar steel that represented our version of a ribbon.

From the start, even prior to its opening, we were very intentional in promoting the new clinic in every way we could—making the clinic staff highly visible in employee meetings and offering opportunities for interactions. This included inviting them to our annual Christmas party and summer picnic, offering basic primary care visits in a conference room for a couple months before the clinic construction was completed (in response to employee requests), welcoming clinic staff to our free coffee bar and encouraging them to roam about the business so that they were visible and available.

Forward five months: the tenured CFO at Merrill Steel, Mike Klussendorf, walked into my office with a quizzical smile and shared what he had just learned in the first quarter financial review meeting. We had already achieved a return on our $250k investment!

We certainly had hoped for cost savings, but we did not expect them so quickly. As you might imagine, the owners were pleased, and gave me the proverbial nod to go forth with more healthcare innovations. Every new healthcare service or point solution we added, which were typically provided at no cost to members, redirected patients from the expensive pinball-machine referral methods of the large hospital systems to alternative high-quality, cost-effective care, each reaping new returns on investments. We were building the plane as we were flying it. We learned daily, and we admitted that there was much we didn't know. We kept asking questions that were difficult to answer.

The rewards we were delivering didn't feel like low-hanging fruit; it was more like we were tripping over fruit. Everywhere we looked there was opportunity. We were onto something.

Others Take Notice

Forward five years: we continued to learn and our plan was performing well. Our premiums were affordable (approximately $50 per month for a single individual and $160 per month for a family), employees were able to keep their Health Savings Accounts (HSAs), our deductibles were reasonable (HSA minimums), our low maximum out-of-pocket limits protected our members' financial stability, a host of new no-cost services were now available to members, and a revised wellness program was in place that enabled members to earn enough HSA dollars to more than cover their deductible. Overall, we had reversed the trend. Both the plan and participating members had saved millions of dollars by shaving significant non-value-added costs in areas of medical claims, pharmacy claims, workers' compensation and stop-loss insurance premiums. Things were going swimmingly.

Other employers in central Wisconsin began to take notice and get involved in the movement. They began participating in the healthcare best practice group sessions. Through the education and sharing of best practices offered within this group, many employers were inspired to begin their own healthcare improvement journeys. Central Wisconsin became the most active region for employers taking control of their health plans, even though it also had the fewest local independent providers.

As we progressed and employers around us also began to get in the game, my world began to change. Unexpectedly, I began to receive phone calls and emails from organizations, notifying me that I had been chosen for an award. The first was in 2019, when I was selected as the central Wisconsin SHRM HR Professional of the Year. In 2020, I was given The Alliance Healthcare Transformation Award. Also in 2020, I was given the National Employer/Purchaser Healthcare Excellence Award, an award that was previously won by Disney, Boeing, and Walmart. Later, after leaving Merrill Steel, I was selected for the Be the Beacon award by the Free Market Medical Association (FMMA).

Interesting things were happening in my personal life as well. My wife Denise and I serve as the champion foster parents for Marathon County, Wisconsin. In 2020, we were chosen to receive the Wisconsin Governor's Foster Parents of the Year Award. This was an amazing stretch of time in my life. I am humbled to have been recognized in so many ways and I am honored to be able to share my learnings with you. I see myself as a salt of the earth kind of guy—an Iowa farm boy with calloused hands, who stands up for what is right and is not afraid to try. People say, "There is nothing but corn in Iowa." However, I always tell them, "That is not true – we also have soybeans."

To not be afraid to try means we cannot be afraid to fail. The more times a person tries, logically, the more times he or she will fail. It goes with the territory. But with each fail, comes a lesson learned, and the more a person learns, the better chance the person will succeed on the next try, and the next try, and the next try. Thomas Edison failed 1,000 times before he found the best filament for the light bulb. The great physicist Niels Bohr wrote, "An expert is a person who has made all the mistakes that can be made in a narrow field."

In my acceptance speech for the Be the Beacon award in 2022, this same thought was on my mind. I shared my sentiments about the importance of trying. I said,

I saw a large mural once that was painted on a lobby wall of a successful family-owned company. It has been forever painted in my mind's visual. It said, "He who toils here hath left his mark". In college, I remember reading a research study that greatly impacted my view of life. The study involved residents who had been resigned to nursing homes – elderly men and woman who were aged and frail, living day to day, unable to do much living, more or less waiting to die. Researchers asked these elderly residents to reflect on their life and to share their biggest regret. What did they say? The theme of their answers was clear. They wished they would have taken more chances.

I can truly say that I have lived my life with this philosophy. If I make it to be old and frail, sitting in my rocking chair, I will probably have made many more mistakes than the average person but I will not have the regret that I played life so safely that I never got in the game. Whatever we do, we must try. Henry Ford said, "Whether you believe you can or you cannot, you're right."

For the past several years, I have gotten regular invites for speaking events and conference talks. Others ask to hear my story and my methods. They ask, "How did you do it?" Inquiring minds want to know. I've always been glad to share. It became apparent, over time, that the complexity of both the problems and the solutions have made this answer difficult to articulate. It's like, "Great question, what are you doing for the next four hours?" This was frustrating for me. I knew the answers to all the questions, and I was excited to share, but I felt overwhelmed with the notion that a lot of education would be required before I could discuss the solution. I felt like the mosquito that happened upon a nude beach. After taking a look around, one mosquito looked over to another and said, "I know what to do, I just don't know where to start!"

But after much reflection, research, and practice, I was able to successfully develop the concept of the Employer Healthcare Success Formula. This still involves a complex answer, but I believe it is the simplest and most efficient way to teach these concepts and equip an employer to redesign and reconstruct their health plan.

So what is this formula? Simply put, it is a template to follow; a detailed sequential journey map you can use as a guide to help you create your own healthcare success story. Through much experience, I can tell you this: if you are willing to put in the work to go through all the steps, and to endure the toils and spoils of a transformational journey, the stage is set for you to build something great. Problems can be opportunities in disguise: the greater the problem, the greater the opportunity to do good things.

The formula is shown below:

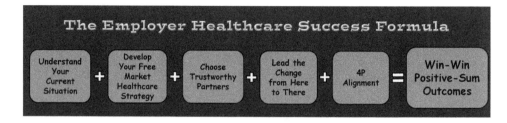

The Employer Healthcare Success Formula Overview

In the following sections, I provide an overview of the formula and action steps. In subsequent chapters, I'll break each of these down and do a deep dive into their details and inner workings. I believe each action step is critical to the overall success of the journey. It may be possible to work on several things at once, but the order of implementation is intentional and of empirical and practical relevance.

Understand Your Current Situation

In Chapter 3, I'll discuss a big-picture perspective of how and why employer healthcare is broken. Additionally, I'll provide education on a variety of important healthcare topics. These explanations are an amalgamation of textbook and real-life circumstances. Together, they will provide a sound framework with which to view the landscape; they'll enable you to begin to form a strategy for your specific situation, such as your region(s) of the country, the hospital systems in your area(s), the independent providers in your area(s), your employee population, the resources within your company, state-specific regulations, and so on. As we go, I encourage you to ask a lot of questions, search for the answers to those questions, and learn everything you can. Time spent on this step will pay off in big dividends later. Of all the action steps in the formula, this first one is probably the most important. All are critical for optimal health plan performance, but if this step is only partially completed, or it is skipped altogether, there is a good chance you will get off track before you even begin.

Let's talk for a minute about why this is so important. First, it's common for problem solvers to be overly anxious to grasp for solutions . . . as in, "Let's get things back to normal as fast as we can." This is a good motive, but it introduces risk. In rushing to fix a problem, the potential is great to diagnose a problem incorrectly, and if this happens, everything we do thereafter will be a lost cause. By analogy, if a doctor is rushed in an evaluation, and it leads to an incorrect diagnosis, it will result in misguided treatment, wasted time, excessive cost, and the patient's condition will persist.

Second, once we've diagnosed the problem correctly, it is critical we take the time to find the root cause. The basic approach to root cause analysis (RCA) is to keep asking "why" until we cannot ask why anymore (I have included a summary explanation of RCA in the appendix). If we do this correctly, we will find the root cause. If we stop asking "why" too soon, we end up identifying only a symptom of the problem, and if the resultant actions are focused on a symptom, the problem will return again and again and it will never be resolved. Aspirin can cover up a symptom (a headache, say), but we know that the reason or root cause of why someone has a headache is not "lack of aspirin". If a physician takes the time in this case to understand a person's eating habits, for example, she can gather important information. Let's say she suspects that the reason the person is having headaches is because of dehydration. The headache is the symptom, and she can make that go away temporarily with aspirin, but it will keep coming back. However, when she understands the situation fully and properly identifies the root cause, she can solve the problem for good! In this case, the root cause is dehydration and the solution is that the person needs to drink more water. Knowing the root cause, the solution often becomes obvious. This is a simple example. In healthcare we are dealing with some very complex problems, but the thinking and methods are the same.

Develop Your Free-Market Healthcare Strategy

In Chapter 4, we will discuss what an optimal free market for healthcare looks like, and how to develop your employer strategy. Many of the problems of our current broken healthcare system are related to a suppressed market. For the healthcare industry to function well, we must open this market back up. There must be clear visibility of cost and quality; the buyer must have freedom to shop for the best value; and there must be healthy competition of sellers to earn the buyers' business, including real-life consequences for poor service or high cost.

Choose Trustworthy Partners

In Chapter 5, we will discuss how to review and assess our healthcare partners and how to make sure that every healthcare partner going forward is trustworthy and acting in the employer's best interests. The hardest problems to solve are the ones that have been around a while. We get so accustomed to them that we no longer recognize them as problems. Consequently, we develop a "that's just the way it is" mindset. This has happened with employer healthcare, and specifically, with the partners employers work with to provide healthcare for their employees. When we begin to analyze each of an employer's healthcare partners, we find many gaps in trust and service, and we realize there are numerous excessive or unknown costs. Ultimately, we recognize a plethora of win-lose relationships, in which the employer's partners have won emphatically and the employer has lost—dramatically. As we open our eyes to the importance of trust, we see the world anew, and we can work toward assembling a team of winning partners.

Lead the Change from Here to There

In Chapter 6, we will discuss a deep-water topic: what is commonly called "change management." Like any significant organizational change an employer may choose to initiate, such as to implement lean manufacturing or to develop a new product or service line, the biggest predictor of success for a healthcare transformation is how well the change is led.

Experienced transformational leaders understand that the challenges with change are mostly cultural. That is, they are 80% people-related and 20% everything else. If the people willingly move into the change, everything else will fall into place. As you might have observed, employees today in companies are not all that excited about change. They work to provide, not necessarily to be inspired. They see change initiatives come and go, with little follow-through, often without good outcomes, and they begin to see leaders' attempts to drive change as "the flavor of the month." In these contexts, there is no need for an employee to buy in to the proposed change. It will only lead to frustration because it will fade away as fast as it arrived and there will be a new shiny sparkly thing next month to replace it.

Effective transformational leaders are different. They make change possible. They help people transition from an old place (here) to a new place (there) without the car stalling or the wheels falling off. This is not to say the wheels may not wobble for a time. In fact, wobbly wheels are unavoidable, in my opinion. On the way through a transformational process, experienced leaders know that things will never go perfectly and that people's willingness and ability to change varies greatly. We will use Roger's Adoption Curve to demonstrate this concept. Further, we will discuss what effective change management looks like and how you can be successful in the transformation of your healthcare plan, leading your team from here to there.

4P Alignment

In Chapter 7, we will discuss how your new healthcare ecosystem must be guided by a common playbook. I call this 4P alignment. This means, your:

- Partners
- Providers
- Patients

must all be completely aligned and work in concert with your:

- Playbook

This is incredibly important. Alignment is a good predictor of success. Strong alignment leads to great outcomes. Poor alignment leads to infighting, frustrated partners and providers and ultimately disjointed patient care.

Imagine a football team, with each coach and each individual player having his own playbook. The players might be incredibly talented and highly motivated, but if not well aligned, they will each have their own personal goals and their own ideas about how to play the game. Some players might want to run the ball; others might want to pass a majority of the time. For defense, some players might want to blitz every other play; and others might feel it is important to play conservatively and drop an extra safety back into coverage. A house divided against itself cannot stand. A few superstar players would likely have some good stats, but overall, the players would not be able to function well as a team and the team would lose most or all of their games.

If you intend things to run smoothly, your partners, providers, and patients must all be aligned and each must understand their respective contribution to the overall strategy. Each must play their part, day in and day out. They must realize that no one wins, unless everyone wins together.

Win-Win Positive-Sum Outcomes

If we understand and execute the first six parts of the formula well, we can expect to have sustainable, positive-sum outcomes. In Chapter 8, we will discuss what this looks like and how to monitor and steer the ship going forward, once the new strategy and partners are in place.

CHAPTER THREE
Understand Your Current Situation

My grandmother used to tell my grandfather that he had "Cadillac taste and a Chevy income." They have both passed now. That generation lived through the Great Depression and World War II and sacrificed much, and they also appreciated much. They loved their country, and they sure liked their luxury cars—the bigger the better. We are talking about the Cadillacs that looked 47 feet long, with tail fins and a trunk big enough to store a compact car. And the ride—well, the ride was incredible. You could hit a series of potholes and barely feel a thing. That's because, when they bought a Cadillac, it was reasonable to expect more features and greater luxury. We spend more, and we get more. It's a fair-value proposition.

A Low-Value Proposition

The value proposition presented by the healthcare industry today is not so reasonable. Many find it to be unfair and imbalanced: the services received do not match the amount that must be paid. This frustration is compounded by the patient not knowing what the doctor's orders will be, or how much each step of care they receive will cost, until after the hospital sends the bills.

While society may have gotten "used to" this imbalance in value proposition, or at least used to tolerating it, healthcare hasn't always been this way. As little as 20 to 30 years ago, care was available, affordable, patient-centered, and even though there was less medical research and technology available, there was more emphasis on patient relationships, and more attention given to natural remedies, such as vitamins, diet, and exercise. A lot gets missed when the variable of relationships is removed. In today's primary-care environment of rushed visits, the patient's desire to feel helped still remains, as does the doctor's intrinsic desire to offer help. Without proper time for dialogue and diagnosis, both can be inclined to accept quick fixes, incomplete treatment plans, or prescription medications that merely cover the symptoms and do not address the root cause of the malady.

"I'm afraid we've had to move him to expensive care."

The healthcare value proposition has steadily devolved to become a win-lose relationship between the sellers and buyers, with a multitude of players in the middle making a lot of money and adding questionable value. A win-lose relationship is never sustainable, because one of the mutual parties in a relationship cannot continue to "lose" forever. Game theory offers an interesting perspective on this. This theory posits that we can evaluate a negotiation by its outcome, which can be a negative sum, zero sum, or positive sum. Specifically, in the following table, we can associate a value of +1 to a "win" and -1 to a "lose." In the context of distributive bargaining, if one side wins, the other must lose. However, with integrative bargaining, shared wins are the goal.

In a two-party negotiation, we want the formula to be +1 + +1 = 2.

DISTRIBUTIVE BARGAINING			
Scenario	Formula	Summation	Outcome
Win - Lose	1 + -1	0	Zero Sum
Lose - Win	-1 + 1	0	Zero Sum
Lose - Lose	-1 + -1	-2	Negative Sum

INTEGRATIVE BARGAINING			
Scenario	Formula	Summation	Outcome
Win - Win	1 + 1	2	Positive Sum

In 2022, healthcare accounted for almost 20% of our nation's Gross Domestic Product (GDP), which is the highest in the world. We are getting a Chevy at a Cadillac price. It makes me want to grab a megaphone, jump on an oak tree stump, and proclaim to our great country, *"Have we forgotten our foundations? This is America . . . we are different than this . . . resourceful, free, innovative dreamers."* The industry should be striving to offer a Cadillac at a Chevy price, not to "steal the American dream," as health-care thinker Dave Chase puts it.

Self-Guided Education

In my initial learning stage at Merrill Steel, I was like a sponge. I knew I had a lot to learn and I took a "best practice" mindset. I needed a book to learn about how an employer could improve their health plan, and I wanted it to be written from the employer's perspective. I searched on Amazon, I visited local bookstores, and I talked to anyone I thought might know of one. To my surprise, I discovered that published books on this topic are almost nonexistent. I was able to find only one book. This is not what I expected. Nearly every employer is struggling, and only one book has addressed this—uno libro? Ein Buch? Un livre? It was written by John Torinus, owner of Serigraph, a company headquartered in West Bend, Wisconsin. At that time, I never would have imagined that seven years later I'd be writing the second one.

If you're interested in learning more, I recommend the following books. These are the ones that helped me the most. The authors are paladins in the industry and have had great influence in raising awareness of the problems and helping others to fix them.

- *The Company That Solved Health Care: How Serigraph Dramatically Reduced Skyrocketing Costs While Providing Better Care, and How Every Company Can Do the Same*, by John Torinus Jr.
- *The Price We Pay: What Broke American Health Care--and How to Fix It*, by Marty Makary
- *The CEO's Guide to Restoring the American Dream: How to Deliver World Class Healthcare to Your Employees at Half the Cost*, by Dave Chase

To supplement these readings, I talked with all the experts I could find who were willing to talk with me. I realized that many of these people were brokers who were trying to win my account, and I was open with them that I was not shopping for a new broker (that realization would come later). I learned a lot and made some good friends in the process.

Let's begin to dig in and break down the problems that have caused employer health plans to steadily decline. We can do this by discussing each perspective of the dichotomy, of how healthcare is both unintentionally and intentionally broken.

Healthcare Is Unintentionally Broken

Several years ago, I met with a few top-level hospital administrators from a large hospital system for a breakfast discussion at a Cracker Barrel restaurant. I represented the company, and my request for them would be to begin offering bundled surgery prices. I knew this was a big ask, but Cracker Barrel is one of my favorite places to eat, so I had nothing to lose! If you are not familiar, a *bundle* is a group of healthcare services packaged together, such as for a hip replacement surgery. Instead of billing for the anesthesiologist, surgeon, and facility separately, a bundle groups these costs into one set price that is known to the buyer before the procedure takes place. Imagine if that were the norm in healthcare!

They politely listened to my request and did not respond with an immediate answer. They would discuss it internally and get back with me.

I wasn't holding my breath, but I was hopeful they would be open to the idea, even if it meant starting small with a single procedure. I knew if any hospital system would consider it, they would be the one, because so far this particular hospital system had been great to work with.

About three weeks later, I received an email response from one of the administrators. It was almost a full-page explanation on how they would unfortunately be "unable" to bundle their prices for surgeries. I remember seeing the email come in and opening it with anticipation. Their professed inability was frustrating for me to read. I knew that surgical bundling was possible and was already being done, by organizations like the Surgery Center of Oklahoma. Moreover, I knew that surgeries are broken down into three or four parts–surgeon fee, anesthesiologist fee, facility fee, and sometimes additional hardware. I wanted to write them back and say, "You bill for these things separately–can you not add the numbers together and share the total as a single price bundle?" I chose to bite my tongue. I responded with a brief note to thank them for hearing my request and my hope that we could continue to discuss the topic.

This was an uninspiring outcome. There was no indication they would find a way, they would not discuss it further, nor would they commit to future discussions. The question was answered and the case was closed. "Da-dunk": the judge had pounded the gavel. Disappointed, I got back to work implementing other pieces of our strategy.

By sharing this story, I do not mean to imply that I believe the hospital administrators were lying to me. I believe they were being genuine in their response. I say this because I have been told by various hospital administrators across different states that they literally do not know their own costs for services or procedures. Although it seems unacceptable, this appears to be the norm. I have also heard first-hand from hospital administrators that there is a great deal of industry peer pressure, and if a single hospital begins to break the mold, such as to bundle, share prices, or break away from the network mentality, there can be repercussions from their peers or others in the industry. That's not exactly a free market approach. Frankly, it sounds more like the Mafia: "I'll make you an offer you can't refuse." This gives us an idea of why a hospital CEO would be unwilling to risk business or career stability to do what is right.

Here's where the story gets interesting. Two years later, I was having a casual telephone conversation with one of the hospital administrators I had talked with two years prior. She asked how things were going. With no conscious intent to influence, I casually mentioned that we had begun offering patients the option to travel to Oklahoma to utilize the Surgery Center of

Oklahoma. In fact, in the first couple of months we began offering surgeries at SCO as an option in our plan (patient and a companion could choose SCO at $0 net cost with all travel costs covered), three members chose to go there for a hip replacement surgery. Due to the high costs these members would have incurred under the old plan from local providers (previously their only option), they had been putting off the surgery for years and were "living with the pain." The total bundled price for this surgery at SCO was just under $16,000. Locally, in Wisconsin, this same surgery was known to cost anywhere from $60,000 to $80,000 (estimated by adding various post-surgery bills).

Milestones

I will never forget the hospital administrator's response. She said, enthusiastically, "Oh, we'll bundle." I almost fell out of my chair. Say what? Honestly, I was not expecting to hear that. I was inspired. My needle for "impression of humanity" moved a little higher that moment. Throughout our lives, there are "milestone moments" that take place. We all have them. In the 1994 film *With Honors*, the character played by Joe Pesci would pick up a small stone every time a significant moment happened in his life. He would place the stone in a little cloth bag he carried in his pocket. On occasion, he would pour all of them into his hand and recall the specific moment (and emotion) each "milestone" represented. I don't have a bag of stones in my pocket, but I do have some interesting memories. These milestone moments happen unexpectedly and can be good or bad experiences. They stick in our memories and shape future life decisions. This was one of those moments for me. You may also now understand how easily entertained I am.

By being willing to request a meeting and ask a question that had a low probability of getting a "yes" response, I created a spark that would later allow me to achieve a milestone with a large hospital. Thereafter, they kept their word and followed through with their commitment to offer bundled prices for surgeries.

Sometimes it's worth asking a question for which we already know the answer. If I had never made the request . . . if I had never brought up this topic in that Cracker Barrel restaurant, it would not have been on their minds. If it had not been on their minds, they would never have discussed it internally. During those couple of years, they apparently changed their capabilities to be "able" to do it, and they stuck it in their back pocket. It doesn't appear they planned to initiate it, but they were prepared to react if needed. Ultimately, when they learned I was shopping elsewhere, which would impact their revenue, it spurred them into action.

This example highlights how hospitals view the buyer-seller relationship, and furthermore, how different the health industry's thinking is as compared with the typical free-market-minded retail, manufacturing, or other service sector. We will talk about this more in Chapter 4 when we discuss the importance of adopting a free-market mindset and developing a strategy.

They ~~Won't~~ Will Go

I have been told by healthcare experts—those with a vast amount of knowledge, who have spent their entire careers in the industry—that patients will not travel for medical procedures, even a couple of hours. I brought this up in a local employer coalition group meeting once. We were talking about how healthcare prices were too high and how the local hospitals weren't playing nice with the other kids in the sandbox. I said, "We [as in all local employers in central Wisconsin] are paying over $60,000 for joint replacements and the same surgeries are available for $25,000 in Green Bay, less than two hours away." The gentleman who was facilitating the discussion had probably forgotten more about healthcare than I will ever know. He smiled and said, "While I appreciate your enthusiasm, the fact of the matter is that it's too inconvenient. No one will make the drive, even if the procedure is made free or is incentivized. People are only interested in local care." What he didn't realize is that I had just added the Surgery Center of Oklahoma as an option within my employer's plan. I responded, "Well, I have people flying to Oklahoma for hip replacements." The room got quiet. It was a little awkward. I did not say any more. I knew the truth and I was not there to argue.

The rest of the day, I scratched my head and truly did not understand. Why was he so adamantly opposed to new ideas? And why was he willing to throw away over $35,000, so that no one would be "inconvenienced"? I suppose many people just aren't able to believe that things can be better or they are not prepared to do the hard work to lead transformational change. In your travels, I am sure you have or will come across individuals like this. No matter how great the solution, they cannot see the light and they seem to wet-blanket every idea before it has a chance to succeed. Albert Einstein once said, "Some people have a problem for every solution." Show respect to these people, but don't waste your time with them. They either have conflicts of interest at hand or they aren't able to believe. Either way, they will slow your roll—if you let them.

I can tell you from experience, his statement that people would be unwilling to travel couldn't have been more wrong. Time and time again,

I see real-life proof that cost does matter, and patients will travel—not by requirement, but by choice—if your plan design makes it possible.

The prerequisite to successful plan design-based steerage is a lot of communication and education on how the plan works. Members do not have to be coerced or pushed. If the quality of care is the same or better and more options can be provided at no cost to them, they will go. Trust me, they will go. I can't imagine the inconvenience our first hip replacement patients went through to travel to Oklahoma, considering they were required to find a travel companion (travel costs for both were covered by the company), travel about 1,400 miles round-trip on a commercial airplane (we did put them in first class), and bear the inconveniences and discomfort of commercial airport navigation through a terminal, particularly on the return trip with a freshly installed hip joint. But they did. They were given an option that offered financial protection, while receiving a high-quality surgery to restore and revive their standard of living.

Poor Service ≠ Lost Customers

In a free-market environment, not giving customers what they need or want results in lost customers, and eventually, if uncorrected, it leads to no customers. By contrast, in a suppressed market, being unresponsive to customer needs has no consequence, because there is nowhere else to go. It was only when I voiced a natural consequence to the hospital—I was shopping elsewhere (because I had somewhere else to go)—that I got their attention. Without such a natural consequence, I suppose it can begin to feel very normal for a hospital to think that raising top-line sales is the only way to combat inflation or to increase profits, while completely forgetting about their opportunities and obligations to reduce bottom-line expenses. They are left with the impression that things will just "work out," and when necessary, they will raise their prices . . . and no one should question it, as if it is immoral or superficial for someone to scrutinize cost in healthcare. Contrary to the way all other industries operate, some hospitals seem to feel as if they are entitled to patronage. Mix this with an ample supply (a line of sick patients), combined with restrictive networks, and the buyers are the ones who end up paying for all of the dysfunction. Jay Kempton, owner of Kempton Group Administrators in Oklahoma, states, "In no other industry but healthcare are the seller's inefficiencies made to be the buyer's problem."

This example is a reflection of the mindset that a suppressed healthcare market creates. Specifically, this faulty mindset stains everyone's thinking and it affects everyday decisions—big or small. As I have gained more experience,

I have realized how important decisions are. They ultimately shape our life and our future. All too frequently, it seems, hospitals make "not so good" decisions and thereafter, everyone is surprised when things don't go well. Ineffective problem-solving leads to fighting the same fires day after day and one never really catches up. Our family recently got a new puppy—a Golden Doodle named Oliver, or Ollie for short. He is very playful and if he gets a glimpse of his tail, he will go after it, spinning in circles. He never actually catches that tail, but he keeps trying, spinning faster and faster— as if that would help. He is soft, cuddly, and cute. As human adults, we don't look so cute when we chase our tails.

An especially interesting example of this is a growing trend in which hospitals charge for patient/provider interaction outside of the visit. One involved a hospital in Wisconsin. The story was published in local newspapers and it was televised on the evening news. The hospital decided to make a change to their chargemaster. They shared their concern that messages sent by patients to their providers through their online portal had doubled since Covid and it was creating an overburden of administrative work for their providers. Their solution was to add a new charge of $36 - $70 (per message) when patients sent online questions about new prescriptions, prescription changes, or changes to check-ups or long-term care outside of the appointed visit.

Because we are not privy to the specific internal workings of the hospital, nor are we privy to the problem-solving discussions that took place within the hospital walls, we do not know the details of their reasoning. There is value, however, in analyzing this scenario with a hypothetical lens in the context of problem-solving and decision-making.

We might speculate that perhaps the hospital perceived the increase in online communications to be from "high-maintenance" patients, who were wasting the providers' time with excessive or unreasonable requests. The stated solution appears to be an attempt by the hospital to at least be compensated for the higher demand for the providers' time. If this is the case, we might ask: if high-maintenance patients are the problem, what percentage of the total messages are from high-maintenance patients? If these instances are only the exception and not the rule, they risk penalizing the majority of patients for issues that only involve a few people.

Another question is, what effect will this new charge have on patient/provider communication and ultimately, on patient health? We know patients and plans are already having a difficult time affording healthcare, and patient interaction with their providers is already limited. Now, with the patient having to pay for answers to online questions, patient communication and relationship with their provider will likely be reduced. Would the hospital consider a reduced level of communication between the provider and patient a success? Lastly, with the additional money received, will they add additional resources to step in and help providers respond to the increased online questions? If they will, they will have added cost. If they will not, they have not touched the problem they attempted to solve in the first place—provider overburden. It appears a better solution to this problem would be to utilize lean techniques.

Be Lean, Not Mean

By adopting a lean mindset, hospitals could prevent having to take more and more steps backward. Lean methods are more often utilized in manufacturing, but can be equally beneficial in all industries. McDonalds is a good example of a nonmanufacturing company that has implemented lean tools for high efficiency and first-time quality. Their cash registers, for instance, don't have the traditional keys. They were among the first to do this—many years ago. Their registers are equipped with digital touch screens, with pictures and symbols. This makes training much easier and it reduces the chance of incorrect orders. While I am not sure their food is, well . . . actual food, one has to give them credit for how well they have streamlined their processes. ThedaCare Hospital in Appleton, Wisconsin did some work with lean process design many years ago and anecdotal stories revealed some amazing successes. With changes in leadership, it is my understanding they are no longer on this path, but it would be great if more hospitals would consider it.

One reality we need to acknowledge with most hospitals is that there are mountains of non-value-added waste within those big castle walls. One former executive told me that it is not uncommon for hospitals to have "floors of people" for whom no one understands what they do. Such a statement would be ludicrous in the highly competitive manufacturing industry, where the competition fights for single percentages and pennies of cost for each component.

Lean thinking is particularly concerned with time, and whether time is well spent by everyone in a given process or overall organization. A common technique in lean is to analyze every step in a process and categorize it. This can be done with a smaller scope, such as using a job breakdown sheet for a single process, and it can be done with a larger scope, such as using a value stream map to understand a complete supply chain.

Let's take the example of the hospital making a policy change to charge patients for online communications. A better option would be to utilize a lean practitioner to do an analysis of a provider's time. This could focus on one visit, or it could be expanded, to look at a full week. The thinking is the same. The observer would record every step and action and the amount of time it takes the person to complete them. This is typically measured down to the second. It may seem a little anal, but in large operations, such as auto manufacturing plants or large hospitals, shaving 30 seconds off a single process can amount to millions of dollars in a year.

Once all the actions are observed and the associated time it took to perform those actions is documented, the next step is to categorize each action into three categories: value added, non-value added, and non-value added but necessary. With this approach, we are primarily interested in identifying non-value added actions, so that we may reduce or eliminate them. In doing so, we can effectively free up a lot of time for incumbents and we are able to make their job easier, without losing any substance. When someone goes through such an activity for the first time, they are shocked to learn how much of their time is spent doing things that don't add value. Sometimes as much as 30% to 50% of a person's time in a day can be freed up to put toward other value-added activities. We are eliminating what lean calls "Muda waste." This would enable providers to be more efficient, it would allow them greater fulfillment in their life's work, and patients would receive more streamlined and affordable care. A hospital's goal should be to focus on how to reduce cost, not on creative new ways to charge more (that still don't fix the problem).

It is not my intention to imply that the hospital was intentionally lowering the level of care. They were likely just trying to cover their costs. The problem is that the patients, time after time, are the ones holding the bill and paying the price.

Regarding efficiency, a common misunderstanding is that cutting cost is equated with lowering quality. The opposite is actually true. Increasing quality

> Regarding efficiency, a common misunderstanding is that cutting cost is equated with lowering quality.

leads to greater efficiency. Lean professionals understand this. Lean methods identify and cut out the steps that add little or no value, and keep the ones that do, streamlining the process and making it easier to execute more accurately and consistently. Quality, the first time, is the goal to prevent the error of "We don't have time to do it right, but we have time to do it over." The outcome is a well-oiled machine that requires less elbow grease and ultimately, less resources and time to operate.

Another example that often creates more problems than it solves is widespread layoffs. When organizations make these cuts, without lean knowledge or methods in place, much gets missed. If tasks were not analyzed to take out the non-value-added steps, who will do the work these people were doing and what will get missed?

To help explain this concept of value-added versus non-value-added, I'll share a simple example to which most of us can likely relate. Let's say that you decide to clean out your garage. It's been filling up, and there's no room to park your car. You could take one of two approaches. You could say, everything on the left side of the garage must go. You rent a dumpster and make it happen. Then you cry in your beer because you have to repurchase many of the things you threw away. The other, wiser approach would be to sort out which tools and equipment are still useful and which ones you no longer use. You get rid of the antiquated or broken tools that are no longer needed and keep the ones that still add value. With this approach, you meet your goal of making room for your car, and you still have the proper tools needed to maintain your home. You have cut waste, but you haven't lost any function or effectiveness.

One of my dreams is to be the CEO of a hospital – not because leading a hospital is my dream, but because the position would give me the authority and leadership platform to lead a transformational change. While I believe it would be incredibly challenging, I believe it could be an amazing story.

By transformational change, I am talking about utilizing the full package of techniques, philosophies, leadership, and methods that make up the Toyota Production System (TPS). This is the system I learned while working for a Toyota supplier and then directly for Toyota Motor Manufacturing early in my career. Candidly, I would salivate at the chance to join or even just observe a small team of superstar lean experts, such as Michael Hoseus or Jeffrey Liker (assuming they would be interested), doing what they do best. With the proper support and authority, the stories of continuous improvement in S, Q, D, C, M (Safety, Quality, Delivery, Cost, and Morale) would be astounding, and the overall performance of the hospital in all meaningful areas would improve dramatically. If you don't yet know a lot about lean concepts or lean transformations, my guess is you are doubting this statement. That's ok. I did too before I saw it first-hand. A good example of one of these stories was when Toyota first entered the American auto market. They had a joint venture with GM. I won't expound on it here, but you can search for stories or books on "NUMMI" and learn about it if you are interested. It is an incredible, very true story.

TPS lean experts can walk into manufacturing plants—operations that have been scrutinized daily for optimal quality and efficiency down to the second, and help them make dramatic improvements. Imagine hospital systems, institutions that have never had this pressure to survive in a free market, discovering how much better they could serve their respective communities. Sadly, instead of exploring or engaging in this kind of improvement discussion, they have let insurance companies influence them to raise their prices, as if that was the only option. The outcomes of lean analysis would be almost unimaginable. I realize those in the healthcare industry would not likely understand or agree with my statements, and I will not likely ever get such an opportunity, but one can dream.

Healthcare Is Intentionally Broken

Let's delve into the discussion of how healthcare is intentionally broken. It is important we acknowledge and understand the entirety of the healthcare industry landscape, so that we will be able to navigate effectively. The reality is that thus far, this movement has only been a blip on a few employers' radar. However, as more and more learn and join the movement, it will certainly get the industry's attention. When it does, it is my hope that it encourages healthy free market behaviors by all and that the rising tide will raise all ships.

A fellow author and healthcare podcaster, Ron Barshop, makes the statement, "Healthcare is fixed." His statement is a double entendre. And it is no secret that the problems of healthcare are certainly not fixed, as in made better. For buyers, healthcare is broken in many ways. Conversely, healthcare is fixed, as in "intentionally broken" by the industry. They have created a business economy to suppress the free market's potential. For them, things are working just as they were designed.

At a macro level, we are talking about a national problem that will affect current and future generations. Healthcare makes up one-fifth of our economy; in a sense, how healthcare goes in the next couple of decades so will the future of our great country. Imagine the money we could free up that could be reallocated to other needs. This amounts to billions and trillions of dollars.

At a micro level, each employer has the ability to shape their health plan. I am close with leaders at a few public schools in Wisconsin who have led their own healthcare improvement stories, and by saving millions on wasted expense in healthcare, they were able to retain valuable programs that were previously at risk, add new programs, and even build new buildings. Many families and communities have benefitted from their courageous work.

Collectively we have the opportunity to ensure future generations can experience the same prosperity and quality of life that we have enjoyed.

Let's talk about the current status quo in the design of healthcare. We will discuss what is happening, and also which part each of the participants play. As we shine light on the problems, it may be uncomfortable. It's important to remember that we cannot solve problems by hiding or ignoring them. If a detective intends to solve a case, he or she must investigate the crime scene, no matter how grisly. Similarly, to be effective in redesigning a health plan, we must do the same. We must be willing to see things as they really are. Denial is not just a river in Egypt.

The Core Problem

To understand the primary motivations of the industry, follow the money. Willie Sutton, a famous criminal in the 1930s, was once asked, "Why do you rob banks?" He replied, "Because that's where the money is." The healthcare industry's strategy is to limit the buyer's ability to effectively shop by building a one-lane highway to themselves. Buyers include any employer, employee, taxpayer, or institution who pays for healthcare. In the context of this book, we focus on the commercial side, the employee and employer.

The healthcare industry restricts shopping in two ways:

1. Buyers have no visibility of cost or quality. Cost is not known until the coded, piecemeal bills are received. Quality of outcomes is somewhat random; whether the assigned physician was the best or worst in his or her class, both are called "doctor."
2. Buyers are contractually restricted to shop in exclusive networks. Providers readily turn away patients, with an uncanny lack of remorse, when the insurance card indicates they are not "in-network." Patients are left powerless.

This design effectively means "No Shopping Allowed." Shopping is not a novel concept. We are able to shop effectively by evaluating value (cost and quality) for *everything* else: new cars or used cars, haircuts, plumbers, mechanics, groceries, plane tickets, restaurants, gas or televisions. When I buy electronics, I survey the landscape for cost and quality, and often find myself making the purchase at Best Buy. The concept of shopping is built into their name. It implies the greatest value for your money.

The industry's business model is a good one, I suppose—for the seller(s). Imagine owning a business in which everyone was required to shop at your store, you got to bill them afterward for an amount you choose, and if they don't pay promptly, you have grounds to garnish their wages and place a lien on their home. Such a model wouldn't last, but it would be very profitable.

The following diagram represents the current state of healthcare for the majority of employers. Notice there are no intersections or exits on the roads that lead to other sellers.

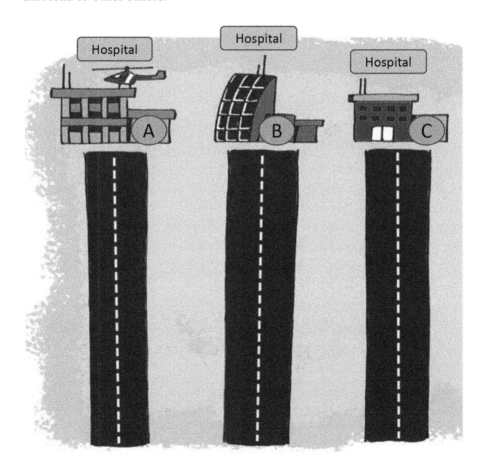

Let's make this a little more relatable. Imagine a scenario in which you were required to utilize one plumbing service. There are many plumbing services in town, but it has been announced that you will now be required to use A1 Plumbing exclusively. Your homeowners' association graciously arranged this structure to "help you" get the "best discounts possible." To do their part, the plumbing companies offered a 20% discount to be a part of this. By choosing a select group of plumbers, for the sake of all members, the homeowners' association also agreed to accept a 5% commission on total billings. Specifically, they divided your neighborhood into four sectors and they signed exclusive contracts with four respective plumbing services to cover each.

Here's the question: In the long term, how would this likely affect each plumbing company's service level, knowing that that even if you are dissatisfied with the quality of their work or their prices, you would still be required to use your same designated plumbing company for all of your plumbing needs? We might suppose a few plumbers would do the right thing by continuing to perform high-quality work at a fair price. However, human nature tells us that a majority would take advantage of your inability to walk away or call another plumber. For the four plumbing services, the level of service would inevitably decrease and their collective rates would increase—at their discretion. There would be no mechanisms in place to stop the trend. Over time, most of the honest plumbers would raise their prices, in order to be competitive at the "market price." This has happened with healthcare. There can be no pseudo free markets.

All Aboard the Healthcare Gravy Train Express!

I've discussed some of the themes and dynamics of the "what." Let's delve into the "who." While I try to keep them somewhat distinct, the who and the what are inherently interconnected.

As we begin to understand who's who in the healthcare industry, we will see the effect of a monopoly-like atmosphere. In particular, we will see the types of power that each of the players have. Analyzing power dynamics will enable us to understand the problems at a deeper level and it will enable you to counter more effectively with your own strategy. I must admit, it feels a little disconcerting that there is a need for the buyers of healthcare to have a "counter-strategy"—that we must guard against the attempted oppression of communities and families from those that we simultaneously trust to care for our health and well-being.

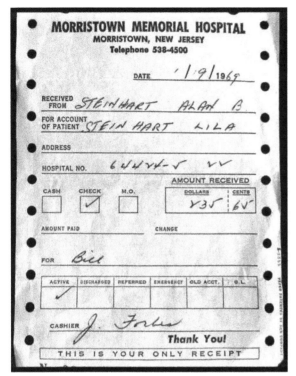

If you were born before 1980, you probably realize that things haven't always been like this. Getting care at a hospital used be affordable, and the bills were simple and understandable, like ones one would receive from a small-town mechanic. This receipt from 1969 for services to deliver a baby was for a handwritten total of $235.65. This one was for a guy named Bill, and they didn't even note his last name. I miss the trust and informality of the "old days."

It feels like our society in general has devalued the virtues of trust and compassion and that many no longer place a high emphasis on relationships, as did previous generations. Today, we may have grave questions as to who we can trust. Fool me once, shame on you. Fool me twice, shame on me. John Torinus, owner of Serigraph, shares, "Some live by a different golden rule—he who has the gold, makes all the rules."

Our Human Nature

During the time Abraham Lincoln lived in Springfield, Illinois, he had a neighbor named Roland Diller. Roland tells a story:

> I was called to the door one day by the cries of children in the street, and there was Mr. Lincoln, striding by with two of his boys, both of whom were wailing aloud. "Why, Mr. Lincoln, what's the matter with the boys?" I asked. "Just what's the matter with the whole world," Lincoln replied. "I've got three walnuts, and each wants two."

Unfortunately, we all have an inherent nature that we must temper and scrupulously guard against. Starting in our youth, every living, breathing person has the potential to be all the things that a well-functioning society despises. If anyone claims to walk above this, the only explanation is that the person is not fully self-aware. Humility helps us see things accurately and arrogance blinds us. We must first choose to be humble to avoid looking foolish. Aldous Huxley said it well: "There is no such thing as a conscious hypocrite."

In 1945, George Orwell wrote a book in which he made this point. He titled it *Animal Farm*. It is a beast fable, a fictional allegory about human nature. Orwell tells a satirical story of barnyard animals who got fed up with an uncaring, tyrannical farmer, until one day the animals decided to take over the farm—so that they could create a fair and equitable society for all animals to be equal, free, and happy. In the story, the animals are able to talk, of course. They devise a plan and are able to successfully run off the farmer and take over control of the farm. Two pigs are the smartest, and they become the leaders. Under their leadership, things go very well – for a while, until corruption bleeds in and eventually, the pigs proclaim, "Everyone is created equal; some are just a little more equal." From there, as you might imagine, things get progressively worse and the newly formed society (the one that was once the reformation of tyranny) is no better than the original. It is a quick and worthy read and it offers a valuable lesson on human nature.

The healthcare industry is now replete with organizations that were once missionally minded, with great cause and virtue of community, who have fallen subservient to despotism. The industry is not alone in going animal farm. It has happened to governments, businesses, charities, and individuals alike. In 1963, the Bronx Zoo had an exhibit called, *"The Most Dangerous Animal in the World."* The title was written on the framed border, and in the center of the exhibit was nothing more than a mirror.

Marty Makary, a great writer on the business of medicine, shares a story of how he reviewed a variety of hospitals' websites. Each website stated their mission, which included their love for the community and how they provide care for those who can't afford it. He would then talk with their CEO, and raise questions about why they had initiated so many lawsuits against patients. Thereafter, he would review the hospital's website again, and found that their mission or charity statement had been changed.

As organizations change from one leader to the next, important pieces of the values and mission can be lost. The original values and mission statements remain public on websites and in other documents, but in many cases, they no longer match the behaviors of the people in the organization. This happened to Enron Corporation in their famous fall. One of their original stated values was "integrity." I had a mentor once who would tell me, "Matt, that paper will lay still for anything you want to write on it." Having a printed values statement on paper does not mean it is being lived out. That intentional and laborious part is up to us.

Amidst the brokenness and financial despair of the buyers, for the folks on board the healthcare gravy train, it's a prosperous ride. It's understandable, if not acceptable, that they would have no interest in changing tracks or doing anything other than protecting and preserving the status quo they have built. Sometimes the industry will make it appear as if they are interested in new ways of doing things, such as through cost control initiatives or community programs. It is common to see commercials on television that create an impression of benevolence, supported by vast marketing campaigns that are intended to create an image of community, caring, and trust. Unfortunately, with many industry participants, these are words spoken but not words lived out. Such initiatives can be a façade, a faceplate standup without anything behind it. Whistleblowers such as Wendall Potter have spoken out and published books, sharing how the industry uses sophisticated public relations and lobbying efforts to shape policymakers' decisions and public perceptions. As Potter shares, "If you are among those who believe that the U.S. has the best healthcare system in the world – despite overwhelming evidence to the contrary – it's because my fellow spinmeisters and I succeeded brilliantly at what we were paid very well to do with your premium dollars."

Who is the Beast?

Who exactly is the beast? The beast analogy is not meant to include all hospitals, all insurance carriers, or the industry as a whole. In the context of this book, the beast represents individuals or entities who have lost their way. The beast is most visible when we see behaviors that are self-serving and solely profit-oriented, instead of ones that lead to shared-win outcomes. "Beast-like behaviors" include greed, selfishness, oppression, monopolism, merciless and excessive lawsuits that garnish wages or place liens on homes, nonprofit entities failing to give substantive charitable care, and ultimately, a mindset of profits over patients.

When healthcare organizations lose their virtue, they become a beast that devours everything in their path. Everyone needs healthcare at some point, the demand is always there. They follow the golden rule John Torinus speaks of—not the one we all learned about growing up: *Do unto others as you would have them do unto you.*" In war, a scorched-earth strategy burns and destroys all in its path, to gather all resources and leave nothing behind. Perhaps the beast-like CEOs of these nonprofit hospitals should go to Wall Street, where many think like this. They could fight it out to their heart's content. Nonprofit healthcare, or healthcare in general, is not the place for a scorched-earth policy. It is a place for trust, empathy, sacrifice, and selfless leadership.

Hospital Systems and Monopolies: It's No Game

In our current structure, hospitals are the primary entities who provide healthcare for American families. Just a few decades ago, it was not uncommon for hospitals to lose money, and to utilize private donations to stay in the black. Today, we see a pattern of acquisitions and mergers between hospitals and many hospitals are eager and willing to buy private practices, particularly if they see them as competition. Despite the news headlines that say how beneficial these ventures are for the community, they are almost never a good thing. Hospital acquisition and consolidation shrinks an already disparate market of medical care choices, and it has an unfavorable effect on the buyers of healthcare and their ability to shop.

Henry Ford once said, "If I could have a monopoly on the service, I would give away the cars for free." The touted positive effects of hospital consolidation include things like improved care coordination, reduced operating costs of up to 30%, increased access to clinics, reduced administrative costs, and improved integration of management. The actual effects of hospital consolidation are not so inspiring. They include things like increased hospital prices of up to 10% or more, reduced competition, increased overhead costs, and less options for healthcare consumers.

While there are a few hospitals across the nation that do things better, they have become the exception. About 3,300 hospitals, out of about 5,000 total, file as nonprofits. If you examine their behaviors related to executive bonuses and lawsuits for collections and garnishments, the tax-exempt "nonprofit" ones appear to be more focused on profit than their for-profit counterparts. Nonprofit entities pay no taxes—no income taxes, no property taxes, and no sales taxes. This tax break is supposed to be in exchange for charity care for low-income people. More accountability is needed for hospitals to keep their nonprofit tax status.

The Fake Price Game

As we look deeper, we see that hospitals and insurance play a game with prices. Various industry executives I have talked with acknowledge this game, and they have shared their distaste for it. I believe many others feel the same. Yet, if this is true, where are the transformational leaders who will change it? Good people don't stand idle and watch others suffer. Is there such a disconnect between those who run things and the circumstances of the middle and lower economic classes that no one cares anymore? Who will show courage and lead change to restore the public trust?

Another topic often discussed is that hospitals are unwilling to share their prices. Price transparency is the most commonly mentioned solution to fix healthcare, and it is a legitimate part of this effort. However, what good is a shared price if it is not bundled? We don't buy a vacuum cleaner as a parts list, nor do we buy a car that way. Surprisingly, hospital systems have taken intentional and public legal actions to keep prices hidden. The American Hospital Association (AHA) and the American Medical Association (AMA) both sued the federal government over a provision in the No Surprises Act, legislation that was meant to increase price transparency. Further, the AHA and other hospital groups filed a lawsuit to stop the transparency rule requiring hospitals to disclose negotiated rates with insurers. To this day, we see many hospitals not posting their prices online, in opposition to what is now the law of the land, or we see them posting data that is very difficult to read or is unclear. Are we then supposed to trust them to care for our physical health?

"I'm afraid we couldn't stop the billing."

Recently, I was supporting a patient who needed a procedure at a local hospital. We had searched for an independent provider, but could not find one. I advised her that she could request that the hospital provide a "good faith estimate," per federal law. She thanked me and about a week later, she responded that the hospital was not willing to share the price. Section

112 of the No Surprises Act states that individual healthcare providers and facilities must provide a "good faith estimate" of the total expected charges to the patient's plan or insurer (if the patient is insured and using his or her coverage) or directly to the uninsured or self-pay patient, upon request or scheduling of a service.

Regarding patients who receive exorbitant medical bills, a colleague once told me that he had conducted some research a few years ago. He reviewed the public court records docket and found that one local hospital system filed hundreds of lawsuits against patients (community residents) in a period of 90 days. Further, a recent study conducted showed that hospital lawsuits over unpaid bills increased by 37% in Wisconsin from 2001 to 2018, indicating this issue is getting worse, not better.

I want to believe the majority of hospital systems still have good intent. Yet, if actions speak louder than words, are these actions consistent with the law-abiding, benevolent image that hospitals present on their websites, or are these actions intended to keep prices secret so that healthcare consumers cannot compare prices? I continue to be hopeful that things will change. Until then, I recognize a beast, one that appears to care more about money than the communities of people they were created to serve.

Let's talk through a hypothetical example of buying a car to bring some of these issues to light. Your car, which was parked on the street in front of your house, was hit by a truck that was passing by. You are now in need of a new car. You go to the local car lot and you are surprised to see that the prices are not marked and there are no window stickers. You ask the salesperson and she clarifies how it works—you meet with a specialist and they conduct a 15-minute interview to determine which car you need. Next, you drive the car home, and in a couple months, you will be sent the bills. You think to yourself, that sounds familiar, but you play along. You need to get to work somehow. You sign the papers and drive the car home.

A couple months later the bills arrive. You find that the pricing is so difficult to understand (it's coded as a parts list) that one would have to be a certified mechanic to make sense of it. If you are from my generation, you have probably misplaced your Tony the Tiger decoder ring, so you are left with many details you do not understand. You see a long list of charges for things like upper and lower control arms, drive shaft, wiring harness, cam sensor, wheel bearings, and mirror heater. You see service charges for shipping, delivery, setting the clock on the car, recycling the air in the tires, and filling the wiper fluid reservoir. The total for the car comes to $162,853. Thankfully, that is not the real price, but you do not know that yet. You panic and call the dealership. You have insurance coverage, but not for anything close to that amount. You finally are able to reach a person after waiting 38 minutes on hold and you are comforted to learn that the car hasn't been "discounted yet." You are looking at the fake price, which allows the insurance company to appear as if they are offering discounts, and it also allows the dealer to write off more money, because repossessed cars that are factored at the equivalent of 800 percent of NADA value makes their charity care appear much greater than it really is. Charity care is key part of the requirement for the dealer to file as a nonprofit entity and to justify not having to pay taxes.

The itemized window sticker arrives in the mail and although you are glad to see the price was discounted significantly to $82,465, that is still far more than you expected and the insurance will only cover up to $65,000. You had talked with your neighbor a couple months ago and learned he had purchased the same year and model of car from another dealer just up the road from your dealer and his bill was $42,000. He has a different insurance company, which apparently has a better contract. You wonder, how can the price for the same car be so different? You see an upcoming out-of-pocket expense of more than $15,000 in your future. Realizing you cannot afford the car, you visit the dealer and are told the car is not returnable. You only have $1,000 in savings and you are living week to week. You begin to wonder how one files for bankruptcy.

You read the window sticker you received in the mail to try to understand. It is titled, "Explanation of Features" or EOF. Some of the charges, as itemized on the paper, are for services that were never provided and for features the car doesn't have. For instance, you were charged $387 for ceramic coating that you told them you did not want, you were charged an additional surcharge of $262 for synthetic wiper fluid, and for premium wheels that are supposed to be standard for that trim level, according to the sales brochure. You call the dealer billing department again to inquire about the mistakes. This time, you wait on hold for 57 minutes. When you finally reach someone, they make you feel as if you are out of line for asking, for not understanding. When you are unable to pay, the dealer calls their powerful law firm to take you and your family to court for collection. You cannot afford a lawyer. The judge rules to garnish your paycheck. You will be paying on this car for the rest of your life.

We Need Answers, Not Excuses

When these issues are brought to light, the typical response from the industry is to give excuses. Hospital systems blame insurance companies, and insurance companies blame the hospitals. None of the entities ever seem to take any genuine responsibility. I used to get really frustrated. I would say,

"Doesn't anyone know how to problem-solve anymore?" Then I realized that these problems were a goldmine for the industry.

One excuse that is commonly given is, "They mean well." These are institutions that are literally responsible for others' lives. People wouldn't break the golden rule by oppressing others or running them over for their own gain, would they? I personally believe that most of the people who are carrying out the work mean well and are just following standard procedure. However, it is one thing to live it and be frustrated, and another to have the power to change it. When questionable things are experienced by hospital employees, it is a normal reaction to conform and to remain quiet, particularly if speaking up would affect their job or require a change in career. Whistleblower laws are in place, but blowing the whistle is an uncomfortable thing to do.

Another excuse given by hospital systems is that they lose money on Medicare, so they must charge much more on the commercial side to make up for it. The Rand studies have not supported this notion, in that no statistically significant correlation has been found between hospital pricing for percentage of Medicare services provided, as related to the percentage of commercial care provided. The most recent of these studies was published in 2022 - *Prices Paid to Hospitals by Private Health Plans.*

Perhaps the most common excuse offered by the industry is that healthcare is "too complicated" to have transparent bundled prices. Part of this is true: healthcare is complicated, but so are a lot of things. Isn't a leader's job to make the complex simple, not to manipulate complexity for one's own gain? A number of independent practices, such as the Surgery Center of Oklahoma in Oklahoma City; Wellbridge Surgical in Indianapolis, Indiana; and Solstice Health in Milwaukee, Wisconsin disagree. They post their bundled prices for surgeries online for everyone to see. Because they minimize overhead (non-value-added steps) and maximize quality, their prices are among the lowest in the country. The truth is, it is absolutely possible to bundle healthcare prices.

In my work at Toyota's flagship American automobile plant located in Georgetown, Kentucky, one thing that really stood out to me is the complexity of automobile manufacturing. Each car is made up of approximately 30,000 parts, and everything converged to result in 3,000 new automobiles rolling off the assembly line, produced at Six-Sigma quality, every 24 hours. Over 8,000 team members worked in complete alignment to make this happen. For health and convenience, they had access to 8 cafeterias, a physical fitness center, daycare, and onsite clinics. About 350 external parts suppliers provided parts for this operation via trucks, trains, and airplanes, if necessary, delivered just in time (JIT). To ensure efficient inventory flow, no part under the 150-acre facility roof was more than four hours old. Would you agree that large-scale automobile manufacturing is as complicated as health care? If you would ever like to see this very large, very complex system that runs like a well-oiled machine, Toyota offers free tram tours to the public.

Amazing People in a Broken System

As we shine a bright light into the darkness, it becomes apparent that the majority of healthcare professionals are not happy with how things are going. Sunlight is the best disinfectant, and as we look more closely, we realize that a few people at the top are making the decisions. A majority of people, including the doctors, nurses, and other support staff who work in hospital systems, choose to work in that industry because they have a desire to help people. They are amazing, good-hearted people, and they too are frustrated with the excessive administration, lack of resources, and the plethora of nonvalue work they are required to perform. Even the best healthcare professionals will prove ineffective in a broken system.

I have experienced this dynamic first-hand through several hospital experiences. In my overnight stay after my tractor incident, the nurses took good care of me. They asked me various questions about my needs and my common response was to ask whether it was included with the room or if it would be an extra charge. They had no idea how to answer these questions, and were adamant to point out that they don't deal with the billing. I could tell this was their rehearsed response. I can empathize. If I were in their shoes, I suppose I might do the same.

As a foster parent, I've had the opportunity to experience hospital care from a different perspective. In these instances, the care is 100% covered by the state, through a Wisconsin state program called BadgerCare. On occasion, my wife and I have needed to take a foster child in for healthcare. It is common for foster children to be exposed to drugs very early in life, many times in utero, and it can cause them to have some health issues as they grow up. One foster child, Noah, whom we adopted a few years ago, has had a few surgeries at a local hospital. One was a tonsillectomy and the other was to put tubes in his ears. In these instances, I witnessed passionate caregivers who showed genuine empathy and went out of their way to help a little boy feel comfortable in preparing for surgery. In carefully observing these caregivers, it was obvious that they were encumbered by a broken structure which they were required to creatively navigate in order to produce good outcomes. This broken structure caused delays, including hours of sitting and waiting. Ultimately, the care experience was acceptable.

In one instance, we were caring for a two-year old girl with breathing issues. She was getting lethargic and we became worried, so we took her to the ER. They admitted her and my wife spent the night at the hospital. Early the next morning, I was surprised to learn that they airlifted her via helicopter to another local hospital, which was 30 miles away. My wife rode with her in the life flight helicopter. We weren't paying the bill, but we did have genuine questions about why they didn't call for ground transportation in the form of an ambulance. Even the receiving hospital questioned the decision to use what seemed to be extreme, unnecessary transportation measures. Her situation was not dire. The sending hospital's response to our question was, "There were no ambulances available." There were no ambulances available at 4am on a Monday morning? That doesn't sound like a busy time for ambulances. In this case, it gave the impression the hospital was taking advantage of state funds. Even as foster parents, we do not see the bills, so we are unaware of what the taxpayers were charged. We are also unaware of who made the decisions.

Rushed Care Is Not Good Quality Care

The quality of primary care has devolved steadily over the past few decades. Depending on who you ask, primary care is able to cover about 75% to 90% of our healthcare needs. In the past, primary care was accessible, relationship-oriented, and effective. Visits between patient and doctor could be scheduled in a reasonable timeframe and they allowed enough time for the doctor to have meaningful interaction with the patient; to listen, properly diagnose, and establish an effective treatment plan. Sometimes the visits even took place at the patient's home, aptly named house calls. The result was a trusting personal relationship with one's primary care physician.

Today, primary care at hospitals is generally structured for profit. Primary care physicians (PCPs) or more often, mid-level providers such as nurse practitioners (NPs) or physician assistants (PAs), act as cogs in the much bigger machine that is designed to do three things—refer, refer, refer. Mid-level providers are qualified to perform their role, but not at nearly the level of quality, competence, and training hours of an MD-level physician. This works well for the hospital because mid-level providers have lower salaries, and due to fewer hours of training, they refer more. These referrals result in more cost for the patient (and plan), and more time away from work and family. Every ailment is attached to a code, which can mean multiple separate charges for a patient for the same visit. It can also mean the introduction of charges to the patient for a preventive visit (which are no-cost to the patient per ACA), when a non-preventive question is asked.

Referrals are where the majority of money is made: imaging, orthopedics, surgeries, and complex care for oncology and cardiology. In many cases, because of the rushed primary care situation, along with real or perceived liabilities, it is estimated by some that as many as 50% of referrals are unnecessary, and research has shown that 20% of all care provided by hospitals is unnecessary.

By design, much of what used to be done in a primary care office is now referred. One doesn't have to be a medical professional to understand this. Even if the provider has the skill to help the person, there isn't enough time! Primary care visits are scheduled every 15 minutes, and after the vitals are taken and the patient steps on the scale, there are about 7 minutes left. Doctors have shared with me that when they enter the room, they have 2 other patients waiting, and all they have time to do is interrupt, prescribe medications to address the symptoms, and refer to specialists. If you talk with doctors, they often don't know if the patient went to the specialist or how it went. They have moved on to many other patients. The patient load for a primary care provider in a hospital system can be two thousand people or more. No matter how talented the provider, no one can provide personalized, high-quality care within this structure. Rushed care equals poor care. As an Iowa farm boy, this reminds of a cattle call. We had Polled Hereford cattle and if we had to tag their ear or give them a shot, we would push them through the chute as fast as we could.

Insurance Carriers: This Boat Always Floats

Several years ago, a former CEO of a hospital shared a story with me. A few years prior, he was talking with an insurance executive and the gentleman vented to him that he has regular nightmares—he wakes up in the middle of the night in a cold sweat, worried that everyone will someday figure out that insurance carriers aren't needed. I do not know exactly what he meant by this statement, but this story made me think. I thought, if it is causing so much internal conflict and stress, why doesn't the insurance executive find a different career? This is easier said than done, I suppose.

Insurance carriers, as the keyholders of the locked provider networks, contract with both fully insured employers and self-insured employers. Insurance may well be the engineer—the one driving the healthcare gravy train. They have pulled the levers to suppress the free market, and subsequently, a patient's ability to shop, by enforcing gag clauses in their contracts and regularly negotiating higher prices with hospital systems.

Insurance has the greatest power within the industry and adds the least amount of value. Insurance is the middleman; they are neither the actual seller or the actual buyer and because they have the luxury of playing the middle, their boat will always float. Low tide or high tide, insurance can't lose in the long term. Insurance companies have talented actuaries and they are good at assessing risk.

While I was at Merrill Steel, I received a call one morning from a leader in distress. This person was an executive at a nearby company and she had just learned that their annual healthcare insurance costs were going to increase 100%. That's right, it's not a typo. Their healthcare costs would go up 100% in one year. I met with the company a couple of times and helped them get to a better place. Today they are a part of the healthcare best practice group and doing better.

Pharmacy Benefit Managers: The Kickbacks Have Kickbacks

The role of a pharmacy benefit manager, or PBM, is to manage all things prescription drugs for a self-insured plan. This can be broken down into two primary parts. The first is pharmacy claims management: they are the entity that processes all the claims for medications on the plan. The second part is managing the relationships with drug companies. Most will claim that they will manage the plan well and lower plan costs will result. However, the opposite is often true. If you have experienced a mosquito-infested muggy summer night in the Wisconsin woods, you may have heard the phrase, "My mosquito bites have mosquito bites."

In the pharmacy world, the pharmacy benefit manager or PBM is the master at disguising all sorts of creative ways to make money. As a result, people in the industry talk about how they get "kickbacks on their kickbacks". We could take this not-so-funny joke further to say their "Revenue streams have revenue streams", owning several of the steps in the vertical supply chain. They have mastered the shell games and it can be very difficult for an employer and their broker to understand where their money is going and how much of it is really bringing value.

Let's talk about how PBMs work so that you can know what to do to develop your strategy. PBMs, serve as the middleman, the intermediary, for prescribed medications between the manufacturer and the pharmacy. Like insurance carriers, traditional PBMs add questionable value and a lot of cost. Pharmacy is now big business. Referred to as "the mafia" by many who understand the depths of how traditional PBMs operate, the worst

PBMs skim, redefine, shave, and tack on charges at every step of the way. The majority of employers "don't know what they don't know." They have no idea of how the money flows, where it all goes, and if they are getting a fair price.

Thankfully, in choosing our PBM partner, which we will discuss in Chapter 5, there are many good choices out there, and working with a transparent PBM can save an employer more than 30% of overall pharmacy spend. You don't have to be a pharmacy expert to do this. In my experience, these transparent PBM's have great systems and prudently monitor the plan well for maximized efficiency. It's a great best practice, and a testament to how "big business" the world of prescription drugs has become.

I will provide a brief overview of PBM revenue. First, I discuss some of the ways traditional PBMs make money. They achieve this by utilizing complexly worded contracts that are often not easily comprehensible.

Rebates

A rebate is a kickback that drug manufacturers give PBMs in exchange for putting the drug on their formulary. For some traditional PBMs, 100% does not generally mean 100%. For instance, the PBMs narrative may be that the employer will receive 100% of the rebates, but in reality, that is simply not true. The PBM redefines the definition of rebate, so that only a portion of the rebates are shared with the self-insured employer, and the PBM pockets the rest. They can do this in all sorts of creative ways, such as taking out money for administration fees, software fees, management fees, education fees, data management fees, and the list goes on. These can be as much as 20%, 30%, 40% or more, greatly shrinking the so-called 100% of rebates given by manufacturers. These kinds of practices are trust breakers in the relationship, which we will talk about in Chapter 5. Personally, when it comes to traditional PBMs, through many frustrating first-hand experiences, my trust for them is low. I wouldn't simply believe them if they greeted me and said, "Hello."

Spread

Spread pricing occurs when a PBM reimburses the pharmacy a certain price for a medication, and then charges the self-insured employer a higher price. Another name for spread is margin, and the opposite of spread pricing is pass-through, in which the self-insured employer pays exactly what the PBM pays.

Administration Fees

Administrative fees are factored into doing business with a traditional PBM. It is often very difficult, even for the keen eye, to discern where, when, and how much money is being charged.

Formulary Steering

A formulary is a list of generic and brand name prescription drugs covered by your health plan. Formulary steering is when a PBM steers patients toward a brand-name drug on the formulary, instead of a lower-cost drug such as a generic. A PBM benefits from this by collecting bigger "rebates."

Rubberstamping

Rubberstamping is when a PBM fails to, or in many cases, chooses not to, implement what are often called utilization management practices, such as clinical review, step therapy, prior authorization, refill too soon, quantity limits, and more. It's really a failure to manage the drug program well, which results in wasted resources, wasted cost for the payers, and higher profits for a PBM.

Healthcare Brokers: Buyers Beware

One of the first and most important decisions an employer can make is to find the right broker. In this section, I talk about broker behaviors: what to watch for, both good and bad, and how to be wise. Traditional brokers lack the skills to maneuver in today's healthcare market, and because a broker lives or dies by being able to build a book of business, one thing all of them are good at is sales. This can make it very difficult to discern if they are really on your side and really able and willing to help you.

I will help you cut through the charm and charisma so that you can make an accurate assessment.

You will notice that I intentionally divide brokers into two camps: what I simply call "brokers" and "traditional brokers." Some go by the term "advisor" or "consultant." In this discussion, the words are synonymous, and for simplicity, I have chosen to use the word "broker." While I know some good ones, I don't feel like the profession as a whole has earned the title of advisor or consultant yet.

By "broker," I imply someone who wants to do the right thing for the employer, even if he or she doesn't yet know how. By "traditional broker," I imply someone who is generally not acting as a good resource to the employer, is self-serving, and has no intention of changing. This could be due to a variety of reasons: Such a person may be

- conflicted by their compensation structure;
- without courage to lead change;
- concerned about losing a client;
- not strategic;
- cozy and comfortable and making good money with the status quo;
- lazy;
- reluctant to interrupt time on the golf course;
- or possible other reasons.

Although it is expected to change over time, a fair majority of brokers are still working in the traditional realm. It may take some disruption to shake their tree enough for them to realize they must change to be able to keep their clients or gain new clients. Interestingly, age doesn't seem to be a factor in this. One might rationally believe that it is the "old fogies" who are resistant to change—the ones sitting with their feet dangling over the water on the dock of retirement, who are planning to bow out in a few years. This doesn't appear to be the case. Almost daily, I observe traditional brokers in their 20s, 30s, and 40s who are change resistant, and I have observed some who are closer to retirement be very effective for the employers they support.

If this message comes across as anti-broker, please know that it is not intended that way. I have many friends who are brokers and several I work with that strive to do things right. The role of the broker is critical and if performed ethically and effectively, it is worth that broker's weight in gold. It is my hope that as the market shifts there will be fewer and fewer "traditional brokers."

How Brokers Make Money

If you would like to know how much your broker makes from your plan, you can now get that information. In the Appendix to this book, there is a template letter you can use for this. Because of the 2021 Consolidated Appropriations Act (CAA), the broker has a legal responsibility to disclose every penny he or she is making from your plan. They are supposed to do this even if the employer doesn't request it. Insurance companies have been creative in the many ways they can make money. Often, employers have no idea of how much their broker is actually making and how.

Ways Brokers Make Money

- Stop loss commissions
- ASO commissions
- Consulting fees
- Per script commissions
- Production bonuses
- Claims analytics
- Performance based bonuses
- Per employee fees
- Retention bonuses (from carrier not to shop the plan)
- Referral fees (DPC, ASC, etc.)
- PBM rebates
- Administration fees
- Overrides
- PEPM from medical manager, PPO, or TPA
- Trips and dinners

In general, any partners that make more money when your claims go up are incentivized to make your claims go up. That's a deep statement. If I were giving a talk, I would repeat that phrase. Incentives shape behavior. If you find this to be the case, you must change the pay structure immediately or change the broker.

Who's Driving Your Train?

I had the privilege of driving a locomotive once, a real train on a real track. It involved a couple of weeks of classroom training, and at the end, I got to sit in the engineer seat of the locomotive. The trainer seated himself just across from me. As I entered the almost antique, majestic locomotive for the first time, one thing that stood out to me immediately was the lack of visibility. It's kind of obvious to me now, but I hadn't realized that the engineer of a train drives completely blind in both forward and reverse. There is a little window to look out, but you can't see anything through it. It gives one a glimpse of the current weather conditions and it lets in a little light. That's about it.

The connection point to attach additional cars may be thousands of feet away. The only way the engineer knows when to go, when to stop, when to speed up, or when to slow down is by ground communication from fellow rail workers. A mistake by the engineer of a train results in—well, you know—a train wreck. This was an exhilarating and eye-opening experience that I will carry with me to my grave. In my first run, I was cruising down a slight slope, feathering the brakes to control the speed, feeling like I was on top of the world. The instructor looked over at me with a serious look on his face and said, "You need to stop ahead and you don't have any air remaining in your brakes to stop." Thankfully I hadn't drunk much water that day or you can guess what might have happened. Before I went into a full panic, he laughed and pulled the emergency brake lever. The train screeched to a noisy halt.

I believe employers feel a lot like this when it comes to their healthcare plan. Technically, I was driving the train, but I was not familiar with the controls. Left to my own devices, I would not have known what to do. Similarly, the employer owns the plan and is ultimately responsible for driving their own train. However, because the world of healthcare is so intimidating and complex, they aren't familiar with all the controls, so they often look to their broker as the instructor. In most cases, the broker is really the one pushing the buttons, pulling the levers, flipping the switches, and driving the train. Employers almost always listen to their broker.

Broker Behaviors

Let's discuss four common broker behaviors. Most of this terminology was shared with me by colleagues who lead healthcare for companies. The types of behaviors are intertwined and a single broker can exhibit any of them at various times. The key is to recognize the common tendencies.

The next chapter contains an additional assessment to measure the effectiveness of your broker. I believe it can be an educational resource on what an effective broker relationship looks like and it can help you determine if your broker is serving you well.

Wet Blanket Broker

This is when a broker acts as a wet blanket to best practices or new ideas. It is the most common behavior from traditional brokers. A wet blanket broker is where good ideas go to die! The motive is to protect the status quo. While wet blanket brokers may talk the talk, they do not walk the walk. Any good coach will tell you that you are either getting better or you are getting worse, and if you have the mindset to maintain, you are slowly getting worse. Brokers who exhibit this behavior may promote themselves as the experts . . . and they may very well be, at least knowledge-wise. They give the impression they have considered all options, but they always end up back at the status quo.

If an employer becomes inspired to make positive change, brokers with a wet-blanket mindset may use fear tactics to squelch their temporary inspiration. They do this until the employer representative gets tired of pushing the rock uphill and goes back to doing his or her normal work. If you talk with founders of healthcare startups—disruptor types who are passionate about fixing healthcare and helping people—they will be the first to tell you about wet blankets. After "reaching the employer" and getting them excited about proven, positive change methods, the employer goes from excited to not responding and soon disappears off the map. The broker has effectively thrown a wet blanket on them.

There are many ways they do this. One way is to talk about extreme situations. They might mention the possibility of a hemophiliac, a premature baby, or a cancer case to create fear about how these diagnoses could blow a self-funded plan out of the water. They might talk about how someone getting lasered on stop loss could expose the company to millions of dollars of expenditure. They might give examples of other employers who have gone self-funded, only to return a year later with regret, and on and on. These are all real issues, but what they don't tell you is that these things can be overcome with smart strategy. Their favorite (and most profitable) place for you to stay is right where you are.

One employer I worked with recently was very frustrated with their broker. Their healthcare costs were high, in excess of $25k per covered employee, and their traditional broker told them they had two options—to stay with their current BUCA or switch to another BUCA (or "Blues, United, Cigna, Aetna" . . . shorthand for the top four insurance carriers). No other options were presented. That's like saying, "Is your favorite color red or blue (although red or blue are both good choices)." I am not a broker, but through the best practice group I help others at no cost. I helped this employer learn how much their traditional broker was making from their account by giving them a CAA template letter (see Appendix). The amount was over $400k per year! And this was with a level of service the employer described as, "They don't attend our enrollment meetings and they won't return our calls."

One important thing to consider is that even if a broker intends to act ethically and genuinely help the employer, there is still one question to ask. Namely, does this person have the experience necessary to lead change effectively and produce good outcomes? In most cases, the answer is no, even for brokers who go through a selection process and are offered better-than-average training. This is why there are so few employer healthcare success stories. I still classify these individuals as the good guys and gals. As long as they are willing to learn and are open to change, they won't catch flak from me. They will only get encouragement and support.

Simply put, if you notice wet blanket behaviors from your broker, consider dropping them like a bad habit. If you do what you have always done, you will get what you've always gotten. Not only are these folks not helping you, they are holding you back.

Weathervane Broker

This type of broker is a smooth talker, making you think they are on the cutting edge and that everything humanly possible is being done to control cost. Some are so debonair they will have you believing that the word "gullible" is not in the dictionary. When you mention strategies, such as those that are mentioned in this book, they are "already aware" of these things and they will act as if they are doing them—but are they? Where and when are they doing them and why haven't they suggested them to you?

They can shift like the wind, and present themselves as whatever they perceive you want them to be. They will buy enough time for you to become distracted with other work and to pay them another year, and another year, and another year. Some may even describe themselves as "disruptive." Unfortunately, few really are. While their façade makes them appear to be forward thinkers, weathervane brokers search for solutions with the same vigor as a thief searching for a policeman.

The best way to see if their talk matches their walk is to check their track record. Have they succeeded with you? Have they succeeded with others? Is there evidence of their success? The proof is in the pudding. Large annual cost increases, or any increase for that matter, particularly over an extended period of time, is not "doing well." Don't be cajoled by this suave charm. If you allow it, they will play you like a fiddle. Catch these behaviors early so that you can make changes as necessary and not lose valuable time.

Professional Check Casher (PCC) Broker

This type of traditional broker is mostly absent. If you were to snap a picture of everyone involved with the leadership of your health plan, they wouldn't be in it. They have a tendency to show up just before enrollment time, if they show up at all. The rest of the year they are off doing all of your proverbial compliance duties. Yet, in reality, the compliance portion is a small part of the role and does not take much time. The only thing PCC brokers do consistently is wine and dine potential clients (with the money you pay them) and cash the checks they receive from the employer and the carriers, with an exclusive goal of maintaining and increasing their book of business. In their time away, they are out trying to win new clients and they spend a fair amount of time on the golf course. Be wise, fellow grasshopper, and find partners that are willing to get in the game with you.

Courageous and Competent Broker

This type of broker is a rare find. They typically have a sense of virtue, an inspiration to seek justice, and a deep-rooted compassion for others. They are willing to fight for what is right and what is fair. They often have a capitalist mindset—one that is based on the notion that healthy competition for cost, quality, and accessibility are good for everyone and are paramount for a healthy free market, where cost is driven down, quality is driven up, and the best outcome is a win-win situation for seller and buyer. These rare brokers have courage and are willing to take educated and strategic risks to overcome strongholds, or to take on the wealthy and powerful entities who are fighting hard to maintain the status quo. Even C & C brokers may find themselves with conflicted pay structures that have been given to them. The test is whether they take the initiative to change, to restructure their compensation to be 100% transparent and eliminate any potential conflicts of interest. These are the brokers that will help employers fix healthcare. They are the few, the exception to the norm.

Carl Schuessler, a new breed of disruptor consultant in Atlanta, Georgia, calls it like he sees it. A few years ago, Carl realized he could no longer make a difference for his clients acting as a traditional broker. He jokes that all he could do as a broker was make his clients "broker." He knew there had to be a better way. This epiphany led him to create what he calls the FairCo$t Health Plan and to create Mitigate Partners, a national network of like-minded advisors. Carl gets a lot of requests to speak, and if you catch him on the right day, you might see him break out the pink pants. He is great at teaching his clients how to eliminate the middlemen and to more actively manage employer health plans, which brings them amazing results. Carl and Mitigate Partners are some of the "good guys and gals" who are challenging Wall Street (insurer-built) health plans by creating local Main Street (employer-built) health plans, to bend the healthcare cost curve. In Chapter 5, I will walk you through the assessment and how to make sure you have a C & C broker.

Who's Working for Who?

Traditional healthcare brokers have done well, purporting to represent the buyers of healthcare (employers and employees), while getting paid by and being influenced more by insurance. We work for who pays us, and insurance often pays them more. This situation must change and all compensation misalignments must be corrected if the payers of healthcare are to get a fair shake.

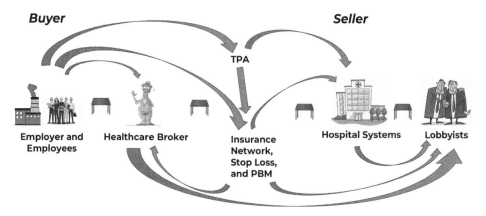

Employers, occupied by the realities of running a business and dissuaded by false assumptions that healthcare "is what it is," have delegated nearly 100% of their benefit strategy to their traditional brokers. Employers sometimes speak of their broker in avuncular terms, as if they are an old friend or relative. And maybe they are, but isn't there also an important role of fiduciary responsibility for the employer? Cajoling employers, traditional brokers have played the good guy/gal role of negotiating a 15% increase down to 12%. This is not representing the employer well, nor is it true success. The reality is that while employer plans have steadily fallen apart, traditional brokers have gone into Christmas break smiling, knowing they just got a healthy raise.

The same compensation alignment expectations must apply to all other partners. In healthcare today, it seems we have a lot of money flowing under the table. All money must flow above the table, where the payers can see it.

Employers, Suit Up and Get in the Game

In this last section, I will close the discussion of who's who in American healthcare by discussing employers' contribution to the hot mess in which we find ourselves. Employers did not "cause" the issues, but they have contributed, because they are the ones who have the power to solve them.

Employers are at fault through their inaction. As the payer, they hold all of the power. But for the past two or three decades, most employers have been sitting on their hands. Employers have delegated the management of their healthcare benefits to their traditional broker, they have not educated themselves on employer-sponsored healthcare plans, and ultimately, they have allowed all of this hullabaloo to go on. They are the check-writers and the gatekeepers, and they have been mostly asleep at the wheel.

Employers must realize there is a significant business opportunity in front of them. Because healthcare has always been thought of as a "benefit," it has not received enough attention from business leaders. That thought is not wrong—it's just incomplete. Healthcare is a benefit, but it is also a cost, because something is being purchased. In fact, no other significant business expense has been "off the radar" as much as healthcare. Healthcare simply cannot remain an ancillary topic to be talked about once, in the fall of each year, then shoved aside and forgotten about until the next year. Tim Schierl, co-owner and co-CEO of Team Schierl Companies in Stevens Point, Wisconsin, states, "Whether or not they realize it, every employer is in the healthcare business. Typically, healthcare costs are an employer's second or third biggest expense. This means, if we can realistically reduce healthcare costs by 10 to 30%, while improving the quality of the plan, it becomes an employer's biggest overall business opportunity."

If Tim is right, it sure beats trying to reduce the office supply expense or trying to squeeze your suppliers even further for another 1% to 3% savings. And Tim is not alone in his realization. Warren Buffet once said, "GM is a health and benefits company with an auto company attached." We also know that Starbucks spends more on healthcare than on coffee beans. I am sure there are many more examples, but the point has been made. Suiting up and getting in this game can reap incredible dividends for your company.

Why Don't Employers See the Opportunity?

In my younger days, I had the opportunity to play basketball in high school, and later, Division 1 basketball at small college for a couple of years. I was athletic and tall (I am still one of those) and one of the things I enjoyed was playing defense. Sometimes I would be the secret weapon to shut down the other team's best player. Coach would grab my jersey, and pull me close, his face was a few inches from mine, and he would say things like, "I want you to guard him well; I want you to be on him like bread on a sandwich, or like white on rice; when the game is over, I want you to tell me what kind of chewing gum he's chomping on." In other words, get in his face, and shut him down. He made his point and I never forgot it. I was on it.

The majority of employers, clearly, have not been "on it" ... but why? One of the reasons is the false impression that cutting costs in healthcare would be synonymous with cutting benefits. Add in the struggles of recruiting and retention, and a comment to cut spending on benefits would likely be dismissed as fast as the last syllable left the person's lips. However, by cutting only the non-value-added things, we cut wasteful actions (time) and wasteful spending (cost), and we keep all the value. These concepts are built into the Employer Healthcare Success Formula, which will allow you to increase the healthcare services offered by your plan (often at no cost to the member) and greatly reduce cost at the same time.

Another reason employers haven't acted is that they are waiting for the government to fix it. A few things come to mind here. First, a mentor once told me, "Never wait for someone else to fix your problems. You will be waiting a long time." Haven't we all waited for the caped hero to fly in and save the day? When I eventually realized it was my responsibility to fix the problem, good things started to happen. Second, even if the government made it a priority to fix the problems, could they? In 2021, healthcare companies spent nearly $700 million on lobbying, the highest ever reported in a single year. This money comes directly from the payers: employers and employers. This means that part of the money you spend in your premiums is working against you to raise your healthcare costs.

Annual Lobbying on Health

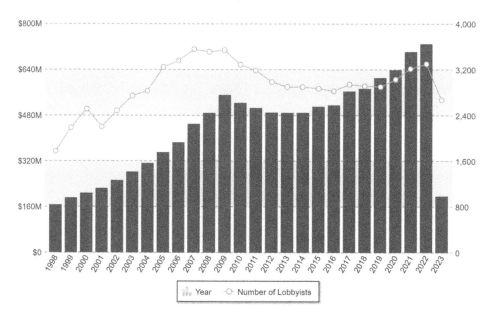

Another reason employers have overlooked this opportunity relates to some interesting dynamics in HR. I can speak to this topic first-hand, as I was in HR for almost 25 years. Candidly, I have always been a little frustrated with my peers and how many seem to have a lack of passion or understanding to make things better. Many HR leaders seem to perpetuate antiquated ways of doing things - never questioning the same old processes that produces lackluster results. Their modus operandi seems to be, "This is just the way HR is done." Often HR people are viewed as the employment experts, and since CEOs don't want to deal with messy "HR people issues," HR tends to carry a kind of weight that makes others have to listen to them, even if they aren't truly respected as impactful leaders in the organization.

Part of this problem is that HR leaders are often pushed into corners, and it may not be "safe" to drive positive change. In his book, Dave Chase points out, "The system has continued because of two directives CEOs have long given HR: Keep people happy and don't get us sued." My response when I read Dave's statement is 1) I agree, and 2) it seems if we look at the long-term outcome of this approach, something is being missed. Are decades of skyrocketing costs and plan degradation "keeping people happy"? When your people stop sharing issues with you, it doesn't mean they are suddenly content. Rather, much of the time it means they have given up and lost trust. I believe this has happened in many cases. If you are not sure, roam about the business and strike up conversations with others on healthcare. As long as it is safe to do so, they will tell you. Be prepared, though: if you ask you need to be prepared to act, if you intend to build trust.

A Raging Capitalist and a Bleeding Heart

A colleague, David Voorhees, once shared with me that he is a "raging capitalist and a bleeding heart." What a great expression, I thought. I suppose this phrase might mean different things for different people. Personally, I am a believer in the American dream, the notion that anyone, regardless of race, socioeconomic status, gender, who aspires to work hard and persist can make something of themselves . . . blended with a genuine deepfelt level of caring and charity: that one should never pursue a dream if it involves taking advantage or oppressing a fellow citizen to achieve it. And it has worked best when government has mostly stayed out of it. Very large "contributions" to state legislators and the funding of lobbyists has come to mean that most anything with government fingerprints on it tends to be low-performing and inefficient, because that money was contributed with a self-serving motive.

It reminds of the time I led a construction crew when I owned a general contracting business many years ago. I had started the business at the age of 19 and I ran it for seven years during my undergraduate and graduate studies. Once in while a customer (homeowner) became inspired and would jump in and help. They always meant well but they were always absolutely in the way and it created safety risks. In one instance, a 65-year-old man climbed on his roof and began unrolling roofing felt! I would joke with my crew about what I should say to customers who "want to help". I would say, "$25 per if we do it, or $50 per hour if you help." Government tends to have the same mindset as the healthcare industry – increasing top-line costs (raising taxes) rather than reducing bottom-line cost (eliminating things that aren't adding value). When was the last time we read a headline that said, "Government lean project is a success. Efficiency increased by 50%, which will enable a reduction in taxes!"

To Regulate or Not Regulate: That Is a Fair Question

I am not generally a fan of government regulation, because just as with industry, the potential for an Animal Farm scenario is ever present. However, I do believe there is legislation we could use to supplement and strengthen the free-market solutions provided in this book.

In Wisconsin, to keep automobile repair shops honest, the state passed strict consumer protection laws regarding upfront estimates, disclosure and return of old parts, and strict penalties for shops that do not comply. In my experience, these are working well. I can tell you that my mechanic is very adamant about giving me a price before service work is done on my car.

Once, I printed this consumer act, grabbed my red pen, and modified the language slightly, plugging in "patient" instead of "automobile," "hospital" instead of "dealer/mechanic," and so on. This sounds a little silly but something like this could really help rebalance the healthcare value proposition. It was very interesting how something so simple could potentially help with these issues—if the right people are motivated to do so. The number of lobbyists the healthcare industry enlists and the amount of money the industry spends to influence laws and regulations is disconcerting. I fear we have many elected legislators who have become more like paid referees. It's hard to play the game when the overseeing powers, government officials who are supposed to be representing voters, have been influenced by lobbyists and financial gifts.

Here are some of the specifics of the consumer protection laws related to automobiles:

- When bringing in your car, pickup, or licensed motorcycle for repairs, you must be offered a written estimate if the bill might exceed $50. If you do not want an estimate, the shop must still give you a copy of the repair order describing what repairs will be done.
- No unauthorized repairs are allowed.
- When calling for additional authorization, the shop must tell you both the cost for the additional repairs and the new total cost of the complete job.
- The shop must return replaced parts to you if you ask for them before repair begins. Warranty parts or parts exchanged for rebuilding need not be returned, but must be made available to you for inspection.
- When work is completed, the shop must provide you with an invoice describing the repairs, replaced parts (specifying if used or rebuilt), and warranties for repairs and parts.

Similarly, there are federal laws protecting consumers when purchasing services from funeral homes. These are enforced by the Federal Trade Commission (FTC) and include the following:

- The right to choose the funeral goods and services.
- The right to receive information, in writing, about funeral services and merchandise before any decisions and purchases are made. This information should come in the form of a General Price List.
- The right to receive information concerning the purchase of any items that are required by law.
- The right to use a casket purchased from someone other than the funeral home.
- The right to have alternative containers available from funeral providers that perform cremations.

In these two examples, it becomes apparent that the Wisconsin consumer is protected from fraud and price gouging for automobile repairs. And with funeral services, the not-so-funny joke is that our estate is afforded more protection after our last breath – after we are pronounced dead, without a pulse, than when we are living and in need of healthcare services. I wonder if these industries could benefit if they enlisted more lobbyists?

A Seat at the Table

Thankfully, some legislators do seem to be taking note. In many cases, they have been deceived by what I have come to realize are fake debates between insurance and hospitals.

In 2022 a few kindred-spirited colleagues and I were invited to testify before a Wisconsin Senate committee. We felt it was important to share the employer perspective regarding an attempt by Wisconsin hospital systems to monopolize J code drug sourcing and infusions. We were able to gather over 100 signatures from supportive Wisconsin companies and we included them in a letter to the Senate Committee. This may have very well been the first time that employers "showed up" at one of these hearings. We had something to say—many things to say, really—things that legislators needed to hear. As it turns out, they had been reading books and doing some of their own research as well. Great job! It worked. A "white bagging" bill that had overwhelming momentum and support going into the hearing was stalled as a result of the whole truth being spoken. White bagging is a term that refers to infused drugs being delivered by pharmacies to the provider who will perform the infusion, as opposed to the provider sourcing it directly, and marking it up multiple times. A drug that is infused every month, for instance, can be marked up from $10,000 to $40,000. This adds significant cost for the patient and the plan.

The hearing started at approximately 9:00 a.m., and although I didn't know when my name would be called, it was approximately 4:00 p.m. before I got the chance to speak. This meant I had plenty of time to observe the setting in the room, and listen to the testimonies of insurance executives, hospital executives, cancer patients, healthcare insurance brokers, and employers. It was difficult to read faces, because it was a time in which masks were required. I could still see everyone's eyes, however, and a lot can be gleaned by watching the eyes alone.

Before this hearing, in which employers were now effectively represented, it had always been the hospital systems on one side and the insurance carriers on the other, to have what appears to be "the great fake debate." Ironically, on this bill, employers sat on the side of the insurance carriers. In visiting the Madison capitol building that day, I met a gentleman who works for the insurance industry and we became friends. He called me a few months afterward and I was able to help him find an affordable provider for a family member who needed a serious medical procedure.

After going through this Senate testimony experience, I began to see a new perspective and I wrote the following reflection of my thoughts:

> For the past few decades, the sellers of healthcare services (hospital systems) and the intermediaries (insurance carriers) have sat at a table and negotiated, writing in gag clauses to keep the prices hidden. The payers (employers and employees), the ones writing the checks, have not been offered a seat at that table. Because the ACA medical loss ratio provision only allows insurance to keep a respective 15%/20% of premiums collected, insurance carriers' profits increase only when claims go up. This means both parties at the "negotiation" table, hospitals and insurance carriers, want healthcare costs to go up.

Important Concepts to Understand in Employer Healthcare

Thus far we have discussed some of the thematic problems with healthcare. Further, we have discussed "who's who" in the healthcare industry and how the structure they have created has affected employers' ability to offer high quality, affordable health plans. For the remainder of this chapter, I discuss some technical concepts in healthcare and important things one needs to know to lead a successful healthcare improvement journey.

Types of Healthcare Insurance

Determining how you will insure your plan is an important decision for an employer. Even self-funded employers typically need to purchase some form of external insurance. The only exception is very large employers who have cash flow and revenue to absorb 100% of the risk.

There are three primary methods of insuring a health plan:

Fully Insured

I frequently say, regarding the fully insured option, "There is no way to win long-term being fully insured." By *win*, I mean to achieve favorable and sustainable outcomes. It is not my intent to be flippant. Unfortunately, I am just sharing what I believe is a true statement in today's healthcare landscape. If anyone is aware of a way to win in the long term being fully insured, please look me up. I will be the first to raise my hand to listen and understand.

A few decades ago, things were very different. Employers could purchase health insurance for their employees without having to know a lot about it. They could get a renewal that was typically the same price, and follow that path year to year. Perhaps not having to know a lot about it was the beginning of the end. Any time we are purchasing something and don't understand what we are buying, we open ourselves up to be taken advantage of.

Chapter 4 will serve as a guide in developing your overall strategy. Part of this will require you to make decisions on which type(s) of insurance you will purchase and who will be your carrier. Although usually some insurance is necessary, it is important to emphasize that your primary focus should not be on "purchasing insurance." Instead, your focus should be on purchasing healthcare. Insurance is in the middle. This distraction, or misalignment of focus, is a common mistake employers and traditional brokers make. At the end of the day, this blunder will result in an ineffective strategy. Ideally, the fewer entities involved between seller and buyer the better. Don't let yourself be hoodwinked. Insurance carriers will be glad to eat your lunch and then take your milk money—if you let them.

When considering a transition from fully insured to self-funded, the incumbent insurance carrier and traditional broker will often make this transition seem impossible. First, as you try to obtain level-funded or stop loss insurance quotes, the incumbent insurance carrier will tell you that the claims data "is not available." I always find it interesting to hear that news. The reality is that it is very "available." They want to prevent you from switching, which means lost revenue for them, so they will conceal information, reduce their renewal, or do anything else they can to keep you from switching. Many argue that the claims data for fully insured plans is the employer's data and should be accessible, but as we have discussed, complex contract clauses and deep pockets to pay for lawyers keep these things hidden.

Second, switching to self-funding also typically means lost revenue in commissions and other compensation for traditional brokers and it will require more of their time and more work. Managing a self-funded plan requires the broker and employer to put several partners in place that come conveniently packaged with a fully insured plan, such as a third-party administrator (TPA), PBM, network, and more. Once the self-funded plan is running, the increased time and work subsides, but the transition is one that many traditional brokers try to avoid. One way traditional brokers commonly avoid such a transition is to provide actuarial quotes that forecast plan costs increasing as much as 30% or 40%. With good strategy, this is simply not true. These calculations are often done without any consideration of how the self-funded plan will save cost.

Another reason traditional brokers may avoid this transition is that they are not strategic. They were trained to sell insurance, and that has put the most food on the table. Within the industry, they are called a "producer". This much space is needed to provide the definition. This makes partnering with a broker who is willing to work and truly recommends the best decisions for your plan (and not their own pocketbook) a critical decision. Not only will the wrong broker not help you move forward, the wrong broker will hold you back. How to choose the right broker will be discussed in detail in Chapter 5.

Level-Funded

Level-funding is an option in the self-funded insurance world that blends the simplicity of a traditional fully insured plan with the flexibility of a self-funded plan. There is a fair amount of freedom and choice for an employer with these plans. This includes the ability to shape the plan design in a bespoke manner for the group making the move to self-funding. Most fully insured options offer a certain number of pre-set plan designs with little to no flexibility. Level-funded plans are typically offered by the same insurance carriers that offer stop-loss insurance and are not part of the BUCA carriers' game. Level-funded plans can be a good stepping-stone for employers who desire to transition from fully insured to self-funded, particularly small employers with 25 to 150 employees enrolled in the plan. These numbers may vary, based on opinion or risk perspective, but it gives you an idea.

Choosing the level-funded path requires the employer to establish working relationships with independent healthcare partners. These partners include a stop-loss carrier to provide protection against potential catastrophic claims, medical claims processing services performed by a TPA (a third-party administrator), pharmacy claims processing performed by a PBM, and the establishment of a network for provider coverage. With level-funded plans, the employer pays a set amount each month, similar to a fully insured premium. A smaller portion of the set amount is premium that goes to the stop-loss carrier, with the majority of the assets serving as funding dollars for incurred claims. The TPA pays the claims directly throughout the year, with the stop-loss carrier paying any claims that exceed the available funding dollars of the group, and at year-end, if the claims exceed the amount the employer paid, there is no further action. Conversely, if the claims do not exceed the premiums paid, the group retains any excess funds. The potential for retaining money can be enhanced by the way the plan is designed and the type of cost-containment vendors that are deployed.

It is important to understand that level-funded plans are not created equal and there are various contractual features to consider when choosing a level-funded option. One of the better ones I am aware of is offered by TPAC, a Managing General Underwriter (MGU) located in Minneapolis, Minnesota. They offer a level-funded product called Spaggregate®, which was developed in 1999 as the first level-funded product. They offer a unique system for automatically moving premium dollars to pay large claims and a contractual agreement that ensures 100% of the savings stays with the employer group (no split with the carrier and the end of the contract). TPAC has written thousands of these Spaggregate® policies across the United States and have helped nearly 200,000 people in the process.

Self-Funded

Self-funded, also called self-insured, is a way for the employer to absorb a share of the risk, and if the plan performs, share in the reward.

Also called reinsurance, stop loss insurance is necessary for most companies that choose to self-fund their healthcare plan. With effective partners and an effective strategy, self-funding offers an employer the freedom to shape the benefit plan and to focus on purchasing healthcare wisely. It puts the company in the driver's seat. For most companies, stop loss insurance makes all of this possible.

Let's talk about how a stop loss policy works. Stop loss insurance is designed to pay only when medical claims exceed a certain amount, either for an individual member, called individual specific deductible, or for the plan as a whole, called aggregate specific deductible. With this approach, the company establishes a separate bank account: a pool of money that is designated for healthcare costs only. Money is deposited into this account in several ways: the company's premium portion, the members' premium portion, copays, deductibles, and stop loss reimbursements (if applicable).

Individual stop loss is focused on each member, or "covered life," of the plan, sometimes referred to as "belly buttons" on the plan. It is set at a certain amount for a specific amount of time, such as a plan year. For instance, if the individual specification is set at $50,000, the company would cover all medical expenses covered under the plan for that member up to that amount. Thereafter, for the remaining time period, the stop loss insurance covers the costs.

Aggregate stop loss takes all the members on the plan into account and is set at a number to protect the employer from risk should there be high claims from many members. For instance, the amount might be set at 125% of expected claims, and it would kick in if the group reaches that amount in the specified time frame.

"Lasering" is a technique from a stop loss insurer in which an individual is excluded from the coverage or is set at a higher rate. All of these factors can be adjusted higher or lower in order to dial in a final premium that is acceptable to the employer. The concept of lasering can be a scary thing for employers, in that they worry that they may become exposed to high costs. Some stop loss carriers offer the option that no lasers will be added without the employer's agreement. In some cases, it may be wise for the employer to utilize a laser, in order to keep stop loss premiums affordable.

A common mistake self-funded employers make is to act as if being insured is the ultimate end-all strategy. This means, they have changed the way in which they take on risk, but they haven't changed anything else. In this case, the employer's plan is still purchasing healthcare exactly the same way, which is convenient, but expensive. The carrier still performs all the duties associated with medical claims processing, pharmacy claims processing, and their network. Additionally, they are glad to determine the plan design, which naturally steers care to their network, and all other services associated with the plan. It's a relatively easy, clean purchase, but the outcomes have shown to be unaffordable and unsustainable.

It begs the question: If an employer changes the way they fund their plan, yet change nothing else, why would they expect to improve? I have heard stories from brokers and employers about companies that had previously transitioned to become self-funded, but after a year or two, they switched back to fully insured because "it didn't work". This is an honest mistake and I suppose a "good try" (with good intentions at least), but it frustrates me to hear these comments. It was not the self-funding piece that caused them to fail, but a lack of other important strategy pieces. It makes me want to use the sign on my wall that has a target in the middle and a title above it that says, "Bang head here". Thankfully, it's just a funny sign. I haven't actually used it – yet.

The miss here is that being self-funded is only a piece of the financial strategy, and it leaves out the other two very important pieces: the medical strategy and choosing trustworthy healthcare partners. These three pieces together form an employer's overall healthcare strategy. Without all three components of the full strategy in place, the employer should not expect to perform better. They might do better or they might do worse, but it would be more of a roll of the dice than anything.

This can be likened to removing collision coverage from your car insurance policy, and keeping the comprehensive and liability coverage. You have changed the way you insure your car, you have reduced your insurance cost, and you have taken on some of the risk, but your car will not perform any differently or you will not be less likely to get in an accident. Such as, you have done nothing to improve the driver designation, safety, braking, airbag restraints, or handling of the car and thus, you have not reduced your risk.

Captives

A captive is made up of a group of employers (plan sponsors) that have grouped together in numbers to secure stop loss insurance. Everyone seems to have their own opinion on captives. I personally believe there is great opportunity and benefit. Important things to consider for a captive include: who is managing the captive, who owns it, how does the captive operate financially, who are the members of the captive, and what, if any, requirements are there of members? If structured well, a captive can be a great advantage to lessen and minimize stop loss insurance costs. The biggest advantage of a captive is the ability to pool like-minded employers together, namely ones who are executing strategy to manage the cost and quality of their health plan. Stop loss carriers insure the ocean and all the fish in it. A captive is more like a pond that selects which fish can swim in it. Through this selectivity, the captive has a much better chance of effective risk management, and therefore a better chance to keep premiums low and return greater dividends from an overcollection of premiums, which is returned to captive members if the collective plans perform well.

Pricing Models

There are two prominent pricing models in healthcare: top-down pricing and bottom-up pricing.

Top-Down Pricing

Top-down pricing is the model most commonly used today. In this model, it is difficult, if not impossible, to decipher how much you are spending and how much you are saving. The approach is concentrated on the notion of "discounts," but the unit prices are not shared. This means that a 40% discount off one hospital's prices could be significantly worse than a 30% discount off another. It assumes the hospital prices are the same, which is not the case.

The industry has pushed the top-down pricing model for decades, as if it was the only option. They have done this very effectively, because it feeds the beast and conceals all the pricing and claims information a buyer needs in order to shop effectively. It makes it very easy to hide money.

Additionally, with a top-down model, hospital systems will push "exclusivity" in their contract. In other words, if you sign up to be in their club, and agree not to shop anywhere else, they will give you a great discount! For instance, a hospital might say, "If you sign an exclusive contract with us, we will discount our chargemaster price by 40%." I don't know about you, but for years I thought, wow! "That sounds pretty good. Where do I sign?" For decades, traditional brokers have successfully sold this offer to employers, and because we trusted our traditional healthcare broker, we believed we were getting the best deal possible. But were we?

For effective shopping, we rest on the notion that we must have visibility of cost and quality. In this context, we'll focus on price and value. We must know what we are spending and what we are getting. With top-down pricing, we don't know either. Without transparent pricing, a stated discount of 40% loses its salt. In other words, 40% of what? It might as well be a discount of 98%. The discount is meaningless unless we can tie it to a clear, set price. This truth has somehow gotten missed over the last few decades.

With hospital systems, which are often affected or controlled by insurance, the nontransparent pricing is intentional. Once, I called a local gastrointestinal provider. I stated our network and asked how much a standard colonoscopy costs. To my surprise, they would not share a price with me. The receptionist asked if I wanted to speak to her manager. I said "Sure," and reiterated that I was not calling to play games, rather, just to understand the price so I could openly refer more employers to them. I shared that I considered them a preferred provider and that I lead a best practice group with over 250 employers, and I would be glad to share their practice. Again, the manager would not share the price and asked if I wanted to talk with their CEO. I said "Sure" and I found myself talking with the CEO. Again, I mentioned that I believed they are the kind of provider that we want to work with and I asked for their specific price. I realized, that although excuses were given, she was not allowed to share the price, likely due to hospital system restraints or insurance contracts. The illogical answers she gave made her look defensive, as if she had something to hide.

For instance, I said, "You do 10 to 12 of these same procedures a day. If you don't know the price structure, how in the world do you know how much to bill"? She replied that it is "too complicated" and there might be one or two or even three polyps. That didn't sound very complicated to me. I told her my automobile manufacturing story and how Toyota puts 30,000 parts into each car and essentially, uncomplicates it. I told her that this process sounds pretty complicated to me, much more than a single colonoscopy with a variation of three polyps. She didn't appreciate my analogy or my humor. I never did get a price. However, in these types of conversations I remind myself that every person has a conscience, and it is my hope that my simple question caused her to lose some sleep. I mean that in a good way, but how can we trust someone who expect us buy from them, yet openly refuses to tell us the price? Maybe you can, but personally, I cannot trust that person, regardless of what constraints they may be under or what contracts they may have signed.

Bottom-Up Pricing

The bottom-up pricing model is one that is becoming more popular, particularly among those who realize that top-down pricing is not useful. Bottom-up pricing allows us to assess value and shop wisely. Unlike the top-down model, this approach ties prices to a stable reference: the most common being the government Medicare rate. For the technical data experts reading this, I am aware that the Medicare rates fluctuate slightly based on region; however, for all practical purposes, it is a solid reference point. The issues with American healthcare are probably among the most complex (and impactful) in our country to solve, so it is important we don't get "analysis paralysis."

Bottom-up models refer to healthcare prices as a percentage of the Medicare rate. One hundred percent of Medicare is a good rate. When negotiating a contract, whether it be a network one or a direct one, it is best to speak in reference-based language. Unlike the meaningless discounts in the top-down model, we reference prices for services as a percentage of the Medicare rate. To compare prices, we might find ourselves saying something like, "With this provider, we are paying 150% of Medicare. In most areas, with a national average of over 200% of Medicare, that would be a great rate." In some of the highest cost states, such as Wisconsin, we commonly see rates as high as 400% or more.

Reference Based Pricing (RBP)

RBP is a newer technique that has surfaced in the last decade. RPB is a unique strategy of high risk and high reward. With this strategy, members go to the hospital system for care, and all bills are processed and paid directly by the TPA. They pay the provider and the member is responsible to pay them. The interesting thing with this approach is that the TPA does not pay the provider the full amount that was billed. Rather, they pay them a chosen percentage of Medicare. For instance, a hospital bills a patient an amount that equates to 300% of Medicare. The bill is processed through the TPA first, which gives them a chance to intercede. The TPA sends a check to the hospital with an amount equivalent to say, 160% of Medicare, and on the check it is printed that if the hospital cashes it, it means they have accepted payment in full.

In some areas of the country and with certain hospitals, it is accepted as full payment and the transaction is considered complete. In some areas, hospital systems accept 95% of these payments, and for the remaining 5%, they "balance bill" the patient directly. In many cases, they go after the patient for collections. This has been a hospital strategy to try to get employers to stop using this method. In some regions of the country, such as Wisconsin, hospital systems are denying care at the reception desk (other than emergent) for patients they speculate is on a RBP plan.

In many cases, this strategy can get messy for an employer, with many collection letters and lawsuits, even if the member has paid their portion through their TPA, according to the plan. When the hospital tries to balance bill and go after the patient, the TPA will try to step in and try to protect the member, but it isn't always that easy. In some cases, this approach has saved hundreds of thousands or millions of dollars, but my advice is to be careful, and if you try this method, know the risks and what you getting into. RPB is not a part of the healthcare formula I present in this book and it has not shown to be a sustainable strategy in Wisconsin. It is not something I recommend.

Reference Based Contracting (RBC)

RBC can take various forms, but at its simplest, it is a pre-agreed pricing agreement. This can be through a formal network, or what is called a direct contract. These are beneficial because it is still founded in language and numbers that are tied to a set reference, as in the Medicare rate. Direct contracts have opened up the free market and are a positive way to save money and shop wisely.

While networks and unique contracts are the norm in healthcare, it does create odd scenarios. In what other industry is the consumer charged such a wide range of prices at the same institution as a result of contract agreements? Certainly, there are none as disparately priced as in healthcare.

Let's take an example of three friends who decide to go out for lunch. Everyone is hungry for a good cheeseburger. The waitress doesn't walk up the to the table and ask which food plan each person is on. Further, if restaurants worked like healthcare, this would mean that each person would pay a different amount for the same cheeseburger. One person will pay $10, another would pay $6, and another $5. That would be kind of odd, right? But this is how healthcare works every day. It begs the question and leads us to the ideal—the way we purchase everything else. In some cases, it may be best to say, what is your best, fair cash price for the cheeseburger? Or how about we put the prices directly on the menu and we can all pay $5 for the cheeseburger?

Utilization Management/ Utilization Review

Utilization Management (UM), also called Utilization Review (UR), are umbrella terms to describe the plan's responsibility to ensure all treatment is clinically appropriate and medically necessary, ultimately to prevent "overutilization" of plan services. The specific approval process used to achieve this is called preauthorization, which requires a provider to request and receive approval for coverage from a health plan before a procedure is performed. I will use the term *preauthorization*, and you may see it called other names, such as prior authorization, precertification, or prior approval. UM services are typically charged as a per-employee-per-month (PEPM) line item, billed to the employer plan through the TPA's normal billing cycle. TPAs can perform UM directly, but most often they outsource these tasks to a vendor.

The presumption is, without oversight, there is potential that doctors will miss important details, make mistakes, or order excessive, unnecessary procedures. On the surface, this seems to be logical. The plans need to keep the docs honest, right? One thing is for sure—neither the sellers nor the buyers of care are fans of this process. Providers are not fans because it adds a lot of work to their plate to justify what they are already accountable to do—provide appropriate and necessary care. They are held accountable to this through state board certification requirements and the Hippocratic oath they took in medical school of "do no harm." Patients are not fans because the extra approvals can halt or delay important care, and can often require them to miss more time from work and make additional trips to their provider.

Ultimately, the question becomes, do preauthorizations improve the quality of care for members under the plan and do they control costs by limiting what would have been incorrect or excessive care? Blanket procedures certainly have the potential to add bureaucracy. One might ask, if we can't trust our doctor to recommend appropriate care, why would we go to him or her in the first place?

As a former VP of HR, policy and procedure development is something I am intimately familiar with. As I matured in my career and gained valuable real-life experience (this is another way of saying I got old), I became more of a fan of guidelines than black-and-white policies. I preferred to give leaders some discretion and flexibility to make the best decisions. Through experience, I learned that black-and-white policies often paint leaders into a corner and force them to make bad decisions. If you have ever found yourself saying something like, "I don't really agree with this and it is not fair, but the handbook states very clearly how this is to be handled," you might have experienced the same.

I recall a personal experience once in which a black-and-white process created a very odd customer experience. I had purchased a new refrigerator from Sears. We began having problems with the refrigerator almost from the start, and we called on the repair service multiple times over a period of several months. After about a year of continual problems, the repair technicians gave up, classified it as a lemon, and requested a new replacement. I called Sears customer service as requested and talked to a friendly customer service operator. We arranged for the new unit to be delivered the next day and everything went smoothly. It was about 10:30 am. She then said, "Sir, we will give you a reminder call this afternoon for your delivery tomorrow morning." I kind of laughed, and responded, "It's OK, ma'am, I am getting old, but I think I can remember. There is no need to call me a few hours from now to remind me of a delivery scheduled for tomorrow." She exclaimed, "I'm sorry, sir, it is something I have to do. It's part of our procedure." And sure enough, a few hours later at about 3:00 pm I received another call from Sears, reminding me of a delivery scheduled for the following morning. I told them thank you and didn't bother to reason with them. These were good folks just trying to do their job. They were not allowed to think and use discretion. They were restricted to following a specific procedure, and it made them look foolish. I am dating myself, but Sears was once THE store. It was the place to go for a large variety of products. Unfortunately, their bureaucracy and culture apparently caught up with them. They have been dying for more than a decade and because the free market determines who thrives and who dives.

Like every situation involving people, the potential for this process of UM to go Animal Farm is ever present. UM companies now boast that they save the plan money by denying 15% of requests. However, this statistic is skewed, because often the request gets reworked and resubmitted, and eventually the procedure gets approved for coverage. Hence, the statement that 15% of requests are denied is misleading, and even in those cases, what if the patient was denied important care? From an efficiency standpoint, what would you prefer to buy—something that has been done right the first time, or something that has been reworked three times? Hospitals are required to play the game, or they don't receive payments. We see another example of how the middleman of insurance has assumed the power of the buyer, when they are not really the buyer. Perhaps this is why hospitals don't speak well of insurance companies, even when they own them, as many have purchased insurance companies as a means to steer care to themselves.

Another example of how preauthorizations may cause more harm than good is the black-and-white requirements doctors are required to follow. UM companies use what they call decision trees. For instance, it is not uncommon for patients to be required to try a variety of treatments before a procedure can be approved, such as to take painkillers, go through physical therapy, and so on. I have had patients tell me of the pain and agony they were forced to endure in physical therapy, when their injury was not one that could be healed without surgery. In such cases, the doctors providing the care, who are closest to the patients, are presumed to know less than someone off in the distance, sitting at a desk, with less credentials and training hours, who is limited to following a decision tree.

Healthcare Cost Assessment

As a final step in this chapter, I will discuss the importance of establishing measures that will help you understand, oversee, and improve your health plan. This is a good transitional step to Chapter 4, which is a guide to help you develop your free-market healthcare strategy. You will choose which measures are important for you to establish a baseline (ideally the past 5 years) and which measures you will track as you go forward. In many cases, your baseline measures may match your ongoing measures, but there will likely be some instances in which baseline data is not available, resulting in you tracking a new variable that hasn't been measured in the past.

It Is Better to Improve than Impress

Key Healthcare Measures Packet is my term for understanding your baseline. I have also used the term Health Plan Dashboard. You can name your packet whatever you like. The point is to constantly understand and be in the know about your past trend, along with how things are going currently. Ultimately, we want to answer the most important question in continuous improvement: "Are we getting better or getting worse – and why?"

It's really important to keep all of this simple. Too often, fancy-looking graphs and charts are produced, such as in a slide deck for a board meeting, with a goal to impress. But fancy graphs or pictures don't help you improve. I had a mentor ask me, "Do you want to look good or be good?" There is nothing wrong with aesthetically pleasing graphs, but not for the sake of appearance only. If we had to choose between fancy-looking graphs that don't help us improve, or hand-drawn sketches that lead to problem solving and the movement of important needles, I will choose the latter every day and twice on Sunday.

To accurately assess whether you are getting better or getting worse, it is best to measure year to year, as opposed to month to month. There might be some things that are wise to review monthly, but in most cases, month to month doesn't tell you much. We are not really concerned with seasonal changes or the like. For the current year, it is wise to include a forecast, or year to date (YTD) measure, so you can have the most up-to-date feedback on plan performance. This allows you to make adjustments within the current year as necessary to shape your outcomes. Overall, we are interested in trends and data that can help us solve problems. As the saying goes, "One month doesn't make a trend." Measuring year to year tells us if we are truly improving.

Measuring your health plan's performance, particularly the past performance, can be a scary step for some, as the feeling is that it somehow exposes failure. My suggestion is to keep calm and don't hide problems. Rather, be willing to expose them so you can work on them. We can't work on something if we can't see it. Do more than "see it." Shine a bright light on it. I have mentioned Michael Hoseus, a well-known former Toyota executive who now works independently as a lean consultant. He tells a four minute story called "Scratchy" that makes this point well. When you have time, I suggest you look up this story on YouTube. It shows the importance of exposing problems instead of hiding them. Again, the theme is to "improve", not to "impress."

I was talking with a colleague once and I was sharing how I was putting together turnover graphs. I showed him a sample. He looked at me with fear in his eyes and said, "You can't show that graph!" I asked why. He said, "That graph will make us look really bad." This is a good illustration of how a continuous improvement culture can support your ability to improve. Is it safe to show a bad graph in your company, with the message that you are assessing the problem and that you aim to improve it? If not, there are deeper cultural issues at hand. Hiding problems is never a good way to improve. To improve, we must first take an honest and candid look at where we are, and how we can make things better.

Also, remember, this is a national issue. Some states are worse than others, but all companies have this problem. It's not where you are, it's where you are going. You've recognized an issue (an opportunity in disguise) and you are moving in a direction to do something about it. Be humble and be forthcoming and others will respect you for being willing to take action. I like to view it as a fun challenge. And when you get the urge to quit, remember that the status quo path is how you got here. If you stay on that path, things will only get worse. It's time for the courageous to take action.

Below is a sample of a basic measurement packet to serve as food for thought. It can tell you a lot about where you have been, where you are, and it can help you develop your strategy of where you would like to go. Once you start using it, it can help you monitor the impact your initiatives are having.

When bringing up the topic of measurement, it is not uncommon to encounter some resistance, even if it is quiet resistance (such as people ignoring you). If you are an HR leader, this can gain you some valuable credibility, as "we" are known for not measuring things. At Toyota, the HR team had rooms dedicated to measurement. The walls of these rooms were covered with relevant graphs and information. The healthcare industry does not operate so openly. Cost is not transparent. Quality is difficult to assess. And year-to-year costs are often not graphed or measured at all.

Below is a subset of basic graphs to consider. Data is far better than speculation, because pure data has no bias. I like to say, "In God we trust – all others bring data."

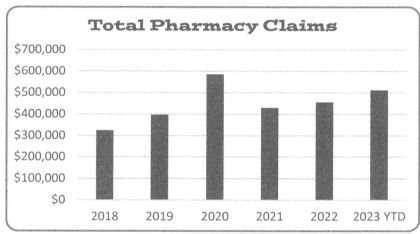

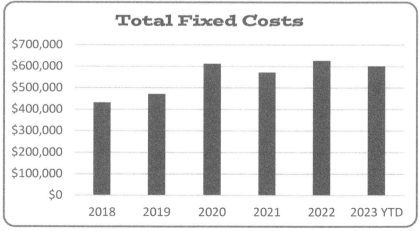

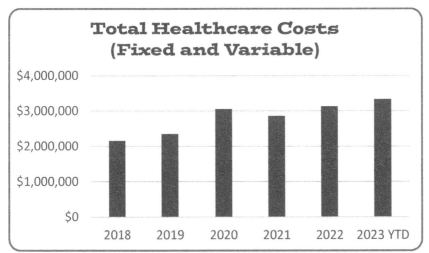

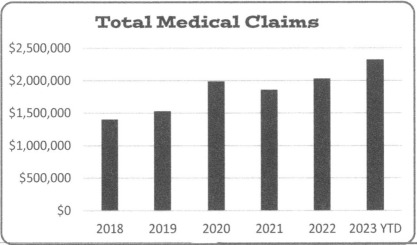

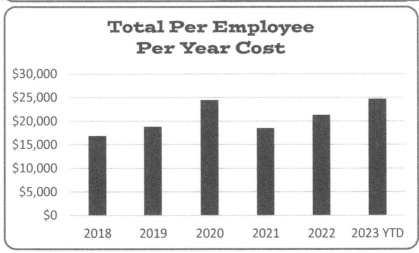

CHAPTER FOUR

Develop Your Free Market Healthcare Strategy

In this chapter, I discuss what a vibrant free market looks like and how you can develop a strategy that will unleash your ability to shop effectively for healthcare in the region(s) where you operate. By knowing how a free market is supposed to look, one can recognize the exceptions: market suppression, restriction, or in some instances, monopolization. Banks utilize this thinking when training new tellers. Instead of showing trainees a variety of counterfeit monies, tellers are shown real money and asked to study it. As their eyes become familiar with the original, they are better prepared to spot counterfeits more effectively. The same thinking applies with a free market.

Free the Free Market!

A fully functioning free market is built on the concept of supply and demand, with sellers competing on quality, cost, and availability—and buyers able to see those things, and having freedom of choice to evaluate and purchase what they want. Fully functioning free markets are not hard to find. Everywhere we look, with the exception of healthcare, we find great examples of mostly self-regulating, fully functioning free markets. Let's discuss an example in the restaurant industry.

Aspiring restaurant owners have many important decisions to make. They choose where they will set up shop, what food options they will put on their menu, what type of atmosphere they will create, and how much they will charge for meals. When ready, they open their doors for business and the public evaluates their choices. If there is adequate demand, and the new restaurant is perceived as offering a fair value proposition, they will likely succeed. Conversely, if the restaurant has a low value proposition—the service is disorganized, the food doesn't taste good, or the prices are too high—consumers will choose to go elsewhere. This natural consequence puts pressure on a restaurant to adjust—to please customers or face the undesired outcome of not having enough revenue to sustain the business. This is a free market economy.

A restaurant that is struggling to make ends meet cannot justifiably say, "We're overstaffed on chefs and therefore our cost is higher," or "Our chef is not very skilled and therefore our food doesn't taste good," or "The food service industry is too complex, and therefore we are unable to determine the price of the food until after the meal is consumed." In a free market, excuses carry little weight. If the customer is not willing to pay for it, an excuse is irrelevant. If the food is delectable, customers might be willing to pay a premium. If the food is inedible, even a very low price may not suffice. Day after day, somewhat unconsciously, customers weigh their options on the value proposition scale and make a decision as to where they will eat. The laws of the natural free market place the onus on the restaurant to offer the customer a desirable value proposition.

Restaurant performance can be at various levels on a continuum. Specifically, if customers view the value proposition scale as more received than paid, the restaurant will thrive, if customers view the scale as balanced, the restaurant will strive, if customers view the scale as less received than paid, the restaurant will scarcely survive, or in many cases, dive. The restaurant is not "entitled" to patronage. Talk to an owner of one and you will find that they are keenly aware of the game they voluntarily chose to play when they became an entrepreneur, a game that involves higher risk and higher reward. Some aspiring entrepreneurs end up losing everything they own, and a few become wealthy. Ultimately, customer choice in a free market will determine where each restaurant falls on the continuum. This is a healthy free market.

Who Has the Power?

Let's continue our discussion on market suppression by examining the power dynamics at play. In any economic situation, we can observe two things—who has the power and how does the money flow? Enter stage left, the star of the show: big insurance. The natural dynamics of seller and buyer have been revised, mediated by an entity who poses as the pseudo buyer, called the "reimburser." The American Medical Association (AMA) established the CPT code system and as of August 2000, it became the law of the land. The AMA represents a small number of physicians, with about 15% of U.S. doctors as paying members. The rule named CPT and HCPCS as the procedure code, to be regulated under HIPAA by the Department of Health and Human Services. It includes transactions and code sets, national provider and employer identifier, security, and privacy.

Insurance utilizes the CPT code system, and if providers don't do things exactly as required, they don't get paid, or they do not get paid in full. This means insurance has efficacious power over hospital systems, and all the ancillary providers who accept insurance are part of their network, which is a large percentage. Moreover, insurance created and controls the concept of "networks," so if a hospital wants to have adequate patient flow, they must concede to the restrictive notion of exclusivity and become "in-network." This gives insurance direct influence over the hospital systems.

I suppose any system that tries to define complex things in black and white has its challenges. Both CPT and ICD codes are utilized. CPT stands for Current Procedural Terminology. These describe medical procedures that are provided during medical consultation. ICD stands for International Classification of Disease. These are used to describe disease. To keep things light and make sure we "have fun," here are a few actual codes:

- W55.51XA — Bitten by a raccoon, initial encounter
- W55.21 — Bitten by a cow
- W56.12 —Struck by sea lion
- W56.22XS —Struck by orca, sequela
- W61.43 — Pecked by a Turkey
- V97.33 —Sucked into jet engine

- W22.02 — Walked into lamp post
- V00.151 — Fall from heelies
- V91.07 — Burn due to water skis on fire
- Y93.D1 — Activity, knitting and crocheting
- Z63.1 — Problems in relationship with in-law

As producers for the carriers, brokers are influenced by insurance, because the carriers determine the various ways in which they are paid and how much. On the other side of the brokers are the employers, who have voluntarily delegated their power to them to manage their health plans. As a whole, most employers are not yet educated on this topic. I used to be among that majority group. When I became educated, I was able to take back control of our healthcare and represent my employer much better.

Let's talk through an example of how these dynamics have affected the buyer and whether it is reflective of a free market. Have you ever had a concern with the quality of care you received at a hospital? Perhaps you were billed for care that you never received, or perhaps you went in for what you thought would be a free preventative visit, and a non-preventative question "slipped out of your mouth" and you were billed for that. How receptive was the hospital in hearing and resolving your concerns? If you waited long enough on hold and you were able to get through, nevertheless you may not have been able to resolve your concern in a way that seemed fair. With insurance in the middle, there is no real incentive for providers if they do, and no penalty if they do not.

As a result, many hospitals don't invest a lot of resources in customer service. It is no longer a factor of their success, because poor customer service doesn't result in lost customers. This is evident in the message, "We are experiencing higher than average call volumes and wait time is increased." But the message always says that. What is the "average"? And if they are ALWAYS experiencing higher than average call volumes, for the sake of patient experience, wouldn't it make sense to match resources appropriately so this message could be changed and customers could be served? Unfortunately, no, because the patient is often not perceived as their customer. When healthcare consumers are dissatisfied with the quality or cost of their healthcare, there is very little opportunity for recourse. If you talk with someone who has had a bad healthcare experience, this will be part of it. Pay your bills, correct or not, fairly priced or not, in a timely manner or get sued. It reminds me of the chapter titled "Carlsbad" in Dr. Marty Makary's book *The Price We Pay*. These types of hospitals practice with a ruthless, merciless mindset. If that chapter doesn't stir your soul and motivate you to get in the game, you are probably not cut out for this.

The "middleman effect" has diminished the natural consequence of a poor patient experience. Complaints can fall on deaf ears because insurance sits comfortably between the seller and buyer, insulating the hospital from the normal conditions of a free market. Over time, it has conditioned many hospitals to be less concerned with patient experience. Maybe your hospital is different. I visited one recently in Iowa, because of my father's passing, and the care was incredible. Iowa fares better in the national cost rankings. Unfortunately, in many states and with many hospital systems, patients have few options and they must keep going back to receive the same lackluster, overpriced service.

In other industries, if you experienced a pattern of unsatisfactory experiences, you would choose to shop elsewhere. Yet, in healthcare, exclusive hospital contracts are mostly the norm. It becomes, "We won't tell you the price, we don't guarantee a good experience, and you can't shop anywhere else." Ultimately, the insurance company is the hospital's perceived customer and perceived payer. They are the entity that the hospitals need to keep happy in order to survive. We work for those who pay us.

Buying a Vacuum

Have you ever done something a certain way for years, or even decades, and then something "clicked," and you saw the world anew? On a day I least expected it, I had a personal revelation. I was helping our custodial team purchase a new commercial vacuum cleaner. Our procedure required me to get three quotes, evaluate the options, and submit a recommendation for approval. I worked with our local industrial sales representative to see about our options. As he explained the features of each vacuum, I took copious notes, knowing I would have to justify my decision. Commercial hand vacuums ranged from $300 to about $500. I thought to myself, "I feel like I can make a good decision in much less time and with less bureaucracy. Are all these formalities really necessary?" I recalled a purchase I had made earlier that day. I realized I had signed a paper to approve the purchase of our stop loss insurance, at a mere cost of – drumroll ... over $700,000! I had worked with the CFO on the decision and considering our options, I believe we made the best choice. Interestingly, purchasing was not involved and there was no specific procurement procedure to follow. Houston, we might have a problem. I wondered: I'm trusted to spend almost three quarters of a million dollars but I can't buy a vacuum cleaner without special approval? In my experience, to my recollection, every company I have worked for in my career does things similarly.

I kept pondering the notion of why health plan purchases are not viewed as "purchases." A purchase is certainly being made, and for a LOT of money, with little procedural oversight. If you know me, you know that I am not a big fan of black-and-white procedures. I am more a fan of employee education, alignment, buy-in, and trust. However, the distinction in this scenario is clear. Healthcare purchases seem to fall into some other category. Companies manage the purchase of office supplies, sometimes down to the notebook or box of paperclips. They require approval to order pens, notepads, and sticky notes—and office supply costs are pennies compared with healthcare. But office supplies are on the radar, and healthcare is completely off the radar.

These thoughts continued to stir in my brain and I began to apply this thinking to another aspect of our health plan. For years, I had been signing a document which locked the health plan into a narrow network, with the understanding that I was getting a better deal. I began to question if I really was getting a better deal. The truth is that not enough information was given for me to answer that question. After nearly two decades in HR, I realized that day I had been tricked—hoodwinked into signing away my ability to shop. I didn't even know how much I was paying. An average unit price that is known is better than a "great discount" off a price that is not known.

BATNA: One Thing You Must Know About Purchasing

In my undergraduate studies, I was an ambitious student with aspirations to gain experience and qualifications so that I would be accepted into graduate school. The department professors noticed this and supported me through a variety of psychology research projects and extracurricular activities. It's amazing how a little hard work and determination can open doors. As a senior, one professor invited me to enroll in a couple of graduate level courses with him. Without hesitation, I took him up on his offer. One of these courses was titled "Negotiation." It was an unforgettable course and it gave me the opportunity to learn about the concept of BATNA, which stands for "Best Alternative to a Negotiated Agreement."

BATNA affects the power dynamics between a buyer and a seller. In short, it is one's willingness or ability to walk away, and the more a person is able to do this, the more power he or she has in a negotiation.

Let's analyze BATNA in the context of buying a used fishing boat. You look on Marketplace. You find a boat of interest and you contact the seller to set up a time to look at it. In this scenario, both the seller and buyer have a level of BATNA. Some listings have the wording, "Don't need to sell." This reflects BATNA power, in that the seller is asking a certain amount and is willing to walk away if he or she doesn't get a desirable amount. In contrast, if the seller needs the money more quickly, the person's power is lower and the price will be more flexible.

This is the power of choice. The healthcare industry has restricted buyers' ability to shop by constructing one-lane highways with no exit ramps. In this scenario, buyers have very low BATNA and are controlled by the sellers. The buyer cannot walk away, because there is nowhere else to go. One can say, I will do without a fishing boat. I will fish from the shore. However, if we are sick and in need of healthcare, we could delay that care, as many already do, but eventually, if the condition worsens, not only will we have to go, the treatment and cost will be more significant. As you implement your strategy to open up the free market, your "buyer's BATNA" will increase, and the resultant level of each seller's quality, price, and overall patient experience will improve as well.

Lessons from the Big 3

The automotive industry provides a great analogy for what we are seeing in healthcare today and for how the strategy described in this book can impact the healthcare market in America. In the 1960s the traditional big three automakers (GM, Ford, and Chrysler) had the American market wrapped up. In 1965, collectively, they had over 85% of the total market share in the United States. On the surface, it appeared as if they were competing with each other, and in some sense, they were, but the sales were there to be had for each automaker and there was not great pressure to improve. In those days, when someone wanted to buy a new automobile, there were primarily three brands of dealerships to choose from.

While at Toyota Motor Manufacturing, I had the opportunity to work closely with a general manager by the name of Ken. Ken had spent his entire career in the automobile industry. As I knew him, he was older and nearing retirement. Many years prior, before joining Toyota, he had worked for GM as a first line supervisor in one of their old-school auto manufacturing plants. His job was to supervise a group of United Auto Worker (UAW) union employees who worked on the assembly line. Things were a little more relaxed then, compared with how manufacturing plants operate today. Ken shared some great stories with me. He said some employees smoked pot on the line and a few even left during work time to go to the bar and return at the end of the day to clock out. He shared with me that he was more strong-willed as a younger man and he was not afraid to confront individuals who were not contributing to the team's success. Although the union members could be very intimidating, Ken shared how he would stand up to them and try to hold them accountable.

When he upset them, which was often, one way the union members would send him a message was by turning his desk upside down. His desk was not in an office; it was out in the open, on the production floor. In those days, it was not uncommon for physical violence to take place or to have a brick thrown through your windshield if you upset the union. Ken was a large man. He stood 6'5" tall, was about 260 lbs., and was once a linebacker on a college football team. He was big and strong, but as I knew him, he was a gentle giant. He joked of how he could not be intimidated, but his stories certainly showed me how difficult it was to lead in that environment.

As you might imagine, the unit efficiency and quality levels coming out of these plants were less than outstanding. He told me, "Half the cars coming off the line didn't start." It wasn't that they were broken, but that they had many missing parts and were not fully assembled when they reached the end of the line. In those days, lean manufacturing was not yet known or a part of the production process, and stopping the line, which had no built-in buffer, was considered the enemy of efficiency. All the loose parts that could not be assembled, travelled with the car. Typically, they were tossed into the passenger seat or onto the passenger floorboard, to be installed later in a separate off-line area after the car rolled off the final assembly line.

Then Toyota came to town. They entered the American market through a joint venture with GM in California (NUMMI). Several years later, Toyota would go one step further and make a big investment in a greenfield startup in Georgetown, Kentucky – affectionately known within Toyota as TMMK (Toyota Motor Manufacturing Kentucky). This plant created and now supports tens of thousands of American jobs. The complex encompassed 1,300 acres of land, with 150 acres under roof, and a fully functional test race track. I had the great privilege of working at this facility in the early years of my career and this is where I learned much of what I know today about leadership, problem solving, and lean manufacturing.

Toyota began taking market share throughout the 1990s and in 2000, they replaced Chrysler as a new member of the big three. Toyota's quality and efficiency methods, collectively named the Toyota Production System, were producing cars of much higher quality, with greater efficiency. Toyota was becoming a real player in the American market. By 2006, collectively, the former big 3 now only had 50% of the market share. In 2007 Toyota surpassed Ford and shortly thereafter, in 2008, they surpassed the giant automaker, GM, to become the largest automaker.

With the introduction of a new competitor, the formerly tired American automobile manufacturing industry was given a wake-up call. No longer was it the case that each automaker could produce mediocre automobiles, with mediocre efficiency, and still thrive. Things had gotten real. They were losing market share fast and all three needed to change or face real consequences. *The market was effectively disrupted.*

By sharing this analogy, I do not mean to imply that the dynamics of the automobile industry were the same as the healthcare industry today. The automobile industry has always had price transparency and buyers have always had the freedom to shop from the dealer of their choice, without restriction. We might say, the automobile industry wasn't nearly as bad. Lou Holtz once took over a football program and started the season with 0 wins and 8 losses. He joked, "Don't be fooled by how we've started our season. We are not as good as our record indicates."

Today, if you look at all the automakers in the world, each practices their own form of lean manufacturing and produces high quality automobiles, with respectable efficiency. Toyota, along with other transplant automakers like Honda and Nissan, raised the bar for the entire industry. Other automakers such as Volkswagen, Kia, Subaru, Daimler-Benz followed. Today we have a plethora of choices, all competing healthily for market share in a free market, and we are all better because of it.

Overview of the Proven Strategy

The small handful of employers in Wisconsin and other states that have utilized this free-market strategy are better off because of it. This elite group recognized and understood the problems, which we have now discussed thoroughly. Next, it asked the question that each of these employers asked themselves, "Is there a way to succeed within the constraints of the current healthcare industry? More simply, is there a way to win with a traditional broker, traditional BUCA networks, traditional PBMs, and modern-day hospital systems?"

Each of us independently arrived at the conclusion that "reform" was not possible. The problems were too big and too far out of our circle of influence.

This question, and the unfortunate answer it produced, indicated that any proposed solution would need to be outside the box—namely, one that didn't yet exist. This new solution would have to be created, tested, adjusted, and tested again until it was proven repeatable. As a result of those pioneers, today, the picture is much clearer and employers are saving millions of dollars, while greatly improving the quality of their health plan. Employers are in a much better position today to fix these problems because the rugged trail has been blazed. As more employers adopt this strategy, this will become the new norm for employer healthcare.

I've labeled it as "Don't feed the beast." I ask the question, why do we keep feeding and strengthening a beast that is trying to eat us? And it could be very tempting to be angry and to attempt to reverse the current win-lose scenario to a lose-win scenario. That wouldn't be sustainable either, nor would it reflect our motive, which is to find a win-win. What good would it do to make an enemy of hospitals? It is my hope they can be an ongoing and future healthcare partner.

If the current situation is to change, employers must take back the control of their health plan. This means no more delegating. If a broker is to be utilized, he or she must be someone who is courageous and competent, and not conflicted by a skewed compensation structure. Leading transformational change is not an easy thing to do. You will not have the energy to pull dead weight, especially if the dead weight is made up of the partners you are paying to help you move forward.

The model is "purchasing healthcare," as opposed to "purchasing insurance," which has pervaded even the self-funded employers. Because many hospital systems currently do not play fair, they are a less preferred option. The overall strategy and specifically the plan design, will be structured to support transparent, high-quality, competitively priced providers, wherever we may find them.

Patient Choice – A Fork in the Road

We start at the bottom of the picture – a fork in the road where the patient can go left on the dirt path or right on the paved road. The plan design, which will be discussed in detail later in this chapter, offers members a choice of providers each time they need care. As you can see, the highway sign is structured to guide members to the paved road.

The dirt path leads to hospital providers who, under the new plan, fall under a very similar cost structure as the plan design was the previous year, with a deductible, plus coinsurance, up to a maximum out of pocket.

The paved road leads to new outpatient options for care. It leads to the Direct Primary Care (DPC) clinic, and through the DPC clinic to other preferred specialty providers in which care is provided at no cost to the patient. To help members understand the new options, the paved road is an addition to dirt road options that members had last year. This helps people realize that they didn't lose choice, rather, they have gained some free options.

Both roads are available for members to travel any time. They can take the dirt road to the hospital today, they can see a preferred provider on the paved road tomorrow, and they take the dirt road back to the hospital the following day. Hence, the fork in the road is not a "set in stone" decision that is elected in open enrollment. The vast number of choices are all part of same plan and members can fluctuate back and forth as desired.

One common example is if a family has a pediatrician they really like. They can continue to see them, if they are willing to pay the cost of deductible/coinsurance/max out of pocket in the middle tier. If the pediatrician makes a referral to other specialty care, the person can choose between the dirt path or the paved road. Keep in mind, in this scenario the default referral for the pediatrician would be the hospital, as required of them. The member would need to be aware of the paved road options and mention this in order to change the course.

This model is structured so that when the plan pays more, the member pays more, and when the plan saves, the member saves—or pays nothing. It is one that supports the notion of consumerism and shopping for value. Currently, the dirt path includes the hospitals. As things progress and the free market opens up, it is my hope that the separation of dirt path and paved road would not be distinctly defined as hospitals and independent providers. Rather, we might see hospitals gravitate to the paved road; and if independent providers lose their way, they will be moved to the dirt path.

The concepts herein are teachable to members, particularly after repetitive communications and ongoing education. The employer or DPC clinic should not feel pressure to get members to the paved road immediately, nor should the employer feel responsible for the hospital's high prices—the hospital is. If any provider wishes to become a preferred provider, as long as they meet the quality and cost requirements, they can be reclassified on the plan. This is a healthy free market. The onus is placed on all providers to have fair, transparent cost and high quality.

The two separate dirt roads to the left—one before the clinic and one after, are intentional. This represents the member's initial choice to go to the hospital or the DPC to receive primary care. Moreover, the member can go to the DPC clinic for primary care, and thereafter, the person can choose the dirt road for specialty care. If you recall, one of the axioms is that "patients almost always listen to the white coat," wherever that white coat may be. It represents authority and credibility. This is an important knowledge nugget as you structure your model to smoothly guide patients to higher quality, more affordable care on the paved road. Once they are in the hospital system and being referred, or pinballed around, they are much less likely to consider outside alternatives. The hospital will always default to internal referrals.

If implemented well, this strategy becomes stronger over time for two reasons. First, as the employer teaches employees and their families about how the new plan design works and how to utilize the available resources to shop effectively for healthcare, member utilization steadily increases. They win, and the plan wins at the same time. This, in itself, is reinforcing, because year after year, it enables the employer to lower premiums. Once this happens, people really begin to appreciate the change and the momentum forward is sustained.

Second, the longer a free market health plan is in place, the more independent practices can be discovered and added to the preferred provider list. This should be a continuous search. Further, the more employers adopt this method, the more doctors will start independent practices. We are seeing this trend in Wisconsin with many new providers in areas of MRI, infusion, surgery, colonoscopy, mammogram, and new DPCs are sprouting up regularly.

The Chicken and Egg Dilemma

The movement has gained momentum, and more employers are transforming their health plans to a shopping model. The more employers move, the more it will encourage doctors to start independent practices. This can be described as the chicken and the egg situation.

First, the chicken (supply of providers): employers are sometimes hesitant to go down this road because there may be a limited number of primary care or specialty options available locally, within a preferred range of a thirty-minute drive or less. Depending on the area, for secondary care, sometimes an hour or two drive is necessary. As more providers start independent practices, availability will improve. As an employer, it is important to note that you do not need to "interrupt" everything at once. You can literally start with primary care only, add imaging, add orthopedic surgery, and so on. For every piece you add, there will be an associated return on investment (ROI).

Second, the egg (demand from employers): because it is early in the movement and only a select number of employers have adopted this strategy, patient flow to independent providers is limited—and if these new independents don't get enough patient flow, they will not be able to sustain operations. In my experience, it works best when both the demand and the supply can grow steadily, together, at a consistent rate. In Wisconsin, thus far we have a relatively even balance. In this scenario, everyone wins and the movement continues to gain steam and get stronger with each day.

This progression does not happen automatically. Healthy disruption of the suppressed free market is needed. As employers or providers go down this path, they will face a fair number of challenges and complexity. Determination, strong problem-solving skills, and a free market mindset will be necessary to succeed. We must continue to smooth out and pave the rough-cut trail that the pioneers have blazed. Employers must be intentional to free up their plan design from the constraints of exclusive networks; they must support independent providers with adequate patient flow. They must make it the new norm.

It is inspiring to see cases in which employers and doctors make life-changing career decisions for the sake of public trust. A great example is Jason Sansone, MD in Madison, Wisconsin. He, along with 10 other courageous surgeons, decided to leave a local hospital and start an independent clinic/surgery center called Orthopedic and Spine Centers of Wisconsin. They opened in February 2023 with the express goal of delivering greater value to patients needing musculoskeletal care. The group feels they are positioned to deliver to the market what it has long been demanding—namely, affordable, high-quality healthcare for the communities they serve.

Craft Your Free Market Healthcare Strategy

If you're ready, it's time to begin formulating your individual strategy. You will never be able to start any sooner than right now! I am excited for you and what you may achieve.

To aid you in covering all bases, I have included a strategy development checklist. This can help you track your progress during your implementation.

Free-Market Healthcare Strategy Checklist

Initial Steps

Read the following books:
- *The Company That Solved Health Care: How Serigraph Dramatically Reduced Skyrocketing Costs While Providing Better Care, and How Every Company Can Do the Same*, by John Torinus Jr.;
- *The Price We Pay: What Broke American Health Care--and How to Fix It*, by Marty Makary;
- *The CEO's Guide to Restoring the American Dream: How to Deliver World Class Healthcare to Your Employees at Half the Cost*, by Dave Chase;
- Develop a first draft of your healthcare measurement packet
- Plant seeds and gain owners/execs buy-in
- Establish a narrative for change

Financial
- Know every direct dollar paid to partners
- Know all indirect compensation of partners
- Assess value of all income (direct and indirect) for partners
- Develop your funding/insurance approach

Medical
- Redesign your health plan to enable shopping
- Find a DPC partner
- Determine on-site or near-site DPC
- Find a network
- Find a TPA
- Find a PBM
- Find a Case Manager
- Develop a communication plan
- Develop start of preferred provider list
- Determine navigation method

The rest of this chapter will serve as a guide for how to do this. Thereafter, the healthcare partners you choose will work with you to effectively carry out your strategy. In Chapter 5, we will discuss how to choose those partners.

You may be wondering - shouldn't I choose my partners first? I have contemplated this question of order, and have come to the conclusion that it is more important to develop your strategy first, because the details and specific requirements of your strategy can shape which partners you will choose. As an example, if your members are spread out across 5 states, you will want to select partners that are knowledgeable and have the bandwidth to support these multistate initiatives. Someone may be ethical and free market minded, but it is also important to assess their capabilities as well. Some partners will have more resources and potential than others. Plus, you will probably read this book all the way through before you begin, so you will have the knowledge in your brain before you officially start. You can always refer back to specific chapters as needed.

One possible exception to this order would be to consider selecting your broker first. You may want to work with a broker by including the person as an expert resource in the process of developing your strategy. While these kinds of brokers are still rare, the best are wise advisors and will be able to do this. You get to choose the how, the when, and the who of your strategy. Ultimately, your leadership and the quality of your decisions will determine your path for whether you will be successful.

Designate an Internal Champion

Through my studies of the other employer healthcare success stories, one thing that stood out immediately was that each had an internal champion who led the cause. In a couple cases, there was an influential sidekick that walked alongside the champion. By stating this I do not mean to diminish credit for others who contributed; I'm pointing out themes and best practices. Employer healthcare success stories are still relatively uncommon, and there are various examples we can study that have happened across the country over the past five to ten years. I was a champion of one of these stories myself in Wisconsin, along with others like Pat Blackaller (Rice Lake Schools), Will Walker/Mark Gelhaus (Walker Forge), Jake Nolin (Rice Lake Weighing Systems), John Torinus Jr. (Serigraph), and Michelle Golden (Chippewa Valley Schools). For the newer stories in progress, the same dynamic exists.

It's interesting how these situations are viewed before and after the success. None of these people, including myself, woke up one morning and said, I am glad to share that I am going to save millions of dollars of spend with our health plan and improve the quality and offerings for care at the same time. No one could have known this in advance. Instead, it started with a leader who sees a cause and has an intrinsic motivation to correct an injustice and serve the people they lead. It involved the implementation of best practices, one by one, to eventually mold and shape the pieces to form an aligned strategy.

Your Financial Strategy

Let's start with developing your financial strategy, which will be an important piece of your overall free market healthcare strategy. In the previous chapter, we covered some educational topics, such as the types of insurance, pricing models, and healthcare cost tracking. Here, we'll begin to break it down.

In general, the core tenet of a wise financial strategy in health plan management is to understand *every dollar* you are spending: where it's going, who's receiving it, and if it's adding value. Further, whenever possible, it's important to understand how all of that money flows and how much compensation each partner has received from someone else. We want to get all money flowing visibly "on the table", and remove as much flow of money "under the table" as possible. Since the employer is the only true payer, it is important to remember, even if you're not writing the check or processing the ACH directly to a partner, you are still paying. The employer is paying for everything that's happening, even including when a healthcare partner takes you out to dinner.

Employer Fiduciary Responsibility

This approach—managing every dollar—is not just wise, it is a legal fiduciary responsibility of the employer, one that cannot be abrogated or completely delegated to someone else. If you have an employer-sponsored health plan, you are legally responsible per the Employee Retirement Income Security Act (ERISA) to take ownership of and manage your health plan in several ways. ERISA is regulated by the Department of Labor (DOL) through a division called the Employee Benefits Security Administration (EBSA). ERISA was signed into law in 1974 to protect workers from abrupt loss of pension or benefits, sparked by Studebaker-Packard Corporation's decision nine years earlier to close their plant in Indiana, which resulted in 4,000 workers losing their pensions.

I mentioned Chris Deacon and the work she did for the state of New Jersey previously. Chris is now the principal owner of VerSan Consulting. She is an attorney and offers great advice on the topic of employer fiduciary responsibility.

An important linchpin for employers in managing their self-funded plan is to have visibility of their claims data. Typically, this has been a struggle for employers. Most of the large insurance carriers make employers go several rounds before they actually gain access, if they make it that far. Usually, the term "HIPAA" is thrown around as a scare tactic. Never mind the fact that HIPAA was as much about standardization of data to make it more accessible as it was about privacy of personal health information. If and when the data is finally shared, it is usually a cumbersome and painful process, riddled with pitfalls and incomplete fields.

Let me tell you, it doesn't have to be this way and frankly, it cannot be this way. Chris Deacon shares this information: "HIPAA is exaggerated, misunderstood, and misused all too frequently. When you actually read HIPAA, 90% of it is directed to carriers and how they are to structure the data in order to ensure its uniformity for the purpose of standardization. 10% of it relates to the privacy of that individual patient health information, and it explicitly states that a self-insured employer is a covered entity that has legal access to claims data, particularly if it is de-identified." There are employer requirements to protect the data, or Personal Health Information (PHI), and most employers consider that obligation sacrosanct, but it is important we evaluate whether HIPAA is being used as an excuse for behavior to which it does not apply.

ERISA requirements of a plan sponsor (an employer) are not aspirational, they are obligatory. Here are the specific, minimum requirements of employers:

- Act in the sole and best interest of plan participants with an exclusive purpose of providing benefits
- Carry out all of your duties as a fiduciary prudently
- Follow your plan documents
- Hold your plan assets in trust for the exclusive benefits of the plan
- Pay only reasonable plan expenses

The last bullet is one in which employers struggle the most. You can find the answers in this book. The Consolidated Appropriations Act of 2021 opened more doors for transparency. One of these is full visibility of how much the broker is making from the employer plan. In many cases, a full-scale review by an employer of their spending can reveal all sorts of interesting things. Particularly with plans that have been in place for a while, you may find you are paying for things that are redundant or things that you are not familiar with.

I remember doing a cost review with the CFO at Merrill Steel, who had been there over twenty years. He had done a great job in managing the benefits before I arrived, and he hadn't conducted an in-depth review for many years. It was his suggestion we do it. The one-page summary from our TPA was a full page of line-items, each having their own fees. We realized that we didn't understand the services for about half of the line items. This exercise served as a wake-up call that we needed to take back ownership of our health plan. For years, like most employers, all of this work had been delegated to the broker. We started by asking a lot of questions. As we learned, we found that some of the items on the page were valuable, but that a fair amount of them were not. Although our TPA at the time (to be changed later) was not happy with the changes we made and their associated loss of revenue, we felt better because this exercise saved tens of thousands of dollars per year. This was another indicator that our partners may have had some financial conflicts of interest. Shouldn't they have been glad that we discovered healthcare spend that was redundant or not bringing us value? Shouldn't they have discovered it for us? Not really, because they weren't compensated on how well our plan performed. They were compensated by line item, and there were a lot of lines.

How Will You Fund and Insure Your Plan?

An important early decision to make is how you will fund and insure your plan. You will need to purchase stop loss insurance to protect yourself against the risk of less common, extreme situations. For the bulk of the claims, the employer will absorb the risk. We don't use our auto insurance for an oil change or to replace an alternator; employers can think this way too. Paying another entity to take on 100% of the risk is expensive, increasingly unaffordable. Employers must be willing to accept some risk, just as they do in other critical areas of the business.

As described in detail in the previous chapter, the choices are:

- Fully insured
- Level-funded
- Self-funded with stop loss insurance

- Self-funded without stop loss insurance (for very large employers only)

If you choose to be fully insured, you could still choose to implement some of the medical strategy (discussed in the next section). Many of the implementations described will not likely prove cost effective, because any potential savings would be reaped by the insurance carrier. Remember, being self-funded means that you take on some of the risk, and in doing so, you give yourself the opportunity to keep some of the spoils.

Interestingly, there is a trend in some regions of Wisconsin and other states for fully insured employers to partner with a Direct Primary Care (DPC) clinic. The primary gains are recruiting, retention, and better overall health for employees and their families. This scenario comes with an added cost, however, because one can only speculate whether potential savings or cost reductions will be reflected in the annual insurance renewals. Being fully insured means you will have limited visibility of your medical or pharmacy claims data. This lack of visibility makes it nearly impossible to implement strategy effectively. It's like shooting at a target in the dark. Generally speaking, the strategies in this book are intended for employers with level-funded or self-funded plans.

If you choose a level-funded or self-funded plan, you will need to establish the necessary bank account(s) that will be dedicated to your insurance plan. Make sure to comply with applicable regulatory requirements. Typically, your third party administrator (TPA) serves as the primary actor for this, or your broker may be able to help you determine what accounts you need and how you will fund them.

Ongoing Health Plan Dashboard

In the previous chapter I introduced a sample for some key baseline measures. You will want to continue to review the graphs regularly. Feedback on plan performance will help you react and solve problems during the year and it can help you identify long-term opportunities. As an example, if you find you are paying high costs for infusions, you can search for alternatives to these treatments and incentivize patients to receive them at independent infusion centers. Infusion drugs are marked up significantly by many hospitals. They are a top money maker, and therefore, a top savings opportunity for employer plans.

Identify High Claim Areas

Below are some of the top areas for cost to keep these on your "interruption" radar:

- Pharmacy
- Infusions (drug costs typically fall under medical claims)
- Emergency room
- Imaging
- Orthopedic surgery
- Oncology
- Cardiology
- NICU
- Colonoscopy
- Mammogram

Ultimately, you can determine which areas are most important to you. Some employers break down categories further, and call this the "money twenty." Some break down the top claims into two columns: frequency and severity, insofar that 100 individual procedures that cost $1,000 each are the same cost as one procedure that costs $100,000.

A Premium Holiday

After you have started, one thing to consider as you approach the last quarter of your plan year is to review the variable costs you have incurred for medical and pharmacy claims, as compared with your funding forecast. If you find that you are tracking well, and you are not aware of any significant claims in progress, you have the opportunity to take a "premium holiday." These go over very well in the Christmas season. A premium holiday means that you temporarily stop the deduction of premiums from employees' paychecks for a specified period of time, such as for a week or a month. Successful years of lower cost can also lead to the opportunity for a premium reduction the next year. At Merrill Steel, plan performance allowed us to freeze premiums for five years, and we lowered them one year. The premium is what people care about most because it is what comes out of the paycheck before any healthcare is needed. You can gain a lot of momentum and support for your healthcare initiatives by enabling employees to take home more of their hard-earned money. Your employees and their families will thank you.

Your Medical Strategy

It can be beneficial to view your medical strategy through a lens of systems theory. More simply, your full medical strategy will be made up of a large variety of interdependent partners and pieces that will need to function as a single, well-oiled machine. I will discuss how to achieve this alignment in detail in Chapter 7.

Plan Design

If you look at the strategy picture, you will see that plan design is represented by the highway sign at the bottom of the picture. By choosing to be level- or self-funded, you have the freedom to shape your plan design to work for you. If you do a good job educating members, the plan design will do 90% of the work for you, meaning that when you explain options to members, you won't have to be pushy or try to make them feel guilty if they choose to go to the hospital. You don't want to give the impression that you're only changing things to save money for the company. Over time, members will realize that they can save equally. The more you communicate and educate, the more members will see the WIFM (or What's in it For Me?). Be patient in your teaching. Members will grasp the advantages of your plan better and better as they experience it first-hand.

For instance, I talked with a member once who was scheduled for an MRI at a local hospital. I shared with her that I had received a preauthorization request, and I wanted to let her know she had other options. I shared that if she kept her appointment to have the MRI done at the hospital, the total cost of the scan would be around $5,000. Her cost would be $4,000, which was her embedded deductible, plus an additional 10% coinsurance of $200. I let her know that there were other providers who could give her the same MRI scan, and with them, her cost would be nothing. She was hesitant. The plan had just gone live a month ago and this was all new to her. It sounded too good to be true, I suppose. She chose to keep her scheduled appointment.

These incidents can be frustrating for the person explaining the options. It was a no-brainer decision, but we must remember that we didn't learn about this concept in one conversation, and she also needed time to understand it. In her mind, she knew her current path would cost her thousands of dollars, but she also knew exactly what she could expect. This is a long-term process. Some will choose the independent care right away and some may take years. Imagine a month later when she gets the large bill. She will continue to think about it, and as she continues to learn about the new options available to her, there is a good chance she will come around eventually. And when she does, she will have done it of her own will and she will be a smarter shopper for healthcare moving forward. Ironically, in this case, her decision to receive the more expensive MRI scan didn't cost the plan excessively more money. It just cost her more money. The plan paid $800, and would have paid $600 for the other choice. She paid $4,200, and would have paid nothing for the plan choice. Most of the excessive cost came out of her pocket.

With simple and innovative plan design, we can change the mantra from "no shopping allowed" to "shopping is encouraged and rewarded"! How cool is that? We achieve this by consolidating what is often two, three, or four health plans into a single plan with a consumerism structure.

The best practice is to implement a tiered structure, typically ranging from three to six tiers. Each tier represents a categorized increment of cost. The simplest would be to have three tiers. One of the employers in Wisconsin who has saved millions chose to break their provider option into six tiers. In my research, six is the most I have seen. We'll keep it simple here. See the sample of a three-tier design plan below:

	Out of Network - Traditional (Mixed Quality, Very High Non-Transparent Cost)	In Network - Traditional (Mixed Quality, High Non-Transparent Cost)	Preferred (Handpicked for High Quality and Affordable Cost)
	All Nonpreferred Providers	Preferred Hospital	DPC and All Preferred Providers
Employee Contribution		Member Responsibility	
Single		$180 per month	
Employee Plus One		$360 per month	
Family		$440 per month	
Deductible	Member Responsibility	Member Responsibility	Member Responsibility
Single	$3,000	$3,000	$0
Family	$6,000	$6,000	$0
Coinsurance	Member Responsibility	Member Responsibility	Member Responsibility
Single	30%	10%	0%
Family	30%	10%	0%
Maximum Out of Pocket (annual)	Member Responsibility	Member Responsibility	Member Responsibility
Single	$6,000	$2,000	$0
Family	$12,000	$4,000	$0

Prescription Drugs	Pharmacy Type	Member Responsibility
Generic	Preferred /Non Preferred Pharmacy	$15 copay
Preferred Brand	Preferred/Non Preferred Pharmacy	$30 copay
Non Preferred Brand	Preferred/Non Preferred Pharmacy	$50 copay
Specialty	Preferred/Non Preferred Pharmacy	$200 copay

The approach is to assign providers to tiers based on their pricing. If you choose to have more tiers, the increments of pricing would be smaller and more defined. For example, you can have a Tier 1 that is no cost to the member. These providers would be the lowest cost. Your Tier 2 might be providers who are just a bit higher on cost, but still lower than the average. Ultimately, all providers can be categorized into specific cost categories. The beauty of this approach is that it rewards providers for being efficient and minimizing cost. If a provider requests to be in Tier 1, and they are currently in Tier 2, you can let them know what their pricing would need to be for you to make the change on your plan design. The onus is on them to reduce cost and maximize quality, to compete in a free market environment. In these discussions, the specific cost must be known. It should be bottom-up pricing, structured as a specific bundled unit price, or as a percentage of Medicare rate, which can be translated into a unit price. As I have discussed, it should not be in top-down language, that is, discounts off of unknown prices.

You can label the tiers with names that best fit your approach. Sometimes employers will just label the columns blandly, as in Tier 1, Tier 2, Tier 3, etc. Sometimes each tier will have a unique name, as in the example above.

The Quality Question

Early in our journey at Merrill Steel, through a series of employee meetings, I educated the workforce about the new provider options in the plan design. A welder in the group raised his hand and said, "So with these new options that are offered at no cost to us, does that mean we go to a Motel 6, knock on the door of room 119 and ask for Vinnie?" His question made everyone laugh, including me, and it got to the heart of the matter about quality. It sounds too good to be true and there must be a catch, right? The answer is simple. There is no catch. The market has been suppressed, we are opening it back up, wise shoppers will find affordable healthcare that is the same or higher quality.

There is no doubt that quality can be a mysterious question in healthcare. There are many variables at play, making it especially difficult to measure. There are also some good examples of quality measures, such as infection rate for surgeries, that can give us reassurance we are making the right choice. One Wisconsin surgery center conducted research on infection rates and found that the average infection rate for hospitals was about five times the infection rate at their independent surgery center.

From a doctor's perspective, each patient is not the same. Each has his or her own demographics and health history, which can have a favorable or unfavorable influence on the outcome. One patient may be young and healthy and as a result, he or she may be less likely to have complications and more likely to heal quickly. The next patient may be older, or have a lot of health issues, and as a result, the patient may be at much greater risk for complications. Ultimately, this question of quality is not one for me to answer. It is one a medical professional must answer. I can only share some advice on how we need to view it from an employer health plan perspective.

Because we are representing the employer plan, we must keep in touch with the medical community and listen to what they are saying. They are the ones who know best about their peers. If any concerns of quality arise, particularly with trends of bad quality, we must make the decision to remove those providers as options within the plan.

In my conversations with medical professionals, I have learned that independent practices adamantly believe they have better processes and overall accountability for quality as compared with hospitals. They believe this for several reasons. First, all of these doctors once worked in hospitals, meaning they have the privilege of first-hand experience in each environment. Second, they state quality of care as one of the noteworthy reasons they left the hospital and started their own independent practice.

Medical professionals have shared with me that within hospitals, the quality is more hit and miss. Patients sometimes feel as if they are rolling the dice. One Wisconsin doctor goes so far as to say that there are "butchers" out there and if one doesn't know how to evaluate the quality of a surgeon, a patient can be at higher risk. One very interesting thing in healthcare is that quality and cost are inversely correlated, meaning when cost is higher, the quality tends to be lower and when cost is lower, the quality tends to be higher.

Ultimately, you will need to evaluate the providers you offer as part of your plan and make sure the quality of care is high. Research and experience have given me the strong impression that independent practices are better equipped to provide more consistently high levels of service for both primary and specialty care.

Reimbursement and Incentives

For cases in which travel is necessary for a patient to see a provider, there are some best practices to discuss. Travel to receive more affordable and/or higher quality care is commonly referred to as medical tourism.

To lessen the financial burden of travel, reimbursements and incentives can be given. Reimbursements are intended to the keep the person "whole," and incentives can be utilized to motivate someone to consider medical tourism, particularly for higher-cost procedures at longer distances.

When an employer reimburses the employee for travel expenses, it is typically done through their normal expense reimbursement process. This helps keep things consistent for tracking of accounting expenses and it minimizes training requirements and administrative burden. Mileage reimbursement is the default, and each employer can specify or add other forms of reimbursement as desired. Additional reimbursement benefits to consider include food expenses, hotel expenses, excused time off, and paid time off. For out-of-state opportunities requiring air travel, it is easiest to schedule the flight for the member and his or her companion. Per diem gift cards or advance payments can also be utilized for food or hotel costs, if desired, and any unspent money on these cards can be kept by the member.

In some cases, it is wise to offer additional incentives. These can be $1,000, $2,000 or more. You can determine the amounts based on the level of plan savings. These must be taxed as compensation and they must ultimately pay for themselves. It is never wise to offer incentives if the plan doesn't win exponentially at the same time. A joint replacement or heart surgery, for instance, would easily cover the cost of an incentive because the plan would save tens of thousands of dollars, whereas a minor surgery might not justify the means to the end. I have seen some plans go so far as to offer a $5,000 or $10,000 incentive to inspire the patient. If the plan is saving $50,000 or $100,000, it can create a shared win. Without the incentive, the WIFM might be too low. We must always consider the person's needs and make sure it is worthwhile for him or her to consider extensive travel.

Can We Keep Our HDHP?

Sometimes, there are cases in which the employer has what is called an ERISA-qualified High Deductible Health Plan (HDHP) with a Health Savings Account (HSA). An HSA is similar to a Flexible Spending Account (FSA), in that pretax dollars are contributed and these dollars can be used for qualified health-related expenses. With a FSA, the employee is allowed to contribute pretax dollars into the account and the account can only be used for qualified healthcare expenses. With an HSA, both the company and the employee are allowed to contribute pretax dollars into the savings account that is in the employee's name. As long as the money is used for qualified healthcare expenses, the employee will not pay income tax on those dollars. As compared with an HSA, an FSA is less desirable, in that an FSA has "use it or lose it" regulations. Since an HSA is a "savings account," even if the employee leaves the company, he or she still owns the account and will never lose the money. Thereafter, it can be saved indefinitely, it can be used for healthcare expenses, or it can be taken out with tax penalty to be used for other things.

For an employer who is implementing this strategy, it is not uncommon to want to keep their HDHP plan and the HSA accounts, particularly if employees have been building them up for years. We had the same scenario at Merrill Steel and we decided to keep ours in place.

However, in doing so, there are some complications related to the plan design—specifically if the employer wishes to offer certain providers at no cost. Although I have heard differing legal advice, most attorneys will tell you that with a HDHP HSA plan you cannot offer primary care through your DPC as free to members, and further, you cannot offer secondary care as free to members. It's a little bit of a head-scratcher when you think about it. The company is paying for healthcare for their employees, and they don't have the option to pay for 100% of it to providers? No HSA money is exchanged in this scenario. It is my contention that this law should be revised.

Specifically, the ERISA regulations for a HDHP HSA plan state two things. The member must pay the "first dollar" for care, and the amount paid for that care must be "reasonable and customary" for the services received. I won't get into the details here, but there are ways for employers to do this legally, and still incentivize members to go to preferred providers. One of those ways, for instance, is to remember that an employer can incentivize an employee at any time, for any reason. If employers want to give away their money, they have the freedom to do so. Sometimes you have to be innovative, within the parameters of the law, to get the outcomes you desire.

Make Primary Care Your Primary Care

The next step is to decide how you will structure your independent primary care, which is commonly referred to as Direct Primary Care, or DPC for short. DPC is the "heartbeat of the medical strategy." In the DPC acronym, the word "direct" implies that it is outside of the typical hospital and insurance realm.

When deciding who will operate your clinic, it is very important you partner with a primary care provider that is independent and not associated with a hospital system. As a word of caution, do not— I repeat, do not—bring in a hospital system to run your onsite or near-site clinic. Early in my journey at Merrill Steel, I was learning and just getting started. I came very close to doing this. It would have been an innocent mistake, but a significant one nonetheless, that would have required correction. A local hospital had offered to provide care at a rate of 100% of Medicare. That is a great rate, and clearly, a reference-based one, considering that hospitals in Wisconsin can charge as much as 800% of Medicare, discounted typically to 250% to 400% by renting a network. I was tempted to take it, until I had a conversation with an independent DPC provider who opened my eyes.

I came to realize that it would have been an unwise decision to invite the hospital to run my clinic, because I learned that hospitals use primary care as a funnel to collect patients for subsequent costly referral. This is how they make most of their money. Some of my colleagues would refer to this as inviting the fox into the henhouse. I came very close to inviting a referral machine onsite that would have likely *increased* our overall healthcare costs!

DPC reintroduces a lot of the quality factors of primary care that we used to experience many years ago. They achieve this first by slowing down. A typical patient load for a primary care provider in a hospital can be as much as 1,500 to 2,000 patients, while the typical patient load for a DPC provider is 400 to 600 patients. It's no surprise that DPC is able to offer things like same-day or next-day appointments, 30-to-60-minute appointments, open communication channels after the visit, and effective treatment plans, among many other things. In the chart below, I provide a juxtaposition: a side-by-side compare and contrast of the differences between primary care received at a typical hospital, and primary care received at a DPC clinic.

HOSPITAL SYSTEM PRIMARY CARE	DIRECT PRIMARY CARE
Discourages seeking of care	Encourages seeking of care
Unknown Cost	No Cost
Weeks or months for an appointment	Same or next day appointment
Rushed visits	30, 45, or 60 minute visits
Missing or disjointed treatment plans	Effective treatment plans
Unnecessary referrals	Referrals to specialists ONLY as needed
No time for relationships	Genuine opportunity for relationships
Abundance of prescription medications	Prescribe meds as beneficial and renew without a visit
Limited or poor communication after the visit	Provider text, email, or phone accessibility after the visit
Complicated billing, by code (don't bring up a nonpreventive issue in a preventive visit)	Unlimited visits and ancillary services covered (labs, crutches, medical supplies)
Unresolved or worsening conditions	Conditions managed or resolved
An empty wallet	Money in your wallet
A not so good experience	A favorable experience

Through DPC, we take the first step to provide far better care and we put the patient on the path to better health. This method offers the patient better primary care, and it opens the door to better secondary care, if needed.

By introducing our own funnel and offering DPC care, we interrupt the large volume of patient flow to the hospital. This is the smoothest model to achieve this. I know of employers who seem to undervalue the DPC interruption model and instead, they try to pull patients out of the hospital once they are entrenched in it. This is not wrong to do. It is sometimes necessary to try, as we will discuss later in this section. However, in the long term, it is a whole lot easier to interrupt patient flow from the start than to try to intervene in the middle or the end. Once in the hospital system, a patient is much more likely to stay in the hospital system. This is because of the axiom, "patients listen to the white coat." They will listen to the white coat at the hospital or they will listen to the white coat at the DPC. A primary strategy for an employer that ignores interrupting patient flow with a DPC is like trying to pour oil into your car's engine without a funnel. It is very messy and most of the oil doesn't go where it was intended.

Hospitals use primary care as a collection funnel, and we counter that strategy by doing the same. Except we will give patients far better primary care, we will refer only when necessary, and when a referral is needed, we will offer voluntary options to receive high-quality care at a preferred provider at no cost to the patient.

To summarize, there are four primary advantages of offering DPC care to your members.

1. Better Primary Care. DPC is the heartbeat of the medical strategy, because almost all other medical care either goes through it or is supported by it. Primary care can cover as much as 80% to 90% of our medical needs. As a result of the atrophy of employers' benefit plans over the past couple of decades, patients now avoid more care than ever before. They do this, not because they are too proud or too busy to receive care, they do it because of a lack of accessibility and because of high cost. They are footing most of the bill. Delaying the scheduling of an appointment to see a provider until the pain becomes unbearable is not a good approach for one's health. On top of that, once the patient finally makes the phone call for an appointment, it can take months to get in, which leads to excessive and costly urgent care or ER visits. By the time the patient receives care, the condition has sometimes progressed to the point in which higher level care is needed. This means more cost for the patient and the plan. With DPC,

patients can visit their primary care provider as often as they want and at no cost. In fact, patients are encouraged, and often incentivized, to have annual physicals or wellness visits to be proactive about their health and to identify potential health conditions as early as possible.

2 *Refer Only When Necessary.* It is estimated that as much as 50% of the referrals that come out of "rushed" primary care visits are unnecessary. This is due to a couple factors. First, if the provider was given more time, there are many procedures that could have been completed in the primary care visit. Second, a rushed environment also increases the chance for misdiagnosis. Even the best providers cannot be effective if they aren't given adequate time. Lastly, it is not uncommon for hospitals to utilize incentive systems that reward providers for making referrals. RVUs (or relative value units), for instance, which purport to measure productivity, often encourage excessive referrals instead. In many cases, providers are continually reminded and are given financial incentives to increase RVUs and hence to be "more productive."

3 *Refer to Preferred Specialty Providers.* Employers who have succeeded in healthcare follow the best practice of "interrupting" the pathway to the hospitals through a DPC. They practice system avoidance by building an alternative system of healthcare. They choose not to feed the beast that is trying to eat them; rather, they feed independent providers who openly share competitive prices and offer high-quality care. DPCs offer a much greater level of flexibility. Sabina Singh, MD, and Vice President of Anovia Health shares, "DPCs are able to be nimbler and more responsive. Great people with good intentions work throughout healthcare, but bureaucracy can slow everything down. For example, if an employer is set up to refer to preferred providers, the DPC provider can facilitate the referral by making a couple of phone calls. This is a win for everyone involved—most importantly, the patient. A large health system would need to discuss the appropriateness and relationship with the specialist, get the approval from the medical staff, redesign the computer software, and educate the frontline staff on the entire process. Referrals may need prior authorization from the insurance company too. Clearly, this takes a lot of time."

4 *Proactive Health and Wellness.* Wellness programs do not have a very good reputation with employers today. I share a similar sentiment, with a couple exceptions. These programs can certainly offer a warm and fluffy feeling, but the reality is that participation is generally low and outcomes are questionable, at best. There are, however, a couple of best practices related to wellness that my research showed are embedded within employer healthcare success stories.

First, a no-cost annual preventive physical has been shown to identify serious health conditions in patients, which enables the patient to seek treatment early. These can range from an early onset of diabetes to more serious diagnoses such as cancer. Second, if you have a DPC in place, incentivizing employees and their family members to have an annual physical, which is sometimes supplemented with a health questionnaire and coaching, can be a great way to get members comfortable with the DPC clinic and staff. If your clinic happens to be onsite, you can even do this on work time, if desired. The intent is to help everyone feel comfortable going to the DPC when they are healthy, so they will be more likely to go there when they are sick. The higher percentage of members that utilize the DPC for primary care, the greater your plan will perform. If I could choose only one metric to predict overall plan performance, this would be it!

Onsite or Near-Site DPC?

One early decision related to your DPC will be to choose the location of your clinic(s). Specifically, this means whether you will have onsite care or near-site primary care. If you have more than one location, this may involve a mix of onsite and near-site clinics. In some cases, it may involve working with more than one DPC provider. Your structure and the location(s) of your employees mostly determine these things for you. Onsite and near-site clinics each have their own advantages and disadvantages.

For an onsite clinic to be a financially feasible, there needs to be a larger group of members (employees and their dependents) concentrated in one area. A plot of land on which a clinic could be constructed, or an open space within a current structure to be remodeled into a clinic, is needed. The biggest challenge in establishing an onsite clinic is cost. One reason for this is because dark clinics don't tend to go over well. It is a best practice to have the clinic open a minimum of normal business hours Monday through Friday. The risk of a dark clinic is that someone seeks care and is not able to get it. In many cases, the person never returns, instead choosing the hospital for care. This leads them back to their old options, which are the habits and pathways you are trying to change.

In such cases, if you can't keep the lights on all the time during business hours, it is my recommendation to switch to a near-site option that may be a little less convenient but more affordable, because the cost is spread across a few employers that use the same clinic. In some cases, DPC clinics are available 24/7, meaning they take calls after hours and on weekends. This is less common, but it is a huge advantage if you can find a DPC provider that is willing and able to do this. It would enable you to interrupt some of the most expensive care, which is urgent care (about 3x the cost) and emergency care (about 5x or more).

Onsite clinics do offer a few advantages. These fall under the umbrella of accessibility, such as for personal healthcare, work-related healthcare, and wellness program care. An onsite clinic is more accessible for new hire orientation tours, new hire drug testing and physicals, and other testing, such as if your company requires respirators, hearing tests, or DOT certification. While all of these things are more convenient with an onsite clinic, they are still possible to do at a near-site clinic. It would just require local travel. A small disadvantage of an onsite clinic is the potential for members to perceive it as part of the company: they may worry about confidentiality. I have had a few employees tell me that certain situations, such as care that requires one to get fully undressed, can make it uncomfortable when they see the clinic staff at the summer picnic or at the Christmas party. This is understandable. This is why we build choice and flexibility in the plan structure. It will not make or break the plan or the patient to have occasional primary care in the hospital, so long as they understand the lower level of care and potential for pinball referral.

Participation with the DPC

One of the questions I get asked a lot is how to increase employee participation in the DPC. This is one of the predictors, if not the most important predictor, of this model's success. I don't have a magic-wand answer for this, but I have learned the best practices. The theme of the answer is communication, which we will talk about much more in Chapter 6, when we discuss change management. The short answer might be, "Any way you can." More simply, anything you can think of to get people in the clinic, through the clinic, comfortable with the clinic, and trusting of the clinic will support your overall efforts to provide the best primary care possible, and to avoid feeding the beast.

This can include incentives, food, games, sharing stories of good experiences (with permission of the patient, of course), videos, new hire orientation physicals and tours, welcoming clinic staff to your coffee bar, inviting clinic staff to your summer picnic and Christmas party, and overall, meshing the clinic into your business and developing relationships with them as much as possible. At Merrill Steel, we had a pregnant mother fall on the ice in the parking lot once and the clinic was able to see her immediately and perform an ultrasound to make sure her baby was ok. This story was powerful, and the patient was anxious to share her positive experience. We got the camera out and turned it into a television commercial. This is a good example of how having a great health plan can support an employer's recruiting and retention efforts.

Physical Therapy and Chiropractic

Physical therapy (PT) and chiropractic can be a great supplement to primary care as a means of treating musculoskeletal issues. Further, these professionals can be a great resource should the patient need to have surgery. The medical professionals you work with will likely have varying opinions of how primary care and musculoskeletal care fit together. Some primary care providers treat PT as a referral option and some see them as a hand-in-hand partner. Some PTs I work with feel strongly that they should be viewed as the "primary care" of musculoskeletal. I have not heard chiropractors say this, but I believe it is fair to say that many feel the same.

Opinions vary on both of these disciplines as to how, when, and if they are valuable. Some primary care providers say, "I don't believe in chiropractors." Personally, I happen to have one leg shorter than the other (about 7mm), and I have received regular care from chiropractors for the past 30 years. A chiropractor was the first to tell me that I needed a lift in my shoe, which greatly reduced my back pain. Chiropractors are my personal go-to for musculoskeletal problems and health maintenance. Chiropractors focus more on spine and joint alignment, whereas PTs focus more on the soft tissues that can affect the way the spine and joints move. PTs are also great for rehabilitation after surgery. Most medical doctors seem to shun chiropractors, in my experience, as if they are not part of the mainstream medical profession. However, many patients say that chiropractors are the best at root cause analysis to genuinely cure the ailment, while also being more forward thinking in areas of nutrition and natural remedies.

How does each fit in your strategy? It's up to you and the medical providers you work with. I prefer to include both options under the preferred provider column in the plan design. This means that both physical therapists and chiropractors are offered at no cost to members. The use of PT typically requires a referral from the DPC, and chiropractic does not. If you are concerned about too much use, I have never had an issue, but you can put in limits if desired, such as 26 visits per year. I would suggest that only adjustments be covered 100% by the plan—with the understanding that the member must pay the cash rate for anything else. The simplest way I have found is to have the patient pay, which is typically between $40 and $50 dollars per adjustment, and submit the receipt for reimbursement.

At Merrill Steel, we partnered with Dr. Voigt Smith, a PT. He worked onsite two days per week, and he was on-call for other days as needed. His office was just down the road and could be used as needed. Along with doing valuable preventative therapy to help people heal, mitigate pain, and prevent surgery, we also used him for post-surgery rehabilitation. And perhaps most importantly, we used him to hold the patient's hand in the middle—in choosing a surgery center, interacting with the surgeon, and preparing for a surgery. He would even go to the person's home if requested to guide them on how the surgery would impact their daily living: things like helping them remove needed items from top shelves in preparation for upcoming shoulder surgeries. This provided members a great experience and it gave them a personable support person who was medically knowledgeable.

How to Interrupt the Secondary Path

We have talked a lot about DPC and how it can improve the quality of primary care as well as smoothly keeping patients on a more cost-effective path. If done well, implementation of a DPC alone can save an employer 10% or more of total plan spend. However, to get the full bang for your buck, it is important to talk about the secondary referral process.

By looking at claim reports, we are able to view hospital pricing within a region. Interestingly, prices vary dramatically for the same procedures across hospitals and even for the same procedures within the same hospitals. At one hospital, a hip replacement can run about $50,000, while at another it can be as much as $80,000. Of course, these are not bundled prices, so we have to do some addition: in this example, we added together the surgeon fee, anesthesiologist fee, and facility fee, with potentially some cost for hardware. Ideally, we would get an all-in price in advance to know exactly how much we are paying.

By examining post-treatment billed amounts from different hospitals, and comparing them with independent provider pricing, which is often bundled, we find some significant differences. For instance, an MRI from an independent provider costs $400 to $600 and that same MRI costs $4,000 to $6,000 at a hospital.

Drug infusions, which are typically billed under the medical plan (instead of pharmacy) are another area in which the stagecoach is getting robbed. As an example, by partnering with an independent infusion center, an employer plan reduced their cost for a series of Entyvio infusions, which is used to treat Crohn disease, from $271,700 per year to $39,000 per year. Most of the hospital markup is found in the purchase of the drug. This is an actual example of real numbers and real savings.

Surgeries are another place the industry cashes in. It is not uncommon to come across, say, a $300k knee replacement surgery. Yet we know independent surgery centers can perform a full knee joint replacement in the range of $18k to $23k. A doctor shared with me once that he performed a half-hour knee surgery on a patient. Everything went well until the patient showed up at his office about nine months later, holding the bill in his hand: $144,000. The surgeon was put in an uncomfortable position, as he had no idea the hospital charged that much. After the patient left, the surgeon looked up the specific surgery in his records and saw that he was paid $900 for that surgery.

I sometimes joke about the astronomical savings a single action can yield in healthcare. Sometimes a 10-minute phone call can save the plan $50k, $100k, or even more—while providing the patient a high-quality, no-cost option for care. The same can be said for brief emails or texts. It's a unique feeling to end a day of work knowing that a brief, caring action just saved the plan tens of thousands of dollars, while giving the patient free care. It can also be frustrating when a patient decides to walk the beaten path to the hospital, and you know that that person will get a $5,000 bill for an MRI in a few months— for a procedure that he or she could have gotten down the road for a plan cost of $600, with no out of pocket cost.

While these savings from voluntary, redirected care may appear hyperbolic, the reality is that these kinds of outlandish charges are common and happen regularly, every day, all across the country. The chart below describes a detailed example of options that could be presented to a patient who needs to have hip joint replacement surgery. We wouldn't typically share this much detail with the patient, as it might be overwhelming. Ordinarily we simply highlight the factors related to their choice. The evaluation below is for teaching purposes, so the reader can review individual member cost and plan cost separately.

Member Choices for Hip Replacement Procedure

MEMBER COSTS	TRADITIONAL Care Path		PREFERRED Care Path			
Treatment	Local Hospital 1	Local Hospital 2	*Local Independent Surgery Center	*WellBridge Surgical - Indianapolis	*Solstice Health - Milwaukee	*Surgery Center of Oklahoma
Primary Care Visit	$300	$300	$0 copay (DPC)	$0 copay (DPC)	$0 copay (DPC)	$0 copay (DPC)
MRI Scan and Read	$4,700	$4,000	$0 copay (local preferred MRI)	$0 copay (local preferred MRI)	$0 copay (local preferred MRI)	$0 copay (local preferred MRI)
Orthopedic Surgery	$0	$700	$0 copay with Travel Reimbursement	$0 copay with Travel Reimbursement	$0 copay with Travel Reimbursement	$0 copay with Travel eimbursement
Total Member Cost	$5000 max out of pocket	$5000 max out of pocket	$0	+$1,500	+$2,000	+$2,500
Quality	Good	Good	Very Good	Very Good	Very Good	Best

PLAN COSTS	TRADITIONAL Care Path		PREFERRED Care Path			
Treatment	Local Hospital 1	Local Hospital 2	*Local Independent Surgery Center	*WellBridge Surgical - Indianapolis	*Solstice Health - Milwaukee	*Surgery Center of Oklahoma
Primary Care Visit	$300	$250	DPC Subscription Covers	DPC Subscription Covers	DPC Subscription Covers	DPC Subscription Covers
MRI Scan and Read	$5,000	$4,000	$0 copay (local preferred MRI)	$595 copay (local preferred MRI)	$595 (local preferred MRI)	$595 (local preferred MRI)
Orthopedic Surgery	$65,000	$50,000	$28,500	$22,500	$19,512	$17,579
Total Plan Cost	$72,600	$56,150	$29,500	$23,095	$20,107	$18,174
	(estimated prices based on post treatment bills)		(prices based on upfront bundled price sheets)			
Quality	Good	Good	Very Good	Very Good	Very Good	Very Good

* PREFERRED provider

We don't remove the old-school options with the hospital system. Those options are still available, but they will cost the member their $5,000 out of pocket max. The four options on the right offer the patient choices that range from no out-of-pocket cost to additional money in their pocket. Imagine actually getting paid to have major surgery. That is how expensive healthcare has become.

Remember, the plan never incentivizes unless that incentive more than pays for itself. In this example, if the patient is open to travel, based on the level of savings, we can offer as much as $2,500 to fly to Oklahoma. We know the quality is great and it is the lowest cost available. Options like Wellbridge Surgical in Indiana and Solstice Health in Milwaukee are also highly competitive, and all of these providers post their prices online. The other local option at the independent surgery center costs the plan a little more, but it requires the least amount of travel. By offering patients several options, with varying costs and reward differences, they are typically inspired because they are given freedom of choice. They are also comforted to know that they will not go broke having a major surgery, which is stressful enough without having to worry about how you are going to afford it.

These interruptions can offer the patient a very rewarding medical and financial experience and an increased standard of living. Typically, the patient will return and share their positive experience with many others, which further promotes the strategy. Across the nation, many options exist for these types of cash-based surgeries:

Surgery Center of Oklahoma – http://www.SurgeryCenterOK.com
THE pioneer in cash pricing for surgery

Surgery Center of Allentown– https://scoallentown.com, Allentown, PA

Christian Healthcare Specialists https://chspecialists.org/

Lonestar Surgery Center – https://lonestarsurgeryctr.com
West University Place Houston, TX

No Insurance Surgery - http://www.noinsurancesurgery.com/
Las Vegas, NV

Pacific Surgical Center – http://Pacificsurgicalwa.com, Longview, WA

QuikSurg – https://www.quiksurg.com, Chattanooga, TN

Texas Free Market Surgery – https://texasfreemarketsurgery.com
Austin, TX

OrthoIllinois – https://www.orthoillinois.com/
bundled-pricing/surgical-procedures

North Texas Team Care Surgery Center – https://www.nttcsurgerycenter.com

---

NW Surgery – https://nwsurgery.net/direct-pay, Houston, TX

Solstice Health – DPC Clinic Oconomowoc & New Berlin
Direct Medical Care Milwaukee (solsticewi.com)

WellBridge Surgical – WellBridge Surgical -
High-Quality Surgical Services - Zionsville, IN

Free Market Medical Association – http://marketmedicine.org/free market-map
Map of free market medical facilities and physicians

One thing to keep in mind, as you help the patient make a choice and schedule a surgery, is to be sure not to waste a surgeon's time. The best practice is to have the discussion with the patient and have him or her choose the provider first, and then reach out to the surgery center to get the ball rolling. In contrast, if you have consultations with a surgeon at one surgery center and the patient later chooses another surgeon, not only will the patient have to repeat the consultation, the surgeon will become frustrated as well. We must help these providers remain efficient to keep their costs down.

Who Helps the Patient Choose the Provider?

A common question with this model is, "Who has those discussions about choice with the patient?" There are two ways to do this. First, in some cases, if you have a clear list of preferred providers, broken down by specialty and location, you can give this list to the DPC. The DPC doctor will refer to the list whenever one of your employees needs any of the procedures that are listed. Like primary care providers in the hospital systems, DPCs are positioned well to refer. However, remember, referring a patient to a specialty is one part, and talking through the detailed options with a patient in the context of their specific employer plan design is another. Most DPCs, if given an adequate list and the right support, are willing to have these discussions, particularly in that all the paved-road options are free. For specific deductible accumulator questions, those can be directed to HR or the TPA's customer call center. How amazing is it that, we can take care of the patients medically, while also supporting them financially?

The other primary method to have these discussions with patients is to use what is commonly called a "patient advocate." Ross Bjella, an entrepreneur in Wisconsin, has been offering this service to forward-thinking employers for the last decade. He founded Alithias, which is a data-driven advocacy company that does both of these things. First, using a database of millions of adjudicated claims, he has compiled a list of high-value providers for a large variety of procedures. Second, he employs Patient Advocates who support DPCs and members with referral navigation.

Alternative Ways to Interrupt

As you can likely see, the smoothest and most reliable way to interrupt or redirect care is by creating our own funnel of alternative primary care, called DPC, and having those white coats guide patients to better care.

There are two additional ways of encouraging patients to consider alternative care that are worth mentioning. I cannot emphasize enough that most of your energy, time, and resources should be spent on strengthening this primary way of interruption, but for cases in which that didn't work, I will discuss two backups.

First, by working with the Utilization Management (UM) vendor, we can gain visibility for preauthorizations, which are a request from a provider, based on a plan requirement, to approve and verify that a health care service, treatment plan, prescription drug, or durable medical equipment is medically necessary. Any time we are looking at personal health information (PHI), as classified by HIPAA, we have to make sure we are complying with the law. This typically means that a select few people within the employer's purview will be provided HIPAA training and an internal HIPAA officer will be designated. PHI should only be viewed by this small group, which is commonly made up of HR and sometimes a CFO or controller-type position.

Through this visibility, we can see when someone is scheduled for a procedure with a less preferred provider. If the procedure has not happened yet, there is a possibility of talking with the patient to make the person aware of a better alternative. For instance, through a preauthorization request, the plan administrator may see that Sue Smith is scheduled for an MRI next Wednesday. In Sue Smith's area, the plan administrator knows that a preferred MRI provider is available. This means that Sue can be presented with another option. She can proceed on the usual path and pay upwards of $4,000, or she can receive the same level of procedure at no cost to her by going to another MRI provider. In these cases, we are not manipulating the patient's experience or sacrificing her health for the sake of plan savings. Rather, we have the opportunity to present a better option to the patient that will give her equal or better quality, at no cost to her.

The other backup option is similar, in that the procedure is again flagged through a preauthorization. However, in this instance, another method can be used to intervene. This can be done with someone who is PHI-certified within the company, such as an HR manager. If this person has trust with the employee, he or she can have this same discussion. The HR manager can use the same line: that he or she was notified that a "preauthorization came through." This can be a touchier situation because we don't want to create an impression that the HR person, or the company in general, is "nosing" in everyone's personal medical information. My suggestion is to handle these on a case-by-case basis and use discretion. The upside is that in many cases, the patient is very glad someone intervened, because it can save him or her thousands of dollars.

Case Management and Disease Management

Case management (CM) and disease management (DM) are common terms used in the industry. Both cover a variety of specialties, and their stated intent is to manage the complex, expensive cases on a plan – the ones in which 5% of plan members account for 90% of the plan's cost. I have seen various statistics on this, and I suppose it varies. Maybe it's that 5% of members account for 80% of the cost, or 10% of members account for 90% of the cost. I also know that 78.6% of statistics are made up on the spot.😊 Whatever the actual percentages, we know this concept is real and it should be on your radar when managing your plan.

When done well, these services can provide your members with a caring patient advocate. If you ask case management companies what their biggest challenge is, they will tell you "engagement"—meaning, the biggest challenge is getting the patient to trust and work with the advocate.

This is where some valuable HR knowledge is useful. How about we change what we call it, to start? Many CM/DM companies use the title "case manager," as in, "Hello, Mary, I am calling from your insurance plan and I have been assigned as your case manager. My job is to review your medical treatments to make sure they are appropriate and cost effective." From the patient's perspective, this often feels impersonal. It can create the impression that it is just "someone from the insurance company trying to save money"—while the patient has just been diagnosed with a life-threatening illness or disease. The individual's tree has been shaken and he or she is already distracted and worried. It is no surprise that status quo case management companies report an average rate of 20% engagement.

By changing the title to nurse advocate or patient advocate, we can begin to work toward building trust with the patient. This will still likely need to be explained, but in a different way. Try, "Hello, Mary, I am with your insurance plan and I will serve as your patient advocate. I recently heard the news about your diagnosis, and I am so sorry you are having to go through this. I am a trained nurse and I want you to know that I am a dedicated resource to help you through this. This means that I can help make sure you are getting the care that you need, and that you are getting covered for that care. Further, I can answer any questions you may have and I can be a confidential resource for you. My goal is to help you and your family get through this and to help you get better. I will give you my cell phone number so that you are able to reach me if you would like. I can take calls on weekends as well."

When effective case management (patient advocacy) happens, the patient gets the best care, the plan spends money more wisely, and there is the best chance for the patient to recover 100%. Protecting the patient and his or her family from financial ruin should not be overlooked. A side effect of cancer treatment should not be bankruptcy! The family already has enough to worry about. We are talking about fathers, mothers, sons, daughters, children, and siblings—fellow human beings. They deserve personalized, caring treatment, not some stranger calling them to place restrictions on care, deny care, or delay care so the person passes away before they receive it (the typical way status quo case management saves money). If you talk with people who have worked in this industry, it happens all too often.

Concerning personalized care, a caveat of the best practice I mentioned to increase the engagement rate is to have someone the patient trusts contact him or her first, in person, and mention that a patient advocate will be reaching out. In many cases, this could be someone in human resources for the employer, particularly if there is a trusting relationship already built. The HR person is on the HIPAA list, so there is no concern there. He or she can connect on a personal level and empathize with the person. Next, he or she can mention that a patient advocate (include the name) will be reaching out to them and can hold their hand to offer support through this process. These are sensitive conversations and should always be handled with great care. The motive is to genuinely help the person, and if done well, it is typically received as such. In my experience, by following these best practices, instead of the bland, impersonal status quo approach, we can flip the engagement rate from 20/80 to 80/20—that is, 80% of patients engage because they trust that you really do want to help.

I wish I could say that the industry standard is the "patient advocate" approach. Unfortunately, it is more of the "case manager" approach. In these cases, we don't see much advocacy or genuine help. We most commonly see "case documentation": there is incredible documentation of what is happening with the case, but not much connection or influence on the care the person receives or emotional support for the patient as he or she goes through a life-threatening experience. Case documentation is typically billed at a range of $100 to $150 an hour, which means they are adding significant cost on top of an already exorbitantly expensive case.

One company that does this well is Veza Health. Founder Cori Zavada employs a small team of caring nurses that serve as patient advocates. They connect with the patient, show him or her genuine care, and help the person traverse the rough and deep waters. It is no surprise that Marty Makary is part owner in this business.

Questionable Hospital Bills

It is important to be an expert on this topic, or to have someone available to help you who is. A reporter by the name of Marshall Allen wrote a book, and the reference is listed below.

- Never Pay the First Bill: And Other Ways to Fight the Health Care System and Win, by Marshall Allen

If you have interest in learning how to skillfully push back against questionable hospital bills, this book can be a great resource for you. Hospitals have a lot of money and partner with legal firms for collections. Allen discusses proven strategies of how companies have fought overbilling, price gouging, and insurance denials. Because the core tenet of the employer strategy shared in this book is to not "feed the beast"—namely, to avoid the use of hospitals and/or BUCA carriers—this isn't an area in which I go into depth. I provide this reference as the best I know of to become knowledgeable in this area.

Emergency Room Cost Control

A big frustration of plan administrators are the costs incurred in the emergency room. Often, when there is no other care available, members go to the ER after hours or on weekends for sicknesses when all they really need is urgent care. This creates a lose-lose situation for the member and plan. For the member, it means sitting in a germ-filled waiting room, and being bumped to the end of the priority list for care, sometimes waiting many hours to be seen.

For cases of true emergency, similar dynamics apply, except in these cases, there are few checks and balances. The potential is there for a lot of care to be provided without the member's awareness. Add in an overnight stay and it is not uncommon for the bills to be in the tens of thousands of dollars. This means a maximum out-of-pocket expense for the member and a hefty bill for the plan.

In the past, there hasn't been much a patient can do about this. The No Surprises Act of 2022 helped things a little, in that it ensured that patients will not be billed out-of-network rates for ER care. However, with the mysterious pricing practices in healthcare, how can one really be sure? The prices are not disclosed in advance and patients are still at the mercy of the hospital's coders and billing department.

Further, when receiving emergency care, the potential exists for hospitals to "upcode." Technically speaking, upcoding is fraud, and it is illegal. However, accountability and oversight are lacking. Each episode of ER care is attached to a level, which is meant to describe the severity of the patient's condition, reflective of the care being provided. Hospitals rate the level of severity of care based on the patient's condition, with most using a rating scale of 1 through 5, with 5 being the most severe. Each increasing level of severity multiplies the factors for the amount the patient is billed. Many patients are left feeling helpless, with very large bills they are unable to pay, and the hospital is prepared to swiftly take them to collections. If you have read my story of being run over by a tractor, you know that I have experienced this firsthand. Ultimately, it felt more like I was run over by the hospital's billing department.

	Al Lewis, a Harvard-trained attorney, has found a way within federal healthcare law to protect patients and the plan from exorbitant ER costs. Specifically, his method limits a patient's exposure for non-elective ER events. His company is called Quizzify.

	Lewis's method is very straightforward. He recommends that, instead of signing the ER's consent to be billed the hospital's normal exorbitant rates, you write in one sentence, which contains 29 carefully crafted words. Doing this enables a patient to cap fees at 200% of the Medicare rate. Lewis notes, "Hospitals can try to deny this effort, but history shows if they try to charge above the 200% rate, they will lose later." Anticipating pushback, Quizzify offers a 24/7 support line with an attorney on demand. "It's not a negotiation," says Lewis. "If they say no, call the number and we explain the law to them on a recorded line and that's the end of it, period."

	What's amazing, Lewis says, is not how well it works, but rather the near-complete lack of interest by larger self-funded employers. He often hears responses like, "Our employees won't be interested," or "We don't want to upset providers," or "This isn't on our strategic plan for this year." Ultimately, this can be a good option to protect members and limit excessive plan costs for ER visits.

CHAPTER FIVE
Choose Trustworthy Partners

An Early Morning Revelation

On a cold winter morning in Wisconsin, I started the day by pouring myself a cup of coffee. This was part of my normal routine, although on this particular day, I went in to the office much earlier than normal. I had woken up about 4 a.m. and almost immediately, the gears in my mind started turning. I was thinking about the healthcare changes we were making and I was excited about some upcoming meetings. Still a little groggy, but unable to fall back asleep, I rolled out of bed, got cleaned up, and made the 22-minute drive to Merrill Steel in Schofield, Wisconsin.

The steaming hot coffee tasted especially good that morning. The temperature reading on the screen of my car read -23 degrees on the way in. Those are the days that you don't dare frown for fear your face will freeze like that. I sat down at my desk and sipped my drink. It was dark—and quiet, which is unusual for HR. The sun had not yet risen and most of the office staff had not yet arrived. Employees in our heavy steel fabrication shop, one of the three best in the country, were already in full swing. Their start time was 5 a.m. On my walk into the office I looked over the fabrication shop and I could see streams of sparks flying off the grinding wheels and the flashes of light from the welders. A handful of employees were already in the office. These were the diehards who had transferred from the shop to desk jobs; they were accustomed to waking up before the birds.

As the caffeine began to stimulate my brain, I had a thought (I know—that's a little scary). I grabbed my favorite blue dry-erase marker, walked up to my giant-sized idea whiteboard, and began listing all of our current healthcare partners. This was not some deep-level strategic exercise. I wasn't fully awake yet. It was a casual train of thought that I acted on, one I would realize later had significant value. I listed out the alphabet soup names of all my healthcare partners and sat back down in my chair to analyze it.

I asked a few simple, rhetorical questions of the current partners:

- Who has a free-market mindset?
- Who realizes there is a problem with healthcare?
- Whose compensation is aligned with our goals?
- Who is willing to support transformational change?

It was at this moment, alone in my office, that I arrived at the stark realization that only one partner on the entire list passed the "fit test": the DPC that we had just chosen. Over the next couple of years, I would facilitate the transition to a completely new set of healthcare partners that aligned better with where we were going. These changes would not be easy to carry out, but they would be necessary if we wished to be successful in living out our strategy. I took an optimistic perspective of the challenge. I told myself that I'd only have to go through this once.

Trust as the Foundation

This chapter is about trust, and specifically, how trust is the foundation of all personal or business relationships. Without it, nothing can be sustained—at least not in a healthy, optimal way. This thinking leads us to the task of evaluating all healthcare partners, current and prospective, as to whether they are trustworthy and effective.

For the past several decades, employers have been inconceivably lax on holding healthcare partner relationships to a high standard of trust. It seems we are accustomed to evaluating trust with other individuals we do business with: do I trust my mechanic; do I trust my plumber, or do I trust my barber or hair stylist? After all, the scariest word one can hear while getting a haircut is *"oops!!"* If the answer to this "do I trust" question is no, we would instinctively be looking for someone else. If this is true, why have employers not applied these same standards to the healthcare partners they pay to run their health plan?

It is important to take a little time here to break down the concept of trust and thoroughly understand it. Trust is more than a word. It is the bedrock and glue for all relationships. If you don't have trust, you don't have a relationship. Allow me to explain. Think of a person you don't trust who you have a good relationship with. Are there any? Now think of a person you trust whom you have a bad relationship with. This scenario is unlikely to exist. Trust and relationships are closely intertwined, and they cannot be separated.

As you go forward, you will need to evaluate your partners and assess if they regularly exhibit trust-building behaviors or trust-breaking behaviors. It is important to acknowledge that the longer the trust gap has existed, the more "normal" it seems and therefore, the harder it is to recognize. And we can't fix issues we don't recognize as problems—because they are not visible to us. By reopening these "closed cases" you can begin to evaluate the contribution and performance of your partners to make sure they will be a good fit so that you can effectively carry out your new strategy—one that will require more open-mindedness, flexibility, and "out of the box" thinking than ever before.

A mentor once told me that a person's trustworthiness can be measured by reflecting on "accumulating personal interactions." More simply, he said, "When you meet a charmer, you are blown away in the first interaction. However, if that person only has skin-deep character, each consecutive time you talk with that person, you think less and less of him or her." In other words, as you get to know the person better, his or her lack of virtue or substance begins to show through. Conversely, if you meet someone, and each consecutive time you interact with him or her, you trust that person more, the person's virtue and character are becoming more apparent to you. This emphasizes the importance of getting to know prospective partners, taking the time to have breakfast, lunch, dinner (can you tell I like to eat?), visiting them at their workplace, or inviting them to your home, so that you can interact in different environments.

I have always found this idea fascinating—that the more you get to know someone, you ask, "Do I trust this person more or less?" This knowledge has shaped my ability to read people and choose trustworthy partners. It's disheartening that so many in the healthcare industry today have lost their way. Money is a powerful thing and unfortunately, many individuals are "bought and paid for" by the industry.

Let's talk about some specific ways to assess relationships with health partners. This is worded in a context of trust-building behaviors, with the direct opposite being trust lowering-behaviors.

Trust-Building Behaviors

- *Do they keep their word?* One way to assess trust is to see if they keep their commitments by doing what they say they will do. If they expect to miss a commitment, do they communicate in advance and explain? We must be able to rely on others to follow through. Their actions must match their words.

- *Do they tell the truth?* Honesty and integrity are critical in any relationship. When you talk with them, do you find they speak the truth? If the answer is no, particularly if there is a pattern, trust will be low. Trust-filled relationships are built on truth.

- *Do they talk straight?* Do you have any partners who talk a lot, but never seem to say anything? They may speak very well, but it's almost as if they are a talking head, having their own conversation. They don't answer questions directly and after a fair number of attempts on your part to clarify or rephrase your question, you still can't get a straight answer. These conversations frustrate me the most. I call it fluff talk. If you feel there has been a pattern of fluff talk, regular avoidance of real answers and real action, it will be nearly impossible to be productive with this partner in the future.

- *Do they care about you?* One interesting question to ask yourself about a healthcare partner is, "Do they genuinely care about me, my company, and my members?" You will know the answer to this question inherently, without a lot of deep thought. Somehow, we just know if someone cares. A healthcare partner can be competent but still not care about others, and both are required.

Your members will see through this smokescreen quickly. When someone knows or feels another person doesn't care, they won't engage and they certainly won't follow you on a healthcare improvement journey. You will have trouble winning if even one of your partners is self-serving or doesn't care about others.

- *Do they seek shared wins?* Have you ever had a relationship in which the other party played mind games? This can be very frustrating. A simple example of this could be in the formation stage of a relationship and specifically, the establishment of pricing. The typical way this happens is one party offering an inflated price and expecting the other party to negotiate them down. In their mind, if they start high enough, even if they come down, they can still achieve a high margin. I try to head off these bad habits and trust-breaking kinds of conversations. I state openly from the very beginning, "One year from now, each of us will evaluate the business relationship from our own perspective and determine if it is fruitful. If either of us determines that we aren't winning, that party will end the relationship. Therefore, let's be honest with one another now, and not play games. Let's establish a relationship that is sustainable—one in which we will both win." I ask for a fair, sustainable price, and I assess it to make sure it is competitive. From there, it is important that both parties are open and honest and focus on winning together. There can be no games in the relationships with your healthcare partners. You simply will not have the time or energy to play them. Teams should never compete internally. The competition is out there.

- *Are they good team players?* Lastly, it is important for everyone to follow the golden rule—to treat others like we want to be treated. Be very cautious of selfish people because they don't make good team members. The name on the front of the jersey is more important than the name on the back. As you build your assembly of partners, everyone must want to win together and to be flexible so to the member, it comes across as a single, well-oiled machine.

When assessing trust, it is important we recognize that these are not black-and-white assessments. Some gray always exists and we must discern wisely. Try to assume good intent with others when possible. Show grace when it's appropriate to do so, perhaps even when they don't deserve it. But when pattern-like gaps are present, we must act quickly to correct them or be willing to make difficult decisions to "right the ship." For cases in which a partner change is necessary, ideally you want to change one time. This means it is important to allot an appropriate amount of time to assess prospective partners in order to make sure they are a good fit. This is easier said than done, and I will discuss best practices for how to select new partners later in this chapter.

The Conscience Is a Funny Thing

A great deal of money flows in various directions in healthcare, and the complexity of those flows means that few really understand it. Money that is not seen can become subject to the greed of the unscrupulous. How can some people allow themselves to run over others in pursuit of their own gain? It seems that if we should trust an industry, it would be the healthcare industry. These are the entities we literally trust with our health, welfare, and lives. When the lights come on and people see behaviors that indicate a motive of profits over patients, it can be disturbing. I suppose the answer goes back to our human nature, and Orwell's animal-farm allegory. While we are all imperfect, the question remains, why do some people seem to live their lives with more virtue, and some fall off the integrity wagon? We might understand this further by looking at our conscience and how it works.

Conscience is a funny thing. We all have one. Some choose to listen to it, and some may not. Our conscience is an inner voice, an unspoken prompt that tells us when something may be off, or when we should take action to make something right.

I read a story once about a new college campus being built. The contractor shared a best practice that they would not install the concrete sidewalks until the campus was in operation for a few months. The college administrators didn't understand. Why wouldn't they just install the sidewalks right away so they could complete construction and wouldn't have to come back? They asked for explanation. The contractor said, "We plant grass, and let the students form the paths. The students will take the best routes between campus buildings and as a result, they will naturally wear down the grass of the ideal walk paths. Once it is clear where the students walk, then we put in the sidewalks. If you put in the sidewalks first, you will end up with dirt paths elsewhere and have to redo everything." The college administrators smiled and agreed that their approach made a lot of sense.

The reason I share this story is to show how our conscience is like grass. If we step on grass once, it bounces back up to its original position. Similarly, if we violate our conscience once, it tells us something is wrong but it is still healthily in place. However, like grass, if we violate it repeatedly, over and over, eventually we do not feel the internal prodding that we have done wrong or that we need to correct something. Like grass, it has been trampled, and it dies.

Choose Trustworthy Partners

Let's begin by discussing the process of evaluating your current partner roles. You should not assume that new partners will be needed. If you are fortunate, you will only need to realign your current ones, or you will only need to change some of your partners. While it is good to be optimistic, more times than not the industry players are so habituated in their ways, and their consciences have been so thoroughly trampled, there is a high probability that you will need to change several, if not all of your partners in order to be successful in the long term. It's not that we want to stir this pot or create all this change, but again, you will not have the energy to pull the dead weight of the people you are paying that are supposed to make your life easier—not harder. Ultimately, you will decide who stays and who goes.

> The bulk of the legal compliance of your employer-sponsored health plan mostly falls under your TPA's umbrella.

Choose a Trustworthy Broker

The first and most important assessment is to fill your need for an expert advisor. This role is unique, in that whomever you choose will help you determine who your other healthcare partners will be. If you make a bad choice at this stage, you could lose a lot of valuable time and energy.

Traditional brokers, especially the largest ones, often paint a dramatic picture for employers: if the broker is not expensively retained, compliance requirements will be missed and company executives will be wearing orange. While this notion can make company executives feel comfortable when they hire such a broker, it is misleading. Traditional broker tasks, including shopping the market for ancillary benefits, can typically be completed in a nominal amount of time. This means, when it comes to basic compliance and the purchasing of ancillary benefits, employers could be overspending by tens or hundreds of thousands of dollars each year.

As a result of the issues with traditional brokers and their unwillingness or inability to help employers create successful health plans, there is a growing trend by employers to structure this role internally, such as with a full-time employee. I will talk more about this option later in this chapter. However you decide to structure the role, this is the person who will be a key leader for your health plan. This person will teach, mentor, and guide others. Further, this person will facilitate brainstorming meetings, lead discussions on plan design, conduct partner assessments, help you choose new partners as needed, co-champion implementations, and help you develop employee communications.

Broker Role

We begin by summarizing the need. An employer's need can be summarized in the following categories:

- Legal Compliance
- Issue Resolution
- Ancillary Benefits
- Strategy and Implementation

With the exception of ancillary benefits, the other aspects of the role are intertwined and are difficult to separate. I will do my best to explain each independently.

The bulk of the legal compliance of your employer-sponsored health plan mostly falls under your TPA's umbrella (discussed in the next section). The broker plays a support role here, and should be knowledgeable concerning the laws and regulations that are applicable to the plan.

Another portion of the role is issue resolution. This could be to help a member deal with a billing issue, to facilitate insurance coverage, to answer plan-related questions, to work with providers, or to address other issues that may arise in the administration of the plan.

With a level- or self-funded employer plan, there is often a need for ancillary benefit insurance to be purchased, or brokered, such as dental, life, vision, AD&D, and more. All of these are important, but they aren't nearly as complicated as healthcare, nor are they as corrupted: you can call your dentist and ask the price of a filling or a crown, and they will tell you! Similarly, you can call your eye doctor and ask the price of a vision exam, or how much a typical pair of glasses costs, and they will openly tell you. The issues are not with ancillary benefits, and as a result, they can be purchased fairly and efficiently without a special strategy.

On occasion, the stop loss insurance may be brokered, and if it is, there is a good chance the broker is collecting a commission of 10% or 15% on the premium. This is not inherently wrong, but it does raise the yellow caution flag for two considerations. First, it could result in the broker getting a raise when your claims go up (misaligned commission incentive) and second, it may not be the best bang for your buck. For instance, if your stop loss insurance premium is $500,000, would it be better to quote it yourself and save 10% to 15% of that cost? You could employ a person for a whole year for that amount of money. Most often, the TPA is the one doing the actual quoting of the stop loss. Quoting stop loss is relatively easy and straightforward and for an experienced person, it does not take a lot of time.

This leaves us with the health plan advisement for strategy. If you contract with an external broker (and pay them a fair amount), this is where you will get your money's worth. Remember, this is not a topic that most brokers are comfortable discussing. For years, and even decades, the mode has been to blame the industry and go with the flow—to paint a picture showing that nothing can be done. Those kinds of answers are no longer acceptable.

Broker Compensation

In previous chapters, I have talked about all the ways traditional brokers are compensated, both in direct payment from the employer and indirect payments made by the ASO/TPA, or PBM. Whoever is getting paid, wherever they are getting paid, remember, the employer and the employee are the ones ultimately writing those checks.

To understand the root of the problem, we can analyze a broker's early career experience. New brokers are typically hired by a firm and given support to pass the state certification process. In Wisconsin, a brief course is required and the prospective broker must pass a 50-question state exam to become certified. Interestingly, the state certification training is 100% in the box and does not prepare a broker for the self-insured model. For example, in the 490-page study manual for the Wisconsin state broker certification, self-insurance is mentioned once and fills a half page of information, which mostly consists of the definition: "A business that pays its own claims." Knowing this background gives us an understanding of how healthcare brokers are shaped and molded early in the education and employment experience to fit into the system—into the insurance box. They are specifically and intentionally taught to "sell insurance." For Wisconsin, it is interesting that Blue Cross Blue Shield is mentioned a few times in the study guide and in the actual test questions. No other insurance company is mentioned.

After certification, brokers typically start work, with a fair portion of their pay structured as variable; meaning they are immediately thrust into a situation in which they must sell insurance if they wish to achieve a sustainable income and put food on their table. And the more they sell, the more they make. Concerningly, health plan sustainability, affordability, and particularly a reduction in healthcare costs for the employer, are not stated goals. In fact, such an achievement would typically reduce a broker's commissions, and therefore, a broker's overall compensation. It is important to note that the individual brokers did not design or request this compensation system. It was given to them, yet we see many examples of how it can affect behavior throughout the span of a career.

Once started, the pressure is on to begin building a "book of business." This approach to rewarding brokers has worked very well for the insurance industry. It has not worked for employers, however. Employer plans have steadily degraded and they continue to decline. Renewal increases of 10%, 20%, 30%, 50%, or even 100%, means the broker has been getting a matching percentage of raise in their commission. Employers can no longer work with any partners that become wealthier while their plan falls apart. A broker's performance should no longer be judged on his or her book of business, rather, performance should be evaluated on the overall outcomes of the employer's healthcare plan, and proper incentives tied to shared-win outcomes. As the employer healthcare success story formula indicates, everything must add up to equal a positive-sum outcome of $1 + 1 = 2$. In this instance, the broker wins and the employer wins. It is a sustainable outcome in which everyone wins moving forward.

One interesting action I recommend for all employers is to find out how much total compensation your broker is making from your plan—every penny. Thanks to the Consolidated Appropriations Act, which took effect in December of 2021, employers now have a legal right to obtain this information and brokers have a legal obligation to share it. Technically, you shouldn't have to request this information. Your broker should be providing it annually as part of their normal process. If they are not, an early red flag just popped up as to whether you are working with a trustworthy partner.

Overall, any broker you work with must be fully transparent with ALL compensation. Their compensation can be structured as net of commission, which means the broker agrees to work for a set amount and return any subrogation (commissions, overrides, or rebates) to the employer (the plan). It can also be structured as PEPM (per employee per month), which is similar, and fluctuates monthly based on headcount. This is not a charge for all employees—only employees "on the plan." Each plan varies, but the average number of members per employee on the plan is about 2.1. With this method, broker compensation is tied to the size of the plan. There is nothing wrong with incentives—we just need to make sure that incentives are tied to plan performance, and not plan degradation, which has been the case far too long.

Ultimately, the compensation must be structured in a way that the broker does not make more money if the claims go up, and ANY scenario that may create a conflict of interest for the broker *must be eliminated*. Everything must be 100% transparent.

Broker Effectiveness

One interesting question to ask an employer to determine a broker's effectiveness is, "If you had the opportunity to hire a full-time internal employee to do that work, would your hire be your current broker?" This is a great hypothetical question because it requires the employer to assess the value the broker is providing.

Newer external models, like Health Rosetta, co-founded by Dave Chase, Sean Schantzen, and Melissa Taylor, are shifting the paradigm from the traditional broker to what they call a *benefit advisor*. In their model, the advisor is still a licensed broker, able to perform the same tasks, such as compliance and quoting of ancillary insurance benefits. Most importantly, they take it to another level by encouraging advisors to "architect a winning plan," as some advisors put it. With the right advisor, this model has shown to be effective, saving employers significant dollars while improving the health plan design and cost for members. Health Rosetta now has thousands of certified advisors nationwide.

One particular challenge of all brokers who wish to make a noteworthy difference is that even if they are dedicated, have good knowledge, and are willing to put in the work, they remain an outsider. More simply, many have not worked directly for an employer in the manufacturing, retail, distribution, or service industry and they may not have the political prowess, cultural awareness, leadership skills, employer-specific knowledge, or simply the time required to lead a company on a successful healthcare improvement journey. If they have worked internally for an employer, they face the challenge that it is more difficult to lead from the outside. This emphasizes the need for an internal champion that I have discussed. When a strong internal champion partners with a competent and courageous broker, great things can happen.

Broker Evaluation

To aid you in evaluating your most valuable healthcare partner, your broker, over the past many years I have designed a tool to assess broker performance. Figure 5:1, called the Broker Assessment Tool, is intended to give you practical insight into what a superstar broker looks like.

Figure 5:1

		Broker Assessment Tool
INSTRUCTIONS:		**Rate each statement 1 to 5, with 5 being high.**
Rating		My broker and I have regular and candid communication. We can talk about anything, even the hard stuff, and our relationship is much deeper than an occasional lunch or dinner meeting. I trust that he or she is always working in the best interests of my company.
Rating		My broker sends me a graph packet regularly to help me analyze meaningful healthcare measures, such as medical claims, pharmacy claims, and fixed costs.
Rating		My broker guides me on a path to improve our healthcare spend and trend. We have saved money already or are on track to save more in the next year or two.
Rating		My broker is fully transparent and sends me a summary of every penny he or she makes from my plan. This includes direct fees paid (PEPM) as well as all commissions, overrides, per scripts, rebates, etc.
Rating		My broker does not have conflicts of interest in his or her current structure of compensation, including under-the-table payments of commissions, overrides, rebates, etc.
Rating		My broker helps me develop a healthcare strategy and communicate the strategy to the workforce; we have a clear idea of where we are going in the next 5 years.
Rating		My broker is free-market-minded and supports providers and vendors who practice free-market principles (i.e,. bundled procedures, transparent price, high-quality outcomes).
Rating		My broker is open-minded and is not a wet blanket to new ideas, even if those ideas are "out of the box."
Rating		My broker regularly attends best practice conferences and other relevant conferences to become educated and stay abreast of the latest methods that support my company in offering affordable, high-quality healthcare options.
Rating		My broker supports my company to align with some of the best free-market-minded partners, eliminating under- the-table money and revenue streams, such as with an independent TPA, independent PBM, independent network, independent clinic, and competitive stop loss carrier or captive.
Rating		My broker keeps in touch with me and is available to come onsite regularly for brainstorming and plan-design discussions, provider assessments and selection, strategy development, and employee communications.
Rating		My broker works with our TPA and legal counsel as necessary to make sure our benefit plan is compliant with ERISA, ACA, CAA, IRS, COBRA, etc.

Rating		There is good equity for services provided by my broker. The amount my company pays is equal to the level of service my company receives.
Rating		Overall, my broker supports us well and we are genuinely succeeding in offering a world-class healthcare plan for our employees and their families.
TOTAL SCORE	**RATING SCALE**	
Score	56-70	Your broker is walking on water. True partnerships like this are rare. With a strong internal champion, you are poised to do great things.
Score	42-55	Your broker is better than average and has some opportunity to improve. Shore up the gaps to reach your potential.
Score	28-41	Your broker is more traditional and has opportunities in several areas. You will need to decide if you can shore up the gaps or if it will be better to choose a new one.
Score	14-27	Your broker is very traditional and is holding you back more than helping you. A broker change should be in your near future.

This assessment tool is not intended to make the decision for you. It is intended to guide you in making good decisions for your most important partner. For cases in which you decide to make a partner change, at the end of this chapter I offer a proven selection model. As a former executive and HR leader, I have developed this model in much the same way I developed the healthcare success formula—through best practices of other employers and first-hand trial-and-error experience. As an added benefit, it may offer you valuable insight on your selection methods for how you hire employees.

To evaluate which broker role structure is best for you, internal or external, let's go over the advantages and disadvantages of each:

External Broker

- *Advantages:* People often follow their passions and strengths. There are some very effective brokers in the industry. Partnering with them can gain you instant insight, wisdom, experience, resources, and sometimes negotiating power, such as with stop loss. If the brokerage firm has many clients, they can leverage those numbers with the reinsurance company to get better rates.

- *Disadvantages:* In partnering with an external healthcare expert, you will be one of many clients they support. This means limited availability, very limited onsite time, and typically higher cost, at least on a level of dollars-per-hour support.

Internal Healthcare Officer

- *Advantages:* Although it is increasing in popularity among employers, "going broker-less" is still more the exception than the norm. Hiring for this position internally gives you the flexibility to choose the level, title, and duties of this role. In most cases, we are talking about the management of your second or third highest business expense. With that said, it seems logical this position should report to the CEO or president. I believe it is less than ideal to have this position report to the current VP of HR or the CFO. Any scenario in which the boss may consciously or unconsciously hold them back, particularly if the person has managed benefits in the past, must be avoided. They may perceive these changes as if they have failed in the past. It is my suggestion that this position be on the executive team and sit *next to* the head of HR as a peer. For the money an employer spends on healthcare, a competent, strategic person in this role can pay for themselves 10 times over. This will elevate the importance of the role and create an impression that your company is doing something about the systemic issue of out-of-control healthcare costs, and it will give the position appropriate credibility and proper support. It will be important this person does not adopt a traditional mindset and that they have an entrepreneurial spirit, along with a reasonable level of business acumen. This means that choosing a lifetime career benefits person may not be the best choice. Consider someone with a purchasing background, or an up-and-comer within the organization who is willing to take on a worthy challenge for personal development and the good of the company.

- *Disadvantages:* One disadvantage of this approach is that it will take more time and energy to get this new structure established. In this broker-less model, time will be needed to align resources and make sure all bases are covered. Typically, a good independent TPA can pick up many of the basic broker and compliance duties, such as a 5500 mailing. The TPA is already taking care of these duties in many cases.

Whether it be internal or external, the overall challenge is to make sure you have a great person. We aren't just talking about your biggest "HR opportunity," we are talking about your biggest business opportunity. Like any profession or sport, the best players are able to help their teams win and who you select for this role will determine whether you shine. You could say the same for choosing an external broker. How many of them are superstars and how many are really making a difference? There is not a long list of company success stories nationally, but if you look hard enough you can find them. One strategy could be to find those success stories, and then identify the broker or internal champion who led the story, and recruit that person. If you have good recruiting skills and can sell the opportunity with your company, the person may take it. Salary can be very flexible, as this person has the potential to save *significant cost*.

Choose a Trustworthy Direct Primary Care (DPC) Clinic

To find your DPC partner(s), you can start by listing all the available DPC locations in each of the area(s) you have members. It can be a valuable resource, although it is still incomplete. Remember, for reasons of referral navigation, you should consider only independently owned and operated practices. One valuable technique is to make a heat map. There are various free online tools you can use for this. I have used www.mapline.com. You can enter the addresses of the area DPC clinic locations, along with the addresses of your work location(s). The heat map will give you a nice visual to identify how well you are covered and if you have any gaps. You can go further and plug in each employee's address for more specificity, if desired. I typically use a 30-mile range for coverage.

Next, you will want to identify which DPC(s) will be a good fit for your strategy. This is achieved by getting to know the owners and staff of the clinics. This may take some time, and it is important not to rush this process. You can invite them to your business, and be sure to visit their clinic(s) as well. In doing so, remember that the selection process is taking place the whole time—through all interactions, not just in the conference room or in your office—but anywhere and everywhere you talk with them. Your goal should not be to "impress," and theirs not to impress you. Rather, the goal is for each party to get to know each other, who each of you *really are* and not a representative facade of what you think the other desires. It is important for both parties to assess true fit.

While there are many commonalities across DPCs, there is not an established standard for how they are structured or how they should practice. There are many ways of doing things right, and it is important to understand the individual characteristics of each DPC as you get to know them. For instance, some DPCs have near-site clinics, some have onsite clinics, some charge by age group, some have a single member charge (PMPM), some charge a fee for service, some utilize doctors, some utilize nurse practitioners, some utilize physician assistants, some have a mix of mid-levels and doctors, some offer many in-house services (i.e. x-ray, ultrasound, PT, chiropractic, nutritionist, mental health), some offer basic primary care only, some have mini pharmacies, some have 24/7 coverage, some are only open during business hours, and so on.

Along with getting to know the owners, MDs, and staff very well, you will want to evaluate all of these things and see who is the best fit for you. With the DPC clinic being the heartbeat of the medical strategy, finding one you can trust will be critical to your success. Ken Strmiska, COO at Anovia Health in Wisconsin, states, "For most people, healthcare in the United States has become a scary proposition because it is not understandable and it can create catastrophic medical and financial risks when it is accessed. DPC re-establishes the independence of the first level of care from the large multi-specialist hospital network. The DPC provider offers care and, just as importantly, educates and guides patients as needed. The DPC provider is the 'quarterback' of care and the trusted confidant for important healthcare decisions."

How Do DPC's Charge?

DPC clinics charge in one of two ways: fee for service (FFS) or Per Member Per Month (PMPM). Subscription rates are much more common. Some include certain services within the subscription rate, and some pass-through additional services at their cost. While other healthcare partners charge Per Employee Per Month (PEPM), DPCs commonly charge PMPM. With PEPM, we are talking about total employees on the plan. With PMPM, we are talking about total members, or "bellybuttons," on the plan (employees and their dependents). As you might imagine, PMPM is a more accurate assessment because it tells us the exact number of lives covered. If needed, PEPM can be estimated to PMPM. The average number of members for each employee on the plan is about 2.1; however this can vary up or down based on plan cost and plan design, resulting in more or fewer dependents to enroll.

PMPM subscription rates, sometimes called capitated rates, can vary by practice and region. Some DPCs are more community focused and market their subscription rates to individuals, families, and small businesses. These types of DPCs tend to have family rates and different rates by age group. Personally, I have a subscription to cover my family with Genesis Health in Schofield, Wisconsin. The owner, Dr. David Lange, offers full family coverage for $1,000 per year, regardless of the number of family members. This is a good deal, especially for someone like me with a large family. Other DPCs that focus more on self-funded employers tend to have one set rate for all members. This is done to simplify the billing, for cases in which there may be several hundred members at a time. PMPM rates vary greatly, with the low end starting at around $30 PMPM, ranging up to $100 PMPM or more.

Variables that influence the subscription price include the number of DPC competitors in the area, the level of provider utilized (mid-level or physician), the breadth of services included in the fee (i.e., imaging, lab work, etc.), the population in the area, the state or region, and more. If the ancillary services such as X-ray and lab work are not included in the fee, typically they are offered at a pass-through cost to the employers.

The other way DPCs charge is fee for service (FFS). Some say that charging FFS incentivizes providers to give unnecessary care. This is understandable, but debatable. We certainly do need to protect ourselves against the tendencies of human nature. Administratively, the PMPM subscription model is the simplest, both for the DPC practice and the self-funded plan administrators. Yet, interestingly, FFS models do tend to be lower cost for the employer plan, because the employer plan is billed only for the care that is received. If participation levels increase greatly, which they should, then the subscription model balances those costs. With both PMPM and FFS models, all of the care received at the DPC is typically provided to members at no cost to them. This makes it easy to encourage members to get effective (unrushed) primary care. It is also critical from a plan perspective to interrupt the path to the expensive hospital pinball referral machine. This is the strategic piece we are most concerned about.

Choose a Trustworthy Third-Party Administrator (TPA)

The TPA is the heartbeat of the administration for the employer plan. TPAs have three primary tasks: claims administration, legal compliance, and member support. First, working as an administrative services organization or ASO, they are not the insurer, but instead, process the claims according to the benefit plan. Claims can be auto-adjudicated, or they can be manually reviewed and processed. The outputs we seek here are accurate and timely claims processing and flexibility in payment methods.

The legal compliance part of the role involves making sure the plan is in accordance with regulations enforced by various government entities, such as the Department of Labor/EBSA (ERISA, COBRA disclosure and notification, 5500 mailing), the Department of Treasury/IRS (Taxes, COBRA eligibility and payment), and the Department of Health and Human Services (ACA, COBRA continuation coverage). To keep things simple the government only has three agencies overseeing the COBRA (sarcasm included). More seriously, as confusing and intimidating as this may appear, the key thing to remember is that the TPA employs and/or contracts with resources to do these things well and keep you in compliance.

Lastly, TPAs provide is member support, typically through a call center. Some go as far as to include an online chat option. In many cases, this is a good way to assess the overall quality of a TPA. While I was at Merrill Steel, before switching TPAs I had a question about plan coverage and I reached out to my TPA. My question was whether a preauthorization would be required for a hip replacement surgery. After 5 transfers and about 40 minutes of being on hold, I finally got the answer: if the procedure requires less than 24 hours of hospital stay, preauthorization is not necessary because it is considered an outpatient surgery. Anything over 24 hours would be considered inpatient, and therefore would require one. You may agree that 40 minutes and five telephone transfers to get a basic answer like this is not acceptable and is a good example of traditional TPA service.

Just as we discussed with the broker, you will want to understand how your TPA makes money. It is prudent to ask them about all of their revenue streams, in and out. What actions are being rewarded? Many, for instance, receive kickbacks from renting an insurance network. In this scenario, the employer foots the bill (as they do all bills) and pays for the cost to access the network. The TPA collects this money as a pass-through and pays the network. However, as an incentive for a TPA to recommend or continue using their network, in some cases the carrier gives some of this money back to the independent TPA. As in the case of brokers, it is important to uncover how the streams of money flow, because it can help explain behaviors you may see. All partners need to be acting 100% in your best interests and they cannot have bias in their decisions or financial conflicts of interest that cause them to recommend bad decisions for you. As a corporate employee, with some companies there were rules and policies in which I couldn't accept so much as an ink pen, for fear of creating a conflict of interest with a vendor. These careful practices seem to be absent in healthcare, where incentive payments are common.

Be Nimble and Quick

As an employer, if you are wanting to achieve favorable outcomes with your healthcare benefits, you will need more than a traditional TPA is willing or able to offer. You will need an independent TPA, or one that does not limit your ability to see claims data or to shop effectively, such as through network restrictions. Traditional TPAs, even if independent, are often set in their ways. Any talk of changing processes to reflect those of a free market can be like a foreign language to them—it is out of their world and they are often unable to have that type of conversation.

A high-performing independent TPA is able to provide all the services mentioned above, and they are able to do the basics of blocking and tackling well, such as to process the claims efficiently and accurately. These TPA's are able to become true partners in helping you achieve your desired outcomes. With the strategy discussed in this book, you will need your TPA to be open-minded, nimble, flexible, innovative, and thirsty for positive change. Specifically, they will need to be able to administer a tiered benefit plan that promotes good consumer choices, work with an independent DPC provider, work with an independent PBM, pay claims to network hospital systems, pay claims to independent specialty providers, directly contract with providers, and pay cash-only providers. They will need to interact with a utilization management company for effective preauthorization, and they will also work with a case management company to help manage the care for complex, high-cost claimants.

TPA Transition

If you find it necessary to change TPAs, it can be a difficult but rewarding endeavor. Of all the partners, the TPA transition is probably the most challenging. Much of the difficulty can be prevented by investing extra time and resources to plan the transition. For the current TPA, the transition of claims processing is called a "run-out." From the new TPA's perspective, it is called a "run-in." Like all other partner changes, you should know in advance that the current TPA will likely be upset and a smooth transition may not be on their mind. Remind them that their reputation is at stake and strive for a peaceful transition. One thing they may do is to charge excessive fees to perform the runout. If it is close to fair, it is probably worth paying to have a cordial transition. The typical run-out period for closing out all of the claims for a given year is three months. If your local hospital system is slow to bill, you may choose to extend it to six months. This transition will directly affect all members and your goal should be to have a seamless transition. In all instances, try to keep your relations cordial and strive for the best outcomes.

Choose a Trustworthy Pharmacy Benefit Manager (PBM)

Let me first state that "trustworthy PBM" is not an oxymoron, although the PBM world is one of the darkest worlds I have come across in my

50 years. Pharmacy costs have increased exponentially and this trend is expected to continue. Therefore, we must manage pharmacy with more energy and resources than we have in the past. When deciding on a PBM, it is important that you have functionality for a variety of services if you wish to maximize service and minimize cost. Like all other partners, it is important to understand exactly how much money your PBM is making from your account. As the pharmacy world is nicknamed "the mafia," it will be impossible to track the flow of all money through it, but you can at least know how the PBM is specifically charging you as the employer. Best practices include paying the PBM a per script fee or a PEPM fee. Any other income source should be returned to the plan and all purchases of medications must be structured as pass-through rates. Ideally, they should earn no other money. Although this is rare, some newer PBMs may enable you to achieve this.

The following are what I call *PBM plus services*. These are a set of combined services, enabled by members, the employer, and various others in the pharmacy supply chain working hand in hand, with a goal of reducing total pharmacy spend by 25% to 50% in the first year for both the plan and the member.

Pharmacy Claims Processing and Formulary Management

Processing the pharmacy claims is the core function of any PBM, yet all are not created equal. Having the right formulary is important from the start, supported by a competent staff to perform accurate and timely processing. A good PBM can recommend a good formulary for you.

Pharmacy Copay Accumulator Program

Sometimes referred to as copay cards, copay assistance, or copay coupons, these programs were created by drug manufacturers to lower or eliminate out-of-pocket costs for the member for name brand or specialty drugs. These programs make it easier for the member to access name brand drugs by covering their copay or deductible, resulting in both the patient being able to purchase the name brand drug and the pharmaceutical company selling more drugs. In response, to preserve plan integrity, employer plans sometimes counter so that copay assistance money does not count toward a plan deductible or max-out-of-pocket accumulator, thus preserving the design of the plan as it was intended.

Pharmacy Clinical Review

Clinical programs are designed to encourage the best outcomes for members as related to prescribed medications. Drug prescriptions and usage are monitored on an ongoing basis, in order for informed second opinions to be made regarding adjustments to prescriptions, as related to quality of care and cost. Examples of formal clinical programs include prior authorization, quantity limits, and step therapy.

Pharmacy International Sourcing

Just as the name implies, international sourcing involves bringing in the identical name brand specialty drugs from outside the United States. With the drugs being the same, the advantage of this service is significant cost savings to the plan and the member. Internationally sourced drugs are limited to a 90-day supply. The cost savings with this service can be significant.

Pharmacy Rebate Management

Rebates are paid to the PBM by the pharmaceutical manufacturing company. In reality, they are deals the pharmaceutical company "can't refuse," in order to get their drugs on the PBM's formulary and therefore to have an opportunity to be covered by the benefit plan. Further, when PBMs say they give this rebate to the plan sponsor (the employer is self-insured), often this is not the case and the PBM is keeping some of it.

Pharmacy Patient Assistance Programs

These programs are designed to help people who are underinsured or who have no health insurance afford medications. In some cases, a PBM can structure the formulary, thus impacting coverage for members, to maximize prescriptions available and minimize costs to the plan and the member.

Choose Trustworthy Independent Network(s)

A major tenet and ideal of this strategy is to open the door to an alternative outpatient network. A fair value proposition for consumers is one that reflects wise shopping practices, such as prices being shared in advance, competitive prices, appointments in days or weeks (instead of months), adequate time for patient/provider interaction, and procedural quality.

While it is true that more and more doctors are starting independent practices, a full menu does not yet exist. This means there will be an ongoing need for higher level hospital services, such as for emergencies, inpatient procedures, intensive care, oncology, cardiology, and organ transplants.

This highlights the importance of needing fairly priced contracts with at least one local hospital system for each area in which your business operates. We have talked about how the insurance networks include contractual restrictions that prevent buyers from shopping, so as of now, they are not a feasible option for this strategy. This leaves employers with few other alternatives. If you search your state, you may already have an employer coalition, employer coop, or some other independent network you can join to achieve pricing similar to that of the insurance networks. A worst-case scenario would be that you would need to gather local employers and form your own employer group to negotiate prices directly with one or more hospitals.

In Wisconsin, while we have the unfortunate privilege of being the fourth worst state in the nation for healthcare costs, self-funded employers are very fortunate to have several independent networks available. The largest of these is the Alliance, an employer coop, made up of approximately 300 employers and approximately 110,000 members. As you might imagine, their size gives them legitimate negotiating power. The Alliance contracts with hospital systems throughout the state to allow their self-funded employer members to have good pricing with hospitals. Further, they contract with a majority of the independent providers, positioning themselves as a comprehensive shoppable network. This makes life easier for self-funded employers. If they set up their plan to enable shopping, their need is filled and they don't have to coordinate a bunch of direct contracts with independents. Employers generally don't have the time or resources for this. In joining the Alliance, this is all covered. Cheryl DeMars, CEO of the Alliance, has worked tirelessly to improve healthcare in Wisconsin and has seen a lot of change over the years. She notes, "The Alliance was started by employers so they could pool their purchasing power to contract directly with providers. Being an employer-owned and directed cooperative ensures that everything we do is focused on meeting the needs of our members. It also means that employers have unparalleled access to their data and contract pricing so they can manage their health plans and encourage employees to shop for high-value care." Cheryl is a paladin in the state, and is involved on many levels, including policy reform with legislators. She testified with me before a Senate Committee in Madison.

The second largest independent network, Trilogy Health Solutions, employs a similar model, offering competitive contracts with both hospitals and independent providers. For employers with members throughout the state, these two networks join together to maximize their effect and allow for optimal contracts in all areas. This is noted by an Alliance/Trilogy logo on the benefit card.

Choose Trustworthy Independent Specialty Providers

In line with the model to utilize providers who play fair and have a free-market mindset, it is important to articulate the characteristics of these specialty providers. Providers who practice this way represent the future of healthcare—what healthcare can and should be if we work together to do what is right and create a win-win scenario for all involved, including all plan sponsors, all patients, and all providers.

The following are a set of guidelines that are intended to help you define who should be placed into the preferred provider tier. Unique exceptions may occur, but in general, the goal is to make this as clear and repeatable as possible.

The Provider Openly Shares Prices for Healthcare Services

The best providers show empathy and take the time to understand the patient's perspective. Transparency is the currency of trust, and mutual trust is important in the preferred provider/patient relationship. With pricing, this involves avoiding insurance contracts that introduce gag clauses. For a self-funded employer or patient to make the best healthcare decisions, he or she must be able to effectively evaluate cost and quality. These are missing today in healthcare and preferred providers do their best to remove this barrier to effective shopping.

The Provider Offers Fair and Reasonable Prices

Meshing well with transparency, when prices are shared, they can be properly evaluated. Win-win relationships are the only ones that can be sustained long-term. The aim is not for one party to "out-negotiate" the other, rather, for the provider to openly offer fair prices without any games.

The Provider Bundles Prices and Warranties Service Whenever Possible

Because the insurance coding system introduces so much complexity, whenever possible, preferred providers group their services together, to form bundles. Bundles are beneficial because they give the patient one clear price, thus enabling the patient to make the best decisions based on cost and quality. Optimally, the bundle also includes a base warranty of services performed.

The Provider Performs High Quality Services

The measurement and evaluation of quality in healthcare is a conjectural topic. Naturally, some level of quality oversight comes with being state-licensed and board-certified, but in the remaining gap a lot of questions reside. Some of this is understandable, in that the outcome of a procedure is affected by many input variables such as health conditions of the patient that are out of the control of the provider. However, we are still left with a need for a quality rating of providers. Infection rates for surgeries is an example that can be measured accurately and reliably, and preferred provider surgery centers have notably lower infection rates. Further, we can learn a lot by speaking to physicians within the medical community. Within their grapevine, they know who the best surgeons are, and conversely, who are not so good. Without access to that grapevine, we would never know these things. Ultimately, preferred providers create amazing outcomes for the patient, with minimal infections, complications, or repeat procedures.

The Provider Is Willing to Accept Direct Payments

Empathetic providers put the patient first and offer them a variety of ways to pay for service. Preferred providers are commonly open to working with independent networks that primarily support self-funded employers, or outside of the web of insurance control with non-insurance entities, such as to work directly with a self-funded employer or patient on a cash basis.

Breaking Up is Hard to Do

Transitioning from a current partner to a new partner can be a negative experience. In almost all cases, they seem to take the news poorly. Instead of seeing it as you aligning your partners and strategy, they perceive it as being fired. At Merrill Steel, I changed all partners, and years later, even to this day, a few of those former partners still refuse to talk with me. Although conflict is sometimes unavoidable, I try my best to do so. Sometimes it finds me. When I shared the news to various partners that I would be making a change, I offered to take them out to lunch and I emphasized that it was not personal. I mentioned that they had not failed, but that we were taking a "different path." I thanked them for all they had done. None of this seemed to matter. One previous partner was so upset, they attempted to sabotage the transition to the new partner by creating bad experiences for our members.

Most people are not change agents. Rather, they avoid change at all costs. They tend to do what they are told and adopt commonly accepted ways of thinking, without question. Hence, most of the people working as your current partners are just doing what they were taught. They are going through those motions every day. So, when they hear you are making a change, no matter how you say it or do it, they hear they have failed. The best will receive the news and will maintain the relationship, with hopes you will return. Many will not take it so well. Be prepared for this and expect it.

Lastly, I share this insight in advance as a heads up of what you can expect, and further, for you to remember that just because someone gets upset, it doesn't mean you have done anything wrong. In fact, in choosing a partner or set of partners that is a better fit for your strategy, you are doing what is right and what is necessary.

How to "Select" Trustworthy Partners

Throughout my career in human resources, I worked for a variety of large employers, from Fortune 100 to large family-owned companies. In these roles I was responsible to lead the staffing process for all positions, ranging from entry-level to executive. I took this responsibility seriously and strove to do more than just "fill the role." I wanted to find the best possible candidate available to help our company thrive. Moreover, I wanted to find out what matters most in the selection process and perhaps what matters very little. I wanted to understand the predictors of success. The more I studied these dynamics, the more my views began to change. Instead of viewing candidates as separate parts that work independently, I began to view them in the context of interdependent parts; how well they will fit within our culture and how willing and effective they would likely be in carrying out our strategy.

Coming to this realization dramatically changed my perspective on how to select. I use the word *select* intentionally, to replace the commonly used HR term, *hire*. I use this word as an overarching term to reflect the overall *selection process*, as opposed to using terms like *interview process*, as an interview is one of many tools in the toolbox we use to select, or *hiring process*, which reflects a legal transaction, trading compensation for work. By using the word *select*, we are speaking of all of the methods we use to gather candidates, screen candidates, vet final candidates, and ultimately, make a choice of a partner who will help us win in the future. Remember, it is ALWAYS worth investing the necessary time, money, and resources in your selection process, because the goal is to do it well and to do it one time.

Experience Is Not the Best Predictor of Success

The typical way of selecting is to measure "experience": to make the assumption that the greater the experience, the more effective the person will be. This is logical, but inherently faulty. Why? Because someone can know a profession inside and out, and they could have done it for the past 20 years, but still suck at it! I am not trying to be disrespectful or flippant. But you know I am right. We need someone who can move needles, someone with a passion to be more than "average," and to do something special. We need someone with passion and fire in his or her belly. What does all of this mean? We shouldn't count experience as unfavorable, but by itself, it is minimally valuable.

When reviewing prospective partner candidates, the most valuable, research-based knowledge indicates:

> *"The best predictor of future behavior is past behavior, and therefore, the best predictor of future success, is past success."*

Memorize this phrase. The goal should be to find a proven achiever; someone who doesn't just talk about success, rather, someone who is already doing it before they have the title.

With this knowledge, we can begin to see a healthcare partner's potential as having much more value. The person with potential may have little experience in healthcare. They may be a new broker with only a couple years of experience or an "up and comer" within your organization who has the touch of gold—that is, "Everything he or she touches, turns to gold." For extraordinary challenges, like the one we face in fixing an employer health plan, I am taking the "touch of gold" person every day of the week and twice on Sunday. Toyota Motor Manufacturing gets this concept. It is why they hire teachers who are interested in career change over a person who worked 10 years at a competitor. Why? Because it is easier to teach a motivated person from scratch how to build a car than it is to try to get a person who is set in his or her ways to unlearn what they were trained and required to do for the past decade.

Further, I would suggest dedicating all time necessary to select new partner(s). Because we are so busy, we sometimes practice with the mentality that we don't have time to do it right the first time, but we have time to do it over. You can't afford a lot of misses, resulting in ineffective partners on your healthcare journey. I like to use the analogy, "You have to choose someone to marry, and I will give you one phone call and two dates." If I told you to do this, you would look at me like I was crazy and tell me to pound sand. But is this not the standard we use for hiring? Granted, we don't have the time to get to know someone for a year before we hire them. We would lose that candidate to a competitor. However, we might have more time in this scenario than the average "job fill." It takes time to truly get to know someone.

Many healthcare industry players are great talkers. Ask them if they are good at something, and they will surely tell you how great they are. Can we agree that this method doesn't work? We need to talk with them in all kinds of environments and in all kinds of situations. We need to go hear about some of their work and visit living examples of it. There is nothing wrong with a conference room or office, but if that is the only place available to evaluate someone's fit and qualifications, we are rolling the dice. I used to teach this concept in manufacturing with tours. I would say, "Do you think when I give a candidate a tour that I am just giving a candidate a tour?" Sure, I am, but I'm also measuring how many questions he asks, how he interacts with other employees, how closely he follows along, how he carries himself, and so on. All sorts of things can be learned by getting out of the conference room and taking time to get to know someone.

As we invest time, and sometimes lots of time, we want to make sure we are getting to know the person as he or she really is, as opposed to a show or a façade the person may be putting on. We don't want to start a partnership and find out later that the individual wasn't being genuine in the selection process. This can be overcome by putting the person at ease, and by having a candid conversation with them first thing, saying, "It's important you get to know who we really are and for us to get to know who you really are, because neither of us want to find out later that this is a bad fit. If it is a bad fit, we must know it now to save both of us the heartache. This is a two-way selection process. You are selecting us and we are selecting you. We need to assess that both ways so that we can measure if we will have a long-lasting, highly successful business relationship." I have found that by airing out these things early, I can prevent a lot of showboating, and it also puts some of the onus on the partners to evaluate from their side as well.

Support and Education for Medical Professionals Who Start Independent Practices

As a final note in choosing trustworthy partners, I want to acknowledge some realities that are present with medical professionals coming out of hospital systems to become entrepreneurs of their own practice. First and foremost, this is a great thing and it is needed. And the good news is that we are talking about some very bright people here, who are motivated to learn. They never would have made it through medical school if that were not the case.

Because the healthcare industry has successfully suppressed the market, our job is to open it back up. Having worked in hospital system environments for years, medical professionals often have a need for support and education on topics such as business management, free market competition, employer plan design, the balance of autonomy and insurance partnerships, and change management.

They have forgotten more about medicine than I will ever know, in that their focus has been on effective treatment of patients. A high level of business acumen is not very advantageous in that realm. Yet, when a physician or mid-level provider starts an independent practice, these skills are needed to succeed. As these professionals are bright, savvy, lifelong learners, most are motivated and capable of learning or refreshing these skills quite quickly.

One of these skills is to assess the market to anticipate patient flow. In many cases, talented, ambitious medical professionals leave the hospital system and work to set up their provider facility, get the proper licenses and insurances established and prepare to open for business, only to find out that the industry has locked down the employer plan designs, making it difficult for patients to use them because they are not "in network." Some patients who have high deductibles may be inclined to pay cash for the services, on top of their healthcare plan costs through their employer. Overall, if such practitioners don't find a way to be a viable option within the employer's plan design, they can feel like they opened a steakhouse in a vegetarian community. They can have the best steaks in town, but nobody is showing up at the door.

There are a few organizations that help medical professionals learn the business side, to help ensure their success and to support the overall movement. One prominent direct primary care service provider is Freedom Healthworks, which is a community of independent DPC practices that are all physician-owned. The services that Freedom Healthworks provides are tailored to ease the burden of front and back-office operations, management, and success. An independent solo practice will have to acquire, perform, and constantly improve on business functions in order to stay relevant. Working with Freedom helps practices run as lean as possible, avoiding high expenses, while still maintaining a high level of professionalism in all patient interactions. Their platform is designed to keep doctors in control of patient care while not stressing about the business activities.

CHAPTER SIX

Lead the Change from Here to There

Change management is a topic that is near and dear to my heart. It was my chosen major in graduate school, it was the focus of my research throughout college, and it is the field in which I have practiced for the past 25 years of my professional career. Unlike the topic of improving employer healthcare, there is much written on this topic. If you are interested in doing a deeper dive than presented here, John Kotter's book, *Leading Change,* is one of the better published works on this topic.

Change Management

Change management is the process by which a transformational leader leads a group of people from a bad place to a good place, from dysfunctional to highly functional, from unsustainable to sustainable, from slavery, through the wilderness, to the promised land. Knowledge of the principles, dynamics, and techniques of change management offers a person the opportunity to change lives. It is the most challenging and the most rewarding aspect of leadership because it transcends all disciplines, all industries, all cultures, all countries, and all times. It involves understanding people at a deep level. Throughout my career I have rolled out of bed each day with something to look forward to, I have found value in my work, and by using proven change management practices, I have led others to achieve things they once thought impossible.

An Early Career Inspiration

Have you ever been part of a large-scale change transformation? Early in my career, I was provided such an opportunity, and it shaped me for life. Just out of graduate school, I had moved to Tennessee to take a new position with Tenneco Automotive, a Tier 1 OEM automotive supplier. In Smithville, we manufactured full exhaust systems for the large Toyota Motor Manufacturing plant in Georgetown, Kentucky. We were an average performing plant, with great people and our fair share of struggles. New product launches tended to overburden us for a while, and we faced the normal everyday manufacturing challenges in areas of safety, turnover, quality, and delivery schedules.

Shortly after I arrived, Toyota sent two mentors to our facility for nearly a year, at no cost, to help us improve. Toyota understood that their supplier performance was an extension of their overall performance. At first, our leaders were not receptive to the "free help." In fact, they were resistant, and they were annoyed that these visitors kept asking why, why, why? If you are familiar with the Toyota Root Cause Analysis method, the "five whys" is a normal part of the problem-solving process to find root cause. In our leaders' minds, they knew their processes better than anyone else and who were these two strangers to come in and act like they can make everything better?

I watched with eager anticipation. After much discussion, much teaching, and a number of escalated discussions, eventually our leaders began to get it. In about a year's time, we became one of the highest performing plants in the company. Through Toyota's effective problem-solving methods, *all of our key metrics were dramatically improved.* Injuries were dramatically reduced, our quality was much better, we were able to meet our delivery schedules regularly, our cost was in line, and turnover became almost too small to measure. We had reduced headcount from over 500 to about 350 employees (through normal attrition) and we were manufacturing significantly more product. We also picked up new customers, such as Honda Motor Manufacturing. After working there about a year and a half, I was promoted. A few months after that, I was recruited to work for Toyota at their flagship facility in Georgetown, Kentucky. To say it was a big operation was an understatement. If a supplier had delivery problems and caused a shutdown in this facility, the charge to them was $100,000 per hour! It was a dream come true for me and the things I learned there greatly impacted me and shaped me for life.

Tumultuous

I am curious. What was your first reaction when you read the phrase "change management"? The notion of change affects everyone differently.

- Did you feel **anxious**, because your previous experience with change has been unpleasant?
- Were you **annoyed** that "someone is always trying to change something," and why don't they just leave things alone?
- Did you feel **curious**; wondering about "possibilities" and what good things may be over the horizon?
- Were you **excited** to learn about new adventures that might be in your future? A new adventure, "Yes!"

Your reaction is based on several factors—your personality, your temperament, and most of all, your past experiences with change in both your personal and work life. If your reaction to the mention of change was not excitement, I encourage you to remember that anything worth trying will not be easy, and often, our initial emotional response is not the best gauge of future experience. If leading others from a not-so-good place to a better place was easy, everyone would do it and there would be nothing special about it. As we delve into this topic, I can tell you assuredly, armed with in-depth knowledge of change management theory, awareness of best practices, a little courage, and support from the top of your organization (what Kotter calls a "guiding coalition"), you are poised to lead others to achieve amazing things.

I also want to be careful not to mislead you. Leading change is not an easy road. It is complicated and often messy. Sometimes things get worse before they get better. Sometimes they never get better. Not everyone is inspired to help people or change the world. I took a college class once called "Adolescence." On the first day of class, the professor walked into the classroom and without saying a word, he turned his back to the class and began writing on the chalkboard (I am dating myself). As the chalked scraped and squeaked, he spelled out, *"T-U-M-U-L-T-U-O-U-S"*. He then turned to everyone and said, "In one word, this describes the period of adolescence—the transition from childhood to adulthood." If you were to pick one word to describe change management, what would it be? Tumultuous could be a good word, because it describes the process of change well.

As I reflect back on my career, my passion and drive to make things better has resulted in good things for many companies and many people. I have been promoted numerous times, I have been chosen for various awards, I have been offered amazing job opportunities, and I have done well financially.

However, at times, especially earlier in my career, this same passion for change and continuous improvement also resulted in less than desirable things, including personal anxiety, high blood pressure, mental distractions from my family, conflicts with peers, bosses who felt threatened, and loss of friends. Having shared both sides of the coin, change management may sound both appealing and scary at the same time. If change management were a pharmacy commercial, it might sound something like this: "For years, I lived with the ups and downs of change management. Then, I talked to my doctor, and he recommended Tumultira. He said it will make everything better. Tumultira may not be for everyone. Ask your doctor if you are healthy enough for Tumultira. Side effects may include nausea, cardiac arrest, headaches, insomnia, and in some cases, patients were no longer able to function in society. See your doctor immediately for inspirational thoughts lasting more than four hours. Ask your doctor if this prescription is right for you!"

As you might imagine, not everyone will see the light or share in your passion to make something better. A transformational leader starts out alone with any new endeavor. It is up to that person to continuously share a compelling narrative, add supporters, and keep the momentum. For many, change is something that is survived, not something one should intentionally initiate. To others, it will seem like unnecessary work that will amount to nothing more than a waste of time. If you were to pay me a nickel for how many times someone said, "It will never work," I would have a LOT of nickels! Many will not understand what you are doing, some may be jealous, and some may be offended. It is important to know and expect these things before you start.

The sides of the scale are apparent. There is risk. There is reward. This is why it is common for leaders to make small, somewhat insignificant changes. It gives the impression that something is being done and it is still safe. The effect is inconsequential, however, and no needles are being moved. This is not transformational change. Transformational change transforms something. With higher risk comes higher reward. I can tell you it has been worth it for me. You will have to decide if it is worth it for you.

That's the Way We've Always Done It

I heard a story once about deliciously cooked ham. Whenever Mary cooked her specially prepared ham, dinner guests couldn't get enough. It was so good that they talked for days afterward with family and friends about how good the ham tasted. There are only so many ways to prepare ham—but this was different. Mary carefully prepared her ham to perfection each time, and always received rave reviews.

One evening, a guest inquisitively asked Mary her secret of how was she able to prepare such a succulent ham? Mary replied, "It's a family tradition. Just before cooking it, I cut off each end of the ham. I have been doing it this way for years and it always comes out delicious." Not understanding her explanation, the guest inquired further, "I see, but how does that make the ham taste better?" Mary said, "I don't really know. I do it that way because that is how my mother taught me to do it."

This discussion sparked Mary's curiosity. Hoping to find some explanation behind the family secret, Mary visited her mother the next day. She asked, "Mom, why do you cut off the ends of the ham before you cook it?" Unfortunately, her questions did not uncover any secrets. Her mom replied, "Well, honey, this is how my mother taught me to do it. It's how I have always done it and everyone has always loved the ham."

The next day Mary went to visit her grandmother. She couldn't wait to ask, "Grandmother, why do you cut off the ends of the ham before you cook it? Does it cook better this way, or does it have something to do with the juices?" "Oh no, my dear," exclaimed her grandmother. "It has nothing to do with those things." With a puzzled look, Mary replied, "But then why do you cut off both ends of the ham?" Her grandmother answered, "Because that's the only way it will fit into my pan."

This funny story illustrates how we can become accustomed to doing things a certain way. We unconsciously default to autopilot and we fail to think about why. The most dangerous phrase a leader can say is, "That's the way we've always done it." If this phrase is used as justification for why something is done a certain way, it will shut down all potential for continuous improvement. As leaders, we must be careful not to use these seemingly innocent expressions or we can unintentionally support the perpetuation of blind traditions that were once supported by good reason, but because many things have changed since, no longer make any sense at all.

Change is a sensitive topic. In my experience, even the mention of change in an organization can stir other's emotions. Sometimes I'll jokingly say, "I think I hit a nerve." It's not like what I said was offensive, but people can still get offended by all sorts of things. This is because the essence of change is psychological. It involves leaving a place that is known, a place that's comfortable, safe, or predictable, and traveling to a new place that is unknown, uncomfortable, risky, and unpredictable. Why would anyone want to do that?

I currently mentor a few other younger leaders. I've shared many things with them that I have had to learn and figure out on my own over the past couple of decades, sometimes the hard way. I share with them that transformational leadership can be lonely at times and I share the great possibilities of how lives can be changed. In this chapter, we'll cover how you can maneuver through this complicated web of unpredictability—to survive, to motivate others to thrive, and to see that the possibilities are greater than the problems—to live out the notion that problems are just opportunities in disguise.

How are Your Enrollment Meetings Going?

In my experience, annual benefit enrollment meetings are unpleasant experiences for all involved. Many employees enter the room and seem to be angry and defensive before they even sit down. HR leaders and brokers who participate in the meetings often get spattered with verbal tomatoes. Why? Because employees have received bad news for the past couple of decades, and no one seems to be doing anything about it. Year after year, premiums, deductibles, and maximum out-of-pocket amounts have far outpaced inflation, often to the point where a person's wage increase is washed away entirely. It is not uncommon to hear of family premiums of $500 or more per month, with family deductibles of $6,000 or more per year, not to mention a greater coinsurance to pay after the deductible is met. In this example, that's $12,000 the employee would pay each year before the insurance even begins to help with the costs. The result is frustrated employees (and rightfully so), who work hard every day to take care of their families. Over time, if problems are not addressed, people tend to check out emotionally and stop caring. They go numb from the neck up, because they are being affected by problems they are powerless to fix, or they check out physically, by quitting their job and joining another employer.

We must remember that not everyone is comfortable speaking in a large group and in those settings, it is more common to hear the opinions of the more vocal employees. Keep in mind, they may be right and they may be wrong, but their perceptions are their reality. Ask them questions, genuinely listen, and make it safe. If you choose to take the time to do this, you have to be good at filtering and finding themes, but there is incredible value in these interactions. Trust is built by taking the time to genuinely care. You'll get a lot of real information, and you'll build credibility, respect, and trust with those you lead. When someone feels heard and knows you care, and that you are truly willing to listen, address problems, and make things better, they will give you their best and they will stay with you.

In your annual enrollment meetings, it is important that the key leaders within your company play an active role.

I understand that, historically, this has not been the case. Company owners and executives must realize that healthcare is not just something provided to employees, it is also typically the second or third largest business expense of the company, yet it has not been managed as such.

Now that we have the company executives in the game (I'm being optimistic), we can begin to assess how the healthcare benefits are perceived in your company. The only way for you to know is to begin asking questions and talking with your employees. You can likely presume that employees are unhappy with the trends in healthcare costs, but what are the specifics? What parts of your healthcare plan do they like? What parts are they concerned about and what things are affecting their family the most? If cost is their biggest concern, which cost matters most: the premium, the deductible or copay, the max out-of-pocket, or all of the above? If quality of care or accessibility to providers is the concern, which are viewed as strong and which ones are not? Does everyone understand the benefit plan and if so, can they explain it to you? It's hard to navigate the trail if you can't read the map. If you can find themes and make things better, you can make a significant impact to your ability to recruit and retain the best talent.

One note if you are an owner or a high-level leader. Although it may not seem like it when you are talking with others, keep in mind that many will likely be guarded with you and may not tell you the full story of how they feel. And just the same, you may have smiled as you read that, knowing that you have some employees who don't have that reservation—at all.

Your efforts in the enrollment meetings can be supplemented by talking with employees individually, outside of the enrollment meetings. I have used the "candid question" approach for to understand employees' perceptions of wage scale, benefits, communication processes, and overall culture. It takes time, but it's far more valuable feedback than group meetings or an employee survey. It allows for two-way communication, to clarify exactly what someone is experiencing. It starts with a simple question, "How do you feel we are doing on _____ and how could we make it better?" Often we overcomplicate things. The best way to understand others' perceptions of a "certain something" is to talk with them. And then be sure to follow up and resolve the issue—or when they stop talking with you, it won't be because they're satisfied but because you've lost their trust.

A final note of advice on this topic: when you hear that that other employers' plans "suck," that's not a good reason for yours to suck, or to suck less. With costs skyrocketing the past couple of decades, employers have passed on a portion of the total cost increases to employees via premium and plan design increases. Year after year, plans have deteriorated. It's been kind of a slow death, but a death by 1,000 cuts is still dying.

At Merrill Steel, I witnessed these dynamics in the enrollment meetings and realized I needed to change the tone of discussion and the format of the meetings. We got to work making changes to improve the performance of our benefit plan, and we were able to freeze premiums and other plan costs for five consecutive years, while simultaneously adding a variety of no-cost healthcare services. I don't know about you, but I have found that good news is easier to present than bad news. We worked tirelessly to create good news. By the second year, employees began to catch on. Not only did they smile, they began to jump in and help find solutions. To this day, even after embarking on new adventures, I still receive messages from employees with attached articles about new strategies to improve healthcare. Healthcare became a positive topic within the company, and it can be the same for you as well.

Transformational Leaders

Memorable movements happen when principled, purpose-driven leaders are called to action. Teddy Roosevelt is a favorite example of this: Teddy was not afraid to try. He said:

> It is not the critic who counts; not the man who points out how the strong man stumbles, or where the doer of deeds could have done them better. The credit belongs to the man who is actually in the arena, whose face is marred by dust and sweat and blood; who strives valiantly; who errs, who comes short again and again, because there is no effort without error and shortcoming; but who does actually strive to do the deeds; who knows great enthusiasms, the great devotions; who spends himself in a worthy cause; who at the best knows in the end the triumph of high achievement, and who at the worst, if he fails, at least fails while daring greatly, so that his place shall never be with those cold and timid souls who neither know victory nor defeat."

Change management is the overall process in which a transformational leader takes a group of people from "here" to "there." This journey can be within a business, when implementing a new policy, a new electronic system, a new way of manufacturing, a new product line, new technology, or a new healthcare strategy. Steve Jobs might be considered an example of a great transformational leader in a business. It can also be larger in scope, such as a widespread social initiative: a cause, such as to promote civil rights, public safety, or religious freedom. Martin Luther King Jr. might be considered a great transformational leader for civil rights. With our topic of improving employer healthcare, we are delving into both realms. Individually, employers are leading transformation with their healthcare plans. Collectively, as more and more employers implement this strategy, we will reshape how America does healthcare. We will wash away the exclusive profit mentality, and put "care" back in healthcare, with a fresh new system that brings back old values.

While it might be more emotionally appealing to say that a high-performing, cross-functional team was formed, and everyone sang Kumbaya as they rowed their boat down the river of change, my research doesn't indicate this. The research on employer healthcare success stories indicates that in almost all cases, a single transformational leader led the journey. In some instances, this person had a sidekick that contributed greatly on the journey, and in all cases, fellow team members contributed by doing a fair amount of the legwork, even if they did it grudgingly for a portion of the journey, not yet being able to see the light. This is not to say that if you have a culture that supports a team approach and this is the method you are accustomed to, that you shouldn't take that approach. Individual or team, it's all good. The key is that employers get in the game.

I once had a member of my team share something interesting with me. This was after we had worked together for five years. She said, "When you first started, you were full of optimism and excitement and you said we could improve all these things. I share with you now that I didn't think it could be done. I didn't believe you. However, I see now that it was possible and thank you for all you have done for our company." I appreciated her honesty. She was like many—she didn't believe. Nothing in her past experience inspired her or allowed her to see that transformational change was possible.

On one particular day, I had another valued member of my team show strong resistance to going forward. She wasn't rude—she just had a reason for why every idea I shared wouldn't work. I was throwing clay-pigeon ideas in the air and she was trap-shooting them down, one by one by one. I had thrown about five to six of these and it became apparent to me that she had no intention to move forward. I cared about her and I needed her with me. I sensed she was digging in her heels and I immediately asked her to shut the door so we could talk. I told her, "I want you on my team and I believe you are very capable. However, I don't need you to tell me all the reasons why something will not work. I need you to figure out all the ways it can work. If you aren't willing to go forward with this, I understand—but you must choose a path. You cannot be on the team and resist my efforts to lead change at the same time."

Flavor of the Month

Throughout my career, I have seen employees react in a variety of ways to change when it is introduced to them. The most common reactions are sarcasm, anger, fear, and anxiety. The easiest and quickest way to "hit a nerve" is to ask a specific group of people to change the way they do things, without notice or a chance for them to give input for how things will be done. In contrast, if the request is for others to change (as in "I won't have to do anything differently") the reaction will not be so strong. For example, if HR changes a policy and it benefits me (and I don't have to do anything differently), I will smile and thank them for it. However, if I am asked to significantly change my process or my normal ways of doing things, it can spark a negative emotional reaction. It becomes personal.

Why? There are many possibilities. With a new way, I might mess up and I could get in trouble. Further, a new way will require me to learn and step back into a novice's shoes, and I am viewed as the expert right now. A new way will be stressful, and I already have enough stress keeping up with normal life, ranging from demanding customers at work, to marriage troubles, to a rebellious teenager, to a car that keeps breaking down. It's like the person is saying, "Stop changing everything. It's hard enough to keep everything going. We don't need to create new problems!"

In today's business world, employees are faced with many pressures. The market moves fast and there are constant demands for new product development, innovative services, cost reduction, and ever-increasing quality requirements. Because of time pressures and a lack of understanding of change management, these changes are often forced upon people, without real explanation or involvement in the decisions concerning how things will be done. Further, all too often, change initiatives that are originally sold to the workforce as "critically important" often end up fizzling out or stalling when the next shiny thing comes along or the priority shifts to something else in the new quarter.

Employees affectionately call this the "flavor of the month." If I have heard this phrase once, I have heard it a thousand times. Employees' impressions of how the company has led change in the past cause them to be reluctant to adopt new changes in the future. At first, they quietly resist, and surreptitiously hope the project fails. If it gets bad enough, they openly resist. Their reaction is not surprising. We are all naturally wired this way. A person will only commit his or her hard work, time, and passion into a new project so many times, particularly if the rug has been continually yanked out from under them in the past. Eventually, they stop caring. As a leader, if this is how change has been done in your company, perhaps you share these same sentiments.

If you have this flavor-of-the-month sentiment in your company, it is important to realize that you can't control any of the past experiences that employees have lived through. What you can do is acknowledge that previous change initiatives haven't been sustained, and as you go forward, ask them to view your actions and tell you if they feel you are walking the talk. Ask them to give their honest opinion of how things are going and to give input on what is going well and what is not going well. Most importantly, involve them in the process so they can help make things go well. Over time, you will earn their trust. More people will buy in and join you on the journey. Once they get in the game, things get easier. Action, not words, becomes the difference. The only way to change their opinion is to prove them wrong by leading change well from that day forward. Thomas Jefferson understood this concept. He said, "Do you want to know who you are? Don't ask. Act! Action will delineate and define you."

I believe how well you do change management will be the greatest factor in making your overall efforts successful or not. Your financial and medical strategies, and your partners, are all critical to your success, but the biggest reason change efforts fail is because "something or some things" went awry with the people side of the change. If we juxtapose a healthcare improvement journey to a lean journey, the dynamics are the same. Just like the Employer Healthcare Success Formula, in lean, the strategy, tools, and best practices are proven and well defined. They are predictable and repeatable. When companies strive to change their way of manufacturing, and inherently, part of their culture, in order to implement lean manufacturing, the biggest determinant for whether the company will succeed or fail is how well the change is led. Like it or not, people are messy. Sometimes when I say this to a person for the first time, they look at me funny, as if I am smoking something. We cannot pretend this away or deny its reality. In accepting this, we gain wisdom, because ultimately, the better we understand people, the better we will be able to lead others through change.

People Are Messy

My HR experience put me right in the middle of messy people situations. I have learned that people are the biggest variable and determinant of an organization's success. More simply, every organization has assets, every organization has customers, every organization has accounting methods, every organization has an approach to doing business . . . and every organization has people. How well the teams work together collectively to carry out a strategy and achieve success will shape the company's future. The companies with the best functioning people team will win in the long-term.

The never-ending challenge in building a strong customer-focused culture is the reality that all people are messy at times. Wherever there are people, there are problems nearby. Conflicts, family issues, financial issues, and health issues arise without warning. Even well-rounded leaders are messy at times. I am messy, you are messy, and we will always have the potential to be. It is our nature. If someone disagrees and claims they have it all together, don't believe them. They are either not self-aware, or they are completely full of it.

This distinction washes away a false stereotype that I believe pervades society. The messy and broken are not just those who have experienced significant trauma, those who are of lower socioeconomic status, those with mental or physical health issues, those who are uneducated, or those who . . . fill in the blank. With an attitude of humility, may we shed our hubris and "be one of them" whoever "them" may be? This is the perspective of a transformational leader: realizing that he or she is not above others, nor is he or she cleaner than others. Rather, this person is a dreamer, a visionary, and a facilitator to get people to be willing to "go," to contribute to the change for a better way. When we are able to realize and accept this fact, it can be an important step for a transformational leader to sprout, to take form, and be what God created him or her to be. During my time in the trenches, I used to jokingly say, "HR would be easy if it weren't for the people." That may be funny, but the truth is that HR wouldn't be a thing if it weren't for the people, leadership wouldn't be a thing if it weren't for the people, and change management wouldn't be a thing if it weren't for the people. Leadership is the biggest challenge we have in our world: to get a large number of independently thinking, opinionated, stubborn, fearful people to go along with something we propose, to be willing to change the way they do things, to encounter and overcome the bumps in the road, and to be a part of something bigger than themselves. An effective transformational leader keeps all of this together and keeps the momentum going forward.

Set the Tone for Change

The first step in a change effort is to establish a narrative, with realistic expectations. The narrative is the story of the reality or problem you are facing, how it is affecting you, and why something needs to be done. It is your "case for change."

With every change, it is important to set the tone that there will be bumps in the road, and for everyone to expect them. So often, it seems even the brightest of people miss this point. They go into a change and literally expect a new process to work perfectly. This is why it is important to set the proper tone; that once the change starts, everyone must play their part, particularly other leaders. If this is not done, or not done well, everyone will just look at the transformational leader and blame him or her for everything that goes wrong . . . as if to say, "Why didn't you make my life perfect and how could you let these problems happen to me?" A colleague once shared with me that he calls this phenomenon "dump your bucket." If the leader is viewed as the only one driving the change, it implies he or she is the only person who can smooth out the bumps in the road. This will cause people to dump their bucket in your lap and say, "You caused this, now kindly fix it." The leader will become overwhelmed trying to fix every problem alone and the change will lose momentum and ultimately fail.

We must get others involved in the change if we expect them to come with us. Bob Pfeiffer, a fellow colleague who consults with employers in the healthcare industry, shares a more optimistic perspective on this. He says, "We must teach everyone to see the obstacles in the change journey differently. We must teach them to say, 'These are not stumbling blocks, rather they are stepping stones in our journey.'"

We're Here Anyway

I've found that humor is a good way to get people to be more open to change. I try to make it fun and keep the mood light. Sometimes I tell a story, in stages, that goes something like this.

> I can't speak for everyone, and maybe you're someone who has nothing to do and all day to do it, but I can say for myself that I am not independently wealthy. And because of this reality, I need to work. Now, for the most part, I can choose what kind of work I do and I have some choice of where I work. But, nonetheless, I have to work—because if I don't work, I'm not able to put food on the table, pay the mortgage, pay the car payment, and so forth. My guess is that you are in the same shoes. You also have to work. Next, can we agree that, on average, we start working at about 18 (some younger) and our career goes until about 65 (some longer). This means we will work for about 45 years. That is a long time.
>
> We have established two things – that we have to work and that we'll work for about 45 years. Here's the main point—if we're going to work that long, we might as well try to do two things. First, we should try to do something special. We're here anyway, and 45 years is a long time to watch the clock. Second, we might as well have fun. Now, by fun I don't mean goof off and eat cupcakes all day (although I love chocolate cupcakes). By fun, I mean accept a good challenge, solve a hard problem, exceed a customer's expectations and overall, do something special.

This speech is a bit "cheesy," but I've found it to work. I am not sure if other states use that word, but it's used in Wisconsin, where we sometimes speak our own language.

I told this story once in a manufacturing communication meeting with about 50 shop floor employees. I was sharing some opportunities we had with safety and how everyone could get involved. Over the next couple of years, they achieved many great things. We improved our safety big time. However, when I shared this story, I got a response I didn't expect. An older gentleman in dirty overalls who was sitting in the back row stood up, and said, "I don't need to be here. I have a lot of money." I responded humorously, "Well, thank you sir – you just ruined my story." He was telling the truth, but he was the only one in the room who could say that. Everyone laughed and his comments helped reinforce the points I made.

What's Your Word?

For many years, I facilitated development sessions for company leaders. Sometimes, as an icebreaker, I would start off the session by asking a question. I would tell everyone to take out a piece of paper and ask them to write down one word that describes their view of "effective leadership." It can be a word with a hyphen, but otherwise, even if several words come to mind, it is important to choose one. You might be thinking, there is no way to describe effective leadership with one word. Like healthcare, it's a complex topic. I agree. However, by requiring everyone to choose one word, it forced them to think at a deeper level and it also revealed something about their individual leadership style. I would ask a few people to share what word they chose and why. It always sparked some good discussion. Typical responses would be things like: communication, engagement, lead-by-example, or vision.

If I were to ask you this question, what word do you choose? Your answer would reveal something about how you view leadership. There is not really a correct answer to this question, and there is not really an incorrect answer. Because of the one-way communication dynamic of this book, I won't get to hear your word (this disappoints me), but you get to hear mine.

My word is "involvement." I choose this word because I believe when people are told what to do, or asked to be excited about someone else's dreams, they aren't nearly as motivated as when they are part of it. When a leader is able to involve others, not only is there less resistance but there's also far more input, ideas, and support from others on how to succeed. I am a big believer that $1+1+1+1 = 8$. For instance, I may share an idea that is mediocre, but it gets others thinking. Then, another person builds on my idea and makes it a little better. And another person does the same, and before we are finished, we have developed a better way to do something—together. Our confidence that it will work is high and there is buy-in to the established method because we included the "experts" in the discussion. The experts are the ones who do the job every day and inherently know it best.

In taking this approach, it is especially important not to be naïve and think that you can please everyone, nor is it wise to try. I learned this lesson many years ago in the school of hard knocks— through experience. I learned that a leader must pick a clear, value-oriented path and stick with it. In doing so, the majority will follow. Courage is the operating system that your convictions run on. As a result, leaders who lead with a mindset of pleasing everyone end up pleasing no one. There is a reason they call it a "backbone." A leader without clear values resembles a spineless jellyfish. However, the best leaders inspire with principle—meaning their values shape their convictions and they lead with virtue. George Washington agreed with this approach when he said, "To please everybody is impossible; were I to undertake it I should probably please nobody. If I know myself I have no partialities. I have from the beginning, and I will to the end pursue to the best of my judgement and abilities one steady line of conduct for the good of the great whole."

Involve the Experts

Over the course of my career, I have seen all too many examples in which leaders didn't believe it was worth their time to talk with the experts and thought they knew better. In one case, a safety leader put in a maintenance request for a guardrail to be installed in a production cell. His purpose was to protect production team members and keep them out of harm's way from forklift traffic. His intent was good, but his method was faulty. The maintenance team installed a new guardrail, but it had to be completely removed during the next shift! Why? Because it was directly in the path of where a forklift needed to go in order to empty the dumpster. You can imagine how this made the maintenance team feel. They had to professionally install a guardrail, and then uninstall it in the same 24-hour period. The manufacturing team wasn't impressed either. They lost production that day because they were distracted by others' actions who didn't take the time to ask them about how things should work in their work area. The safety leader learned a valuable lesson that day – involve the experts.

When we involve others, we not only get the best ideas and learn the best ways to do something, we also get their heart. We can all relate to experiences in which we've been included and excluded. How did we feel in each scenario? When we are included and given a chance to voice our opinion on decisions, we feel respected. The most important phrase a leader can say is, "What do you think?" This shows others that you value their input and you respect them. If they feel valued, they are much more likely to support new initiatives and give you their best.

This is important for those team members who can be difficult at times. By involving members of the team in the change process, it makes it more difficult for someone to play armchair quarterback. More simply, it is easier for someone to complain if he or she is on the sidelines and is not in the game, but once in the game (or allowed in the game), the responsibility factor kicks in and there is no one else to blame and nowhere to run. Any criticism becomes inherently pointed at oneself. As they say, "When you point your finger at someone in blame, three fingers are pointed back at you." If you believe in the concept of involvement, your goal will be to get as many others in the game as possible.

Change Management Models

Several years ago, I worked for a company in Wisconsin called Badger Mining. Badger Mining mines silica sand through surface mining techniques that greatly value the environment. They put the land back the same or better than they found it. That is *what* they do, and *how* they do it is pretty amazing as well. They have a high-trust culture called TEAM that is made up of self-directed work teams. Their culture is one of high involvement. It was molded and shaped by the late George Hess, along with several other family owners who worked in the business. This family-owned company embodies everything a company should in regard to how people are treated, respected—and involved. While working there, my role was to educate, strengthen, and reinforce the TEAM culture. Before joining Badger Mining, I had considered myself a seasoned transformational leader, and an expert on the subject of culture, but I didn't know much about self-directed work teams (SDWT). I can genuinely say that I learned as much from them as they did from me.

Leading at Badger Mining was a great experience, and I am privileged to have been part of a company that was chosen several times as the #1 Best Place to Work/Great Place to Work in the Nation by both SHRM and Forbes. To this day, I agree with notion of SDWTs, and the notion that, "No one has ever disagreed with their own idea." The following decision-making timelines are something I developed during the time I led at Badger Mining. Each provides an interesting perspective from which to compare and contrast different ways change can be led.

The first picture, labeled Autocratic Approach, is the typical way change is led in within companies. From the top down, management makes all the decisions and implements the change rapidly. Once the change is implemented, the earth wobbles on its axis for a while and eventually the change either dies or goes through—with many casualties left in its wake, such as broken trust, frustrated customers, lower efficiency, lower quality, and a sour impression of change management by the employees going into the future.

In contrast, the picture labeled Participative Approach provides a much better context for change management. In this scenario, the ideas for change are discussed openly with the experts, and for a much longer period of time before the changes are enacted. This gives everyone a chance to have input on how things will be done, to measure how it will affect all parties involved, including customers, and it gives the company a chance to polish all processes and decisions before the change is implemented. While the autocratic method may feel faster, it is my opinion that the latter is a far better approach and is not nearly as messy. Relationships are not damaged, processes are refined, and by the time the go button is pushed, everyone is well aware of what the change is and how it will work. It is a much more respectful and smoother way of managing change.

These two philosophies are based on very different value and belief structures. In the autocratic approach, the leader believes he or she is the smartest person in the room and therefore must make all the decisions. In the participative approach, the experts, the people who do the work every day, are involved and they are shown respect. They are intentionally involved in changes that will impact them. I am not a betting man, but if you asked me to bet on which method drives faster and better change, I am doubling down on the participative approach every time.

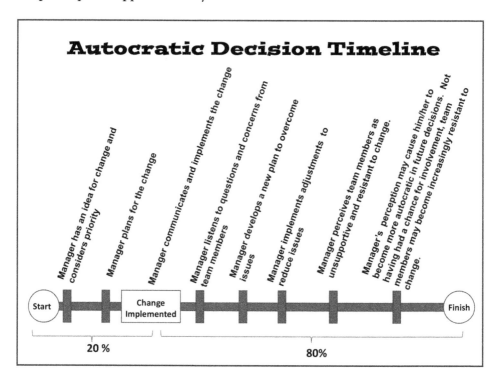

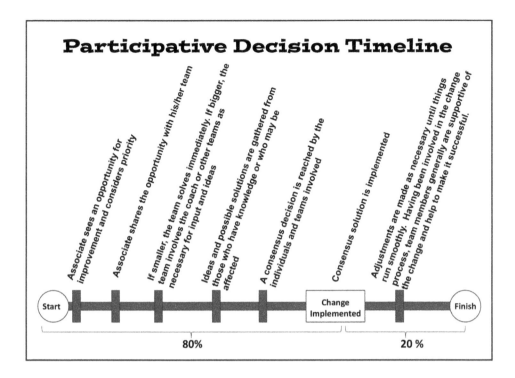

What's Your WIFM?

An effective way to foster involvement is to adopt a mindset of WIFM (what's in it for me), and to remember that people will be more willing to help when their WIFM is higher. This means they know the leader will not take all the credit for a success, the new way will make their daily life better, and conversely, a successful change will not make their life worse. As I am speaking to employees, I always have WIFM in the back of my mind.

Another important thing to remember is that it is common for a leader to talk with fellow leaders about a topic, sometimes for hours. These conversations can stretch on for weeks or months. This is good discussion and can be valuable for developing a greater vision for *where* you want to go or *what* you need to do. It is equally important to have those same conversations with the employees you lead and to be careful not to spring the news on them concerning something that you have been talking about for months but they are hearing for the very first time. You can explain the big picture perspective and the company vision, and then you have an opportunity to involve them in shaping *how* the vision will be achieved. Specifically, how will this impact the way they do things and what will their contribution be? If a leader does not take the time to facilitate these important discussions, the changes will be viewed as "your" initiative and there will likely be a low level of buy-in and support from the team.

We Are All Wired Differently

One important piece of research that explains a person's readiness for change is Rogers' Diffusion of Innovation curve. In his book, published in 2003, Everett Rogers explained how different types of people react to the concept of change. This is illustrated in what he calls the Adoption Curve. His context focuses more on adopting technology; however, it is a good model for us to use to make some basic, foundational points about types of people. Everett Rogers passed away in 2004, shortly after publishing his book, but his research and teaching live on to help us with our change management journeys.

His research shines a light on an important concept for us as change leaders to understand. Namely, we all approach change differently. This truth corrects the mistaken assumptions we make if we believe that everyone views change the same as we do. For instance, if we are innovative and get excited about change, we tend to think everyone views change that way—or at least they should view change like that. Similarly, if we are slower to change, and prefer timely and calculated actions, we tend to assume everyone thinks that way. This is simply not the case. Rogers' adoption curve gives us a framework for different types of thinkers and how each prefers to deal with change.

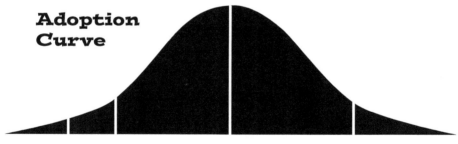

Adoption Curve

INNOVATORS 2.5%
Innovators are enthusiastic, and they desire to be the first to use the latest technology. They represent a tiny percentage of the market.

EARLY ADOPTERS 13.5%
Early Adopters are those who enjoy new innovations and are comfortable taking social risk but are largely motivated by it's potential to drive their success. They are very influential in the marketplace, acting as trendsetters.

EARLY MAJORITY 34%
The Early Majority is made up of pragmatists who adopt new innovations only after it is proven and they feel comfortable that it won't put them at risk. They are the largest segment of the market.

LATE MAJORITY 34%
The Late Majority are conservative thinkers who are risk averse and extremely cautious when using anything new. They not only want to see demonstrable results, they need to be reassured that there is next to no risk. They also represent a large portion of the market.

LAGGARDS 16%
Laggards only use new technology if forced, and then do so kicking and screaming. They are a small audience.

- As you can see in the figure above, 2.5% of people are natural Innovators. These are the visionaries who initiate change, and are able to see the future, far before it exists or before others believe something is possible. They live "out of the box."

- A larger fraction, 13.5% of people, are Early Adopters. Early adopters are similar to Innovators, but they play things just a tad bit safer. They are still mostly "out of the box" thinkers, but they are a little more grounded in their approach. However, let us not mistake them—they are also innovative. This group is naturally driven to initiate change, with something that does not yet exist or something that is very new and has not been fully worked out or proven yet.

- Next is the Early Majority, encompassing a large portion: 34% of people. Those in this group are not innovators. Rather, they are the first to implement new innovations once they have been proven. They have a notably lower risk tolerance than Innovators or Early Adopters.

- The Late Majority also make up a notable portion: 34% of people. They are conservative and calculated thinkers, and prefer lower risk. They are the last big group that willingly goes forward.

- At the tail end we have the Laggards, at a sizeable 16%. These folks are more comfortable with the known, even if it is broken and unbearable. Change is painful for them, and therefore they avoid it, mostly at all costs. They do not "go willingly." It is not in their nature. From the leader's perspective, they mostly must be tolerated and recognized as change resistors. They can derail a change if the leaders do not recognize them and "out lead" them. They must be shown respect, but not necessarily given credibility. They will surface and at times they must be dealt with in the change process. The more awareness we have of the types of people going in, the better prepared we can be to lead the change.

We might all have some laggard tendencies. We as human beings are wired to seek predictability, safety, and comfort. If our goal is to never make a mistake, the surest way to behave is to never change anything, or further, never do anything. However, this mindset also leads to an unfruitful life, one that is monotonous and uneventful, by choice. Wayne Gretzky, the GOAT of NHL hockey, once said, "You miss the shots you don't take."

Let's Embark on the Change Management Journey

We can view this as a full journey, with various stages along the way. Each stage will have its own challenges and milestones. The overall journey starts with what I call "here" and ends with "there." A successful journey is to do all of the necessary pre-journey work to ensure a successful start, to keep the momentum all the way through the long stretch in the middle, and to finish strong to successfully reach our final destination. An unsuccessful journey would be anything that hinders the employer from completing the journey and potentially having to return to the old way. Yet, we also know in healthcare that the current path is not sustainable, so the risk of such a journey is already lessened due to ever-present risk.

In the lean world, the starting point is called *current state* and the goal is called *future state*. Although this mode of thinking uses different terminology, the approach is exactly the same as the one I've been describing here. For our model, we will use the context of a roadmap. I break down the journey into the following stages:

- You are HERE
- New Beginnings
- The Desert Middle
- The Home Stretch
- There – Mission Accomplished

The cartoon map is provided with open spaces for you to sketch out your journey. You can plan out your journey in the way that is best for you and in the format you prefer. I am a child at heart, and I prefer something visual, ideally a cartoon picture. That is just me. I like to sketch out visuals of what Here and There look like, with key milestones to achieve along the way. I have found that most people prefer pictures and stories. They are a good way to make the complex, simple.

I realized this the first time I shared my strategy at Merrill Steel. We had implemented some good single-point solutions, and each had their own ROI, but something was lacking. I needed a narrative, and I needed a comprehensive strategy to go forward. One early morning I typed up a five-page Word document that outlined all the point solutions and all the free-market minded partners. Specifically, the strategy identified how all of these pieces fit together to form a clear and compelling story of where we were and where we would go.

I was so excited. I sent out the summary to a relatively long list of people, including coworkers within Merrill Steel and a host of others in Wisconsin, in Oklahoma, and beyond. My detailed typed strategy was so incredibly inspiring,

Healthcare Improvement Journey Map

You are here!

New Beginnings

Milestones
_____
_____
_____

Desert Middle

Milestones
_____
_____
_____

Home Stretch

Milestones
_____
_____
_____

THERE Mission Accomplished!

do you know how many responses I got? Let me count—one, two, three . . . None. I received zero responses—zilch. Crickets. How could no one be as inspired as I? The reality was that many either did not read it (we are flooded with emails daily and are not inclined to read five-page attachments) or they didn't understand it. I don't mean that in a derogatory way. There is just a reality here that you have probably observed in this book. There are a lot of moving pieces and employer healthcare is complicated.

I scratched my head. If my own team and fellow colleagues were not inspired, I would never be able to inspire welders, painters, accountants, and designers. I needed a new approach. The cartoon pictures you see in this book were what I came up with. I can sketch a little, but my artistic gifts are lacking, so I recruited some help from Mikey Hubacek, the Communications Specialist on our team, and he was able to take my whiteboard sketches and make them look as good as they do. Then, I reshared our strategy, this time in picture form. The response I got from that email was very different. Even Keith Smith from Oklahoma messaged me, saying, "This is great! Can I use this?" I said, "Absolutely, *mi Picasso es su Picasso*." Ok, I didn't really say the last part – but I should have.

You Are HERE

Have you ever seen one of those navigation maps that are placed along interstate roadside rest areas or along walk paths at amusement parks? Typically, there is a colorful map with a big arrow, pointing to a dot with large printed words next to it that say, "You are HERE." If you are at an amusement park looking at one of these maps, you identify the "you are HERE" dot and look around to see how your physical surroundings match the map. Next, you find the place you want to go—your destination— your "there." Let's say the Big Dipper roller coaster is your there. Now, all you have to do is connect the dots in your mind and figure out the quickest and easiest way to get from here to there. As simple as this sounds, early identification of here and there are critically necessary. If you do not know where you are, there is no reference point from which to start, and if you do not know where you are going, as the saying goes, any road will take you there. Ultimately, no one will follow you if you are not able to skillfully articulate where you would like to go. You are welcome to wander and get lost, but no one will follow you on that journey. Both here and there must be identified and articulated before a journey can begin.

Before you share your narrative with all employees, it is important you have prepared well. Preparation is necessary for a successful journey. Those who understand this are in good company. Abe Lincoln said, "Give me six hours to chop down a tree and I will spend the first four sharpening the axe." To help with your preparation, I have included a pre-journey checklist below:

Pre-journey Checklist

- Finalize your Healthcare Strategy
- Determine your Pace
- Gain Stakeholder Buy-in and Support
- Choose an Internal Champion
- Create a Clear and Compelling Narrative

Finalize your Healthcare Strategy

It is critical to have your overall healthcare strategy mapped out. It is made up of the financial and medical components, supported by your healthcare partners. Your narrative is a greatly abbreviated version of this. The progression is natural, in that you won't be able to write your narrative unless you first have a clear strategy.

Determine Your Pace

Before you begin communicating and implementing your strategy, you will need to determine your pace. A mentor once told me, "You can only lead as fast as the people you are leading are willing and able to go." As you look at your overall business initiatives for the upcoming year, this might give you some wisdom as to what pace you should choose. With healthcare likely being among your top three costs, while having the most potential for significant savings, it is my hope that you do not put it on the back burner. Even if it involves hiring an additional person to manage the change, the payoff potential is high.

Here are some guidelines to consider when determining how fast or how slow you would like to drive the change:

	PACE OF CHANGE
Slow	Take isolated steps, a little at a time, with no specific timeline.
Moderate	Take strategic, intentional steps, one at a time, over a period of several years.
Fast	Take strategic, intentional steps, as fast as you can, over a period of one to two years.

Gain Stakeholder Buy-In and Support

Before you begin leading the masses, you will need to make sure you have buy-in from your key stakeholders. They don't need to fully understand everything as well as you do, but they do need to understand it well enough to support you in good conscience. There should be no shortcuts or assumptions at this stage. In the middle of the desert middle, you will need their support. If things get bumpy, you will need to keep them from giving up and recommending you go back to the old way. The only time you should stop your journey is if you see no possible way that you can succeed. This is how it can feel in the desert middle, and in almost all cases, the best decision is to press forward.

Unlike other key areas and top expenses of the business, healthcare has been off the radar for most CEOs. This means, before you request buy-in, there is likely a great need to educate owners, board members, and executives on healthcare and the things discussed in this book. If they're willing, it would be ideal for them to read this book and the others I have recommended. Often, owners and high-level executives do not yet understand the healthcare benefits game, even what it means to be self-funded and how benefit plans work.

This journey will take more than an executive presence and a winsome smile. To be successful, the key stakeholders in your company need to understand and make a genuine commitment. Perhaps most importantly, it will require you to communicate, and to say things in a way that they can understand. So often, we use unfamiliar acronyms, phrases, and terms . . . and we lose our audience in the first five minutes. It is best to be mindful about speaking in terms they can understand.

Choose an Internal Champion

This is the step in which you should decide who will be the point person: the champion for your journey. This person can be anyone you believe is capable. It may be the person reading this book, who becomes inspired to lead the change in your company. Think of who you need as you share this initiative with your employees. This leader can be from any department, with any background. As long as the person is committed to learning, is willing to work hard, is able to lead well, and is passionate about fixing healthcare, he or she can be a successful champion. If this person is not an executive, you will want to make sure you support him or her with the necessary authority to make decisions and to effectively drive the change forward.

Your Narrative: A Clear and Compelling Case for Change

The journey can be kicked off by sharing the narrative with all employees. It is your case for change, a clear and compelling story that educates and motivates others to join you on the journey. The champion and the executives of the company should be able to articulate your story, smoothly and repeatedly, in the course of a few minutes. To give you an idea of how this might sound, I have included a sample narrative later in this next section. You can create your own based on your own situation and strategy.

One critical piece that needs to be in the narrative (more times than not it gets missed) is what I call the "let go" piece. If others are going to join you on a journey to a new place, they must first be willing to leave their current place. This notion is supported by research. A person must first detach from the current state before they will be able to form an attachment to something new.

In our amusement park example, it might look like this: "Hey dad, let's go ride the roller coaster!" Dad replies, "No thanks, the last time I rode on a roller coaster I was terrified and I almost lost my lunch. As I got more comfortable, I did enjoy it, but I was younger then and more adventurous. You kids go have fun and I will sit right here on this bench and see you when you get back." The child says, "Dad, c'mon. Remember on the trip down here how you were talking about how short life is and how we need to have more fun and create memories with family? You talked about how your mom told you how she wished she would have taken more chances – how she would have lived more and worried less? Dad, you can sit on this bench, and watch us ride the roller coaster, see the exhilaration on our faces from the experience of the ride. You can witness our laughter and excitement as we walk back and tell you how fun it was - or you can join us. Think about it. You can sit on a bench any time, but you'll probably never be able to come back to this amusement park and you may never have a chance to ride this roller coaster again. The bench is boring. There will be no stories to tell from it and no excitement in waiting for us to return. What do you say?" Dad exclaims, "Ok, kids, you got me. I will join you. This bench is comfortable, quiet, and predictable, but it is also boring, and I want to make some more memories with you. Let's go!"

In this example, dad was already reflecting on the brevity of life and the importance of leaving his comfort zone (his Here). His kids just reminded him of his own words and feelings and wisdom from his mom – they got him to get off that bench and let go of his Here. When leaders in organizations forget this important step, the change initiative at hand, even if it has a great There attached to it, will likely never be completed, because no one took the time to explain what Here looks like and why we can't stay Here. The reality is that everyone is still holding on to Here with white knuckles . . . and until they let go, any selling attempt to describe how great There is will be felt as an annoyance, as disrespect. It won't work as inspiration.

As obvious as this example may sound, when leaders share their case for change, they often overlook the notion that a person must be willing to leave where they are before they will even listen to ideas about going somewhere else. No matter how great that "somewhere else" is, physically and psychologically, they are still stuck in the here. How does this happen? Let's put ourselves in their shoes. In the corporate world, leaders meet in weekly management meetings.

They talk regularly and frequently. These conversations might happen at a corporate office in Texas, or a manufacturing plant in Wisconsin. They might happen in a company of 100 people, or a company of 10,000 people. Typically, these conversations are in depth, breaking down the pros and cons of a given issue, with everyone in the room sharing their opinion and ideas. These discussions take place over a period of days, weeks, months or even years. The leaders have plenty of time to process, reflect, and work through their emotions. Eventually, the management team collectively agrees: "We can't stay here." Further, they come to agreement about the new place they will travel to and they become inspired and excited about the possibilities. Ultimately, they have worked through the change process together, as a leadership team. So far, this is a good start to a change initiative.

However, what typically happens next is where the train that is just beginning to roll, can derail. The company leaders have decided to proceed with the change and time is of the essence. With good intent, communication meetings are scheduled. In these meetings, having so thoroughly discussed the problems among themselves already, leaders jump straight to the point. They skillfully share how great the new "there" will be with the workforce. To their surprise, the reaction is not excitement. The leaders don't understand, because they are very excited about going there. They comment to each other, "Why wouldn't everyone else be excited about going there?" Instead of shared excitement, the leaders are met with what they see as resistance and grumbling. The employees say, "Here we go— another flavor of the month." The leaders look around and form an impression: "People sure are resistant to change. Why do they have to be that way?" The leaders talk among themselves, scratching their heads. "We talked about how great the opportunity is in front of us and only a few people are excited. Even so, this is an important initiative for our future, so we must push it through. People are just resistant to change."

Sample: Case for Change Narrative

> For the past two to three decades, monumental changes have been happening in our country with healthcare. American healthcare, which was once known for house calls, affordability, transparent prices, and personal relationships, has become big business. Today, it is common to experience rushed visits, disjointed care, hidden pricing, unclear astronomical bills, and superficial relationships. Due to skyrocketing costs, healthcare has become unaffordable for most Americans, to the point where necessary care is avoided. Wisconsin, our home state, has the honor of being the

fourth worst state in the nation for healthcare costs. In seeing these changes, it is no surprise that 2/3 of the bankruptcies in America are related to healthcare and 3 out of 4 of those families had health insurance— or at least had it on paper.

We are seeing these same cost increases affect our company. For the past five years, we have averaged 9% increases in healthcare costs. This means, over a five-year period, our healthcare costs have increased by 45%. No other industry has experienced cost inflation that is anything close to this.

The cause of these out-of-control increases is a result of the healthcare industry's actions. This industry is made up of hospital systems, insurance carriers, and traditional brokers. Each has enjoyed lucrative increases in revenue, while employer plans and employees' lives have fallen apart, because the industry is incentivized to raise costs.

They have done this primarily by creating a system in which there is "no shopping" allowed. They achieve this in two ways. First, there is no way to determine the prices for healthcare services, even if requested. The quality of care is equally difficult to assess. Second, insurance companies have created networks which have restricted a patient's ability to openly shop for the best value. Unfortunately, it has become profits over patients for the healthcare industry.

What does this mean for us? We need to do something, and we need to do it now.

It means we must change our mindset to begin shopping for healthcare services instead of shopping for insurance. Doctors are beginning to start independent practices, ranging from primary care to surgery centers. In Wisconsin we now have over 80 independent clinics in operation. These are doctors who worked for the hospitals and have now made a decision to start their own practice so that they may provide the highest quality of care, at an affordable price. With these new provider opportunities, we will be able to bring back the "old-fashioned level of care" we used to receive years ago.

This means we will be able to offer onsite or near-site primary care at no cost to you and your family, and other services, such as a high-quality MRI for $600, instead of the $6,000 the hospitals charge. Further, we will be able to get a high-quality joint replacement for under $20,000 – a procedure that can cost as much as $80,000 or more at the hospital. By shopping wisely, we can get better care, at affordable prices, and we can begin to repair our broken health plan.

There is much more detail to discuss, but I wanted to at least share a highlight of where we are headed at our company health plan. We feel this is very important and necessary initiative to support you and your families. As we go through this, please ask questions and share openly. We will all go through this change together.

New Beginnings

The beginning of a journey is an exciting time. Your energy level is high and there is hopeful anticipation in the air. The seeds of "we cannot stay here" have been planted and the table is set to begin an adventure, to travel to a new place—a better place. Realistic expectations have been set. Everyone has been reminded that these changes will require some inconveniences and sacrifices because of our tumultuous journey, when we arrive, everyone will be able to enjoy the fruits of the promised land. We wake up afresh, without much worry yet of obstacles or unexpected problems that will arise. We are like warriors who have prepared for battle. "We will overcome, and we will be victorious," we tell ourselves.

A couple of well-known movies in which families take a road trip depict this scenario well. They happen to be comedies. Coincidence? If you have ever seen the movies *American Vacation*, with Chevy Chase, or *RV*, with Robin Williams, you may recall the stages and experiences of their journeys. Filled with this same anticipation, the Griswold family scrapes their luggage off the top of their car as they back out of the garage, not even making it out of their driveway before they encounter the first mishap. The Munros, in the movie *RV*, run over and demolish most of the neighborhood's mailboxes before they've completed the first mile of their trip. It is my hope that your journey gets off to a better start than these, but these examples can help us foresee what can be expected.

Road trips are a great analogy for a healthcare improvement journey. Most of us have had our own Griswold experiences in the family Truckster, so you likely to know the feeling. It's not *if* we will encounter similar challenges (we will); it's more about how we respond to those challenges. Will we be effective problem solvers and lead people well, serving as authentic, caring, and competent leaders? If we set the right tone for our trip, later on when we encounter bumps in the road, road closures, and detours, the people we lead will be ready and willing to adjust and overcome. It is up to us to paint this picture, to anticipate challenges, and create a general awareness that it won't all be unicorns, rainbows, lollipops, puppies, and long walks on the beach. As leaders of change, embarking on a new journey, we will need to be visible, interactive, good listeners, empathizers, persistent, and probably a whole bunch more. The better we communicate and lead, the more favorable the outcome will be.

At this stage, because the general level of education of your workforce on the topic of healthcare will be low (that will change), it is wise to use relatable examples, such as purchasing a car, or buying a flat screen television. The goal is to teach what effective shopping looks like – and to contrast it with modern healthcare. We educate everyone on the tenets of a free market, how it can self-regulate through healthy competition and innovation, and how the healthcare industry has suppressed these tenets.

The end of the journey will mean exit stage left for the beast that is trying to eat us and enter stage right for free market providers. We need to stop feeding the beast and start feeding the good guys and gals who do business in a transparent and caring way. By strengthening the free market providers, we will effectively open up the market.

If I have shared these kinds of examples once, I have shared them a thousand times, individually and in large groups. It will be necessary to have these discussions with your employees, their spouses (and all others who will listen), over and over. Have these discussions—not just until they understand it, but until they become excited about it and adopt the new and better way.

Communication is your greatest tool for getting this "new beginnings" plane off the ground. In educating other leaders, sometimes I will reference the three most important factors of real estate value, which as you know are LOCATION, LOCATION, LOCATION. In change management, we have a similar dynamic. The three most important things are COMMUNICATION, COMMUNICATION, COMMUNICATION. In my experience, a leader will need to share a new concept 100 times, and everyone will *begin* to understand it. Then, the leader will share it another 100 times, and everyone will understand it *a little more*. Eventually, the needle will move and you will see the fruit of your labor. Most of these discussions are with individuals. A few of them are in groups. As exhausting as this sounds, this example is probably more literal than figurative. I am not exaggerating when I choose the number 100. I have found that if we are passionate about the possibilities, and how much it can help people, it is possible to do this. It doesn't have to feel like work, even though someone is paying you for it.

Through my experiences, I have found that communication is one of the most difficult needles to move on an employee survey. For years, even decades, I have studied this topic, trying to improve the survey score on this topic. Unfortunately, all too often, an employer's attempts to improve communication feels about as easy as nailing Jell-O to a tree. The struggle is real.

I remember a focus group I helped facilitate in which there were about 12 voluntary attendees. We had just completed our employee survey process, which was administered every two years. All employees within the company took the survey and our challenge as leaders was to understand and continuously improve our work environment and our culture. We utilized cross-functional focus groups to drill down, ask questions, and to offer employees a chance to share their thoughts. These meetings can be highly valuable, if led well. In one particular meeting, to close the discussion, the empathetic VP of manufacturing asked the group a question. He said, "I would like to go around the table and for each of you to answer this question. In only a few words, if you had a magic wand and could make one thing better, what would it be?" You could see the gears turning in everyone's mind. As we started, it became very clear what everyone thought. We went around the room in a counterclockwise direction. The first person spoke, *"Communication."* The second person, *"Communication"*, the third person, *"Communication"*, the fourth person, *"Can we have free beer at the Christmas party?"*, the fifth person, *"Communication."* And so it went, eleven out of twelve people said communication. We closed the meeting, everyone went on their way, and the VP looked over at me, smiled, and exclaimed, "We communicate more here than I do with my own family. Any ideas of how we can make it better?" Over time, we continued to discuss communication and eventually, we were able to improve our survey score.

One of the ways we did it was by raising everyone's awareness of communication, and by sharing the model below:

This model, while profoundly simple, has been incredibly valuable for me in teaching communication. First, by discussing the topic in detail, it raises awareness. When we shine light on an area, and raise awareness in the culture that it needs to be better, good things happen. Specifically, this model helps improve communication by identifying where the breakdown of communication occurred. More simply, if communication failed, one of these three steps did not happen effectively.

First, was the information sent? If it was not sent, we can identify why communication failed in that instance. An example would be that communication meetings were held, but the meeting with the truck drivers never got scheduled because they are on the road and harder to reach. The information was never sent to them.

Second, was the information received? If it was not received, we can identify why the communication failed in that instance. An example would be that an important email went to spam. It was sent, but the person never received it.

Third, was the information understood? If it was not understood, we can identify why the communication failed in that instance. An example could be that a healthcare meeting was held but all kinds of acronyms were used and everyone was completely lost in the meeting. The information was sent, it was received, but it was not understood. This helps us focus in on where we need to improve and what we need to do differently.

Fourth, was information rephrased back to the sender to confirm understanding? If accurate understanding was not confirmed, we can identify why the communication failed in this instance. One technique we can teach others is to practice empathetic listening. This is not as unique and important a step as the other three, but it can be a good technique to practice to confirm the third step of understanding. I have experienced instances when I genuinely believed I understood what was being sent to me, and with this model in mind, I repeated back to the sender what I heard. In one instance, I repeated the message back confidently, expecting to hear, "Yes, you got it!", and instead I heard, "That is not at all what I said – let me try again."

I would suggest sharing this model with everyone at your company and educating them on how it works. In doing so, you can raise awareness on a common challenge, and help your change management journey go more smoothly.

The Desert Middle

If you have successfully reached this stage, the change has been happening for a while and everyone is beginning to understand the "new way." The narrative case for change has been shared, and shared, and shared. The leadership team is discussing feedback they are receiving in the regular management meetings to try to keep a finger on the pulse.

Follow-up meetings have taken place with the masses to continue to educate and teach people how they can achieve high quality healthcare by shopping wisely through the new plan design. These cumulative follow-up meetings with employees are very helpful. Everyone picks up so much more the second time around, and the third time around, especially if they have some experience of the new way.

The strategy is in motion and communication is your vehicle of change. You have now made it to the middle of the journey—the desert. To make sure I am communicating clearly, by desert I don't mean strawberry cheesecake. I mean hot, barren, sandstorms, and relentless sun. We haven't forgotten to untie the dog leash from the bumper yet, or we haven't looked down the end of the RV sewer hose, but in this middle desert we might get an opportunity to experience some of those things.

Along with getting started and leading others to let go of Here, the middle is one of the most challenging stages of the journey. The anticipation and excitement that once filled our hearts and minds has now faded. I like to jokingly say, once in a while, "Are we having fun yet?" This is particularly important when you're not having fun.

Thankfully, at this stage, the early adopters and the early majority have joined us, faithful and supportive, while the late majority and laggards are weighing down your soul. They can't see the light yet. If it was up to them, they would give up and go back to the known, predictable (and very broken) place of Here. In their mind, they have rationalized, Here wasn't really that bad. You are not yet their best friend. You are the guy or the gal that is messing up their life.

Several problems have reared their ugly heads and things are not as fun and exciting as they were in the beginning. After 100 discussions and many hours of repeating yourself, sharing the strategy in examples that everyone can understand, you begin to tire. The finish line is still too far off in the distance to see it. In the desert, we might ask ourselves, "Is this even attainable?"

You find yourself in the hot desert sun, alone, dehydrated, and tired. Some begin to question your decision as a leader to start this journey, whether your motives were selfish, and if you are competent. Ouch. Yet, this is where we need to remember why we are on this journey. We need to continue to be visible, communicate, teach, listen, and show we care. We all have our own leadership styles which make us uniquely qualified. I have found that humor and encouragement can lighten the tension and keep people upbeat as they go through their day. In my journey at Merrill Steel, while going through the middle, I found ways to keep the mood positive and to lighten the tension. It might be posting a funny comic about healthcare in a place that people will see it, it might be a smile and a pat on the back to thank someone for sharing an article or an idea, it might be a recognition lunch for achieving some key milestones along the way (it is very important to humbly celebrate key milestones), or it might be to show vulnerability: that, as a leader, you are a real person too and although you are seeing the challenges, you care too much to turn back on the journey.

It is very important to be real and to not give up. People are watching you, and any sign of you giving up will be "game over." One nugget I always like to remember is that even though people seem to be dumping their buckets in your lap, if they're talking to you, that means they still have some trust and respect for you. Some just like to keep the pressure on so they can have confidence that the problems will get fixed. When people share their issues with you, it means they think you care and that you might be able to help them. When they stop sharing with you, it means you have lost their trust. Some leaders mistakenly perceive quietness as meaning the problems are fixed. They say, "Well, things are quiet. Things must be better." Don't make this mistake. Keep the lines of communication open, continue to care, continue to problem-solve, and continue to press forward. A positive attitude is contagious and most people, down deep, understand that change is difficult. When you show a positive attitude, it can have an amazing effect on others. My wife went to the doctor and he asked her, "Do you wake up grumpy?" She said, "No, sometimes I just let him sleep."

In the desert middle of the Merrill Steel journey, we encountered our share of desert middle problems. Our new TPA was struggling in the midst of Covid and we were feeling the pain. We were dealing with mostly administrative issues, such as deductible accumulator mishaps, incorrect logos on cards, denials of care by hospitals for incorrect logos, customer service call center issues, and one hospital was calling because they hadn't been paid in six months. Thankfully, the TPA recovered well and over time was able to clean up the laundry list of administration issues. Empathizing with my pain, and also realizing my hard work and efforts, the president of Merrill Steel, Fred Schwalbach, sent me this meme in the middle of our journey. It meant a lot to me that he understood. He knew I was catching some flak, that it was normal and expected at this stage, and I was doing everything I could to resolve the issues. He supported me and lifted my spirits. He encouraged me to keep going. He understood that we were making worthwhile improvements, that transformational change is hard, and that "things would get better." And they did get better—much better, but not before they got worse for a while.

> Six Phases of a Project
>
> 1. Enthusiasm
> 2. Disillusionment
> 3. Panic
> 4. Search for the guilty
> 5. Punishment of the innocent
> 6. Praise and honors for the non-participant

Our memory sometimes plays tricks on us, causing us to have the impression of the "good old days" and that somehow, things were easier in the past. I reflect back on how much I loved my first car. Don't we all? We look back to yesteryear and relish the memories. The smell of the interior, the sound of the engine, and the way it made us feel free when we rolled the windows down on a warm summer day. However, when I really think about it, that first car probably wasn't so special. We tend to remember the good over the bad. My first car was a 1980 Datsun hatchback. It was complete with rusty doors, no power steering, a gas gauge that didn't work (I watched the miles to know when to fill up), an engine that would race continuously at 3,000 rpm's until it warmed up (people thought I was revving it to look cool) and it had the oddest of issues, like, it wouldn't start after it rained. No water was actually getting under the hood – it had something to do with the humidity. The car ran fine once it was going, but after a rainstorm, cranked and cranked and cranked and would not start. I remember looking out the window from my high school classroom, watching the rain start, and think, oh great, I guess I'm stranded again today. Thankfully, there was a kind and cute little cheerleader that would give me a ride and drop me off on her way home. That part wasn't so bad. But as fun as that first car was to drive, I wouldn't want to go back to those days.

Those who are uncomfortable with change can be like this. "Here" was basically intolerable and unsustainable, but in their mind, it was their first car.

The Home Stretch

We step out of the desert middle, take a deep breath, smell the fresh air, and we look over the horizon. The finish line is in sight! We have ploughed forward, even when things seemed impossible. The Red Sea has parted and we have led our workforce through the hardest parts of the journey. We aren't there yet, but we're getting closer.

These are times when it's important to continually review the milestones that have been achieved and remember to celebrate them. These celebrations are times for encouragement, laughter, and camaraderie. They are absolutely necessary and a key part of any successful journey. People get tired, physically and psychologically, and they need a recharge. Celebrating milestones is the best way to do this. These celebrations need to happen with a humble tone, as new challenges remain ahead. It is too early to take our foot off the gas pedal. We must push on and finish the journey.

Perhaps the biggest caution at this stage in the journey is not to celebrate too early – to make sure that you finish strong. It's like a sports team that gets a huge lead early in the game, only to become lax, completely forget about the game plan that got them the big lead, and end up losing the game. It's commonly called a miraculous comeback, but usually it's because the leading team lost their focus. Keep your focus, view the destination, and lead others to finish strong.

There – Mission Accomplished

Smile. Laugh. Hug. High five. Pop the cork on some bubbly (not at work) and celebrate! The planned destination has been reached. You have arrived – you are There. The long journey is over. You can take a deep breath and relax. All obstacles have been overcome. New trails have been blazed, new paradigms have been created and your organization is positioned on a win-win, sustainable path.

Congratulations! You have also built trust with your workforce. No more flavor of the month nonsense. Your next change initiative will be easier. Not easy, but easier, because you have built confidence and you have finished what you started. You have raised everyone's self-efficacy for change and you have helped many people.

You may be wondering, what about the late majority and laggards? Typically, the late majority join somewhere in the last half or even final stretch of the journey. The laggards, well, I'm not sure they ever really join. These folks are often of the "half empty" perspective and many times, they are not happy unless they are unhappy. Show them respect, but don't spend too much time on them, as they will just weigh you down.

The Winner's Circle

If you make it over the finish line and lead a successful change effort, you'll notice a big change in how people talked to you during the race as compared with how they treat you in the winner's circle. While you are running the race, the supporters are few and far between and people are anxious to tell you all of the reasons why you will not succeed. Members of your company, your team, and even your family may tell you it's not possible and that you have embarked on a fool's errand.

After the success, the story shifts. Everyone, including the doubters, are excited that they contributed, proud of how they believed and supported the effort all along. Stacey King, a Bulls teammate of Michael Jordan, commented one night after a game in which Jordan had scored 69 points, "I'll always remember this as the night that Michael Jordan and I combined to score 70 points." Stacey was just being funny, but this is how it feels after a long, treacherous, and grueling change effort. Those that were against you and joined in near the finish line now act as if they were with you the whole race. When this happens, let it be. It's not worth anything more than a smile.

The case study analyses are clear: without the efforts of the champion, the change would not have started, it would not have persisted, and it would not have succeeded. Stay humble and continue to lead others to better places.

Difficult People

As a final note in this chapter, I would be remiss if I didn't discuss the topic of "difficult people." Difficult people can weigh down a leader, and particularly a champion who is already carrying an extra heavy load. It is important to know how to deal with these people, so they don't burn you out or derail your efforts. These individuals sprout from the laggard category, but a few of them are more than just "resistant to change." They are downright impossible.

The Psychology of Difficult People

To lead through change effectively, it is important to understand the psychology of difficult people. First, difficult people are unconsciously consumed with themselves. So much so, they are often unable to help or care for others. If you watch carefully, you will not typically see them ask others how they are doing. More often, they dump their bucket (which is often full) frequently and without remorse.

I read a psychological study a few years ago on happiness. The goal of the researcher was to understand questions like, "Who are the happiest people and what types of things do they do that cause them to be happy"? The results were surprising. The happiest people were not those whom we might guess, not the ones with the most money, the ones who are most attractive, the ones who have the most friends, the ones who love their jobs, the ones with the most kids—or with the least kids. It turns out that the happiest people, according to this study, were the "giving people." Giving people are those who help others in various ways, such as by providing financial help or encouragement to another person. They volunteer their time for nonprofit organizations or they give in smaller ways, such as offering a ride, cooking a meal, or helping someone repair something that's broken. Because difficult people are cognitively and inwardly focused on themselves and the pain in their lives, they take it a step further by sharing their misery. In my experience, I would have to agree with the saying, "Misery loves company."

How to Deal with Difficult People

After starting my career in Human Resources many moons ago, it didn't take me long to realize that the difficult people were consuming an inordinate amount of my time. I was green. There was a lot I didn't know. The joke was that an HR person spends 90% of his or her time with 10% of the people: the difficult ones. I didn't find that joke very funny. I spent a lot of money on my education and worked hard in school to get to this place. This is not what I envisioned. If this is how it was going to be, how could I get anything done? And how could I help the majority of people? Something had to give.

If you are in leadership, you have likely experienced this same issue. As leaders, we carry a lot of weight on our shoulders. In our daily work, we strive to support teams, develop employees, meet goals, improve processes, and serve customers. In addition to our daily work, we need to be strategically minded. We need to look over the horizon to determine where we want to be one year from now, five years from now, or even ten years from now. Yet, often, instead of doing the things we want to do, we find ourselves bogged down in dealing with all of the "urgent" issues that arise from difficult people.

If I didn't find a way to free up my time so that I could encourage, recognize, and develop the 90%—the positive contributors—I would continue to expend my energy spinning my wheels, repeating the same cycle over and over, day after day, without making a real difference.

I began to study difficult people. I wanted to understand their psychology. I wanted to be able to help them to become positive contributors. I had good intent, but this was mostly naïve thinking. Here is what I learned.

First and foremost, we cannot change anyone. We can only change ourselves. A leader's job is to create a healthy environment in which individuals and teams can thrive. This often means holding non-team players accountable, and sometimes it means they can't play on your team any longer, because for the good of the whole, we must have a healthy work environment.

We have all been difficult people in the past and we will all likely be difficult people in the future; at least for moments in time. The difference between the normal person and the difficult person is that difficult people are difficult *almost all the time*. I call these individuals sour grapes. I have empathy for them. However, if you aren't careful, they can ruin your team. These sour grapes are literally unable to have a positive thought. You can give them encouragement, say that it will be sunny and 75 degrees tomorrow, and their response will be that it is supposed to rain tomorrow night. No matter what you say, they will hold fast to the half-empty attitude.

I admit that I've had my moments. I have learned and matured as I've gotten older. I've made mistakes, fallen short, and missed the mark many times. Have you ever returned something to the store and acted rudely to the customer service person, who had nothing to do with the cause of your problem? You too? Have you ever gossiped about someone when they were not around? You too? Have you ever failed to receive honest and good-hearted feedback from a mentor who intended to help? You too? The truth is that we all have—many times. And because we're not perfect, we should show compassion and forgiveness in how we treat others and we should always be respectful to the absent in our discussions. If someone will gossip about the absent to you, what will they say about you when you're not around? Gossip breaks down the foundations of trust. Following the golden rule is the simplest way to solve this, treating others how we want to be treated.

Overall, I try to approach difficult people with an EGR mindset. EGR stands for Extra Grace Required. This doesn't mean I ignore their problematic behavior, but it does mean we will always treat people with compassion and respect, and truly hope in our heart that they will make the appropriate change to their life. Expectations can be powerful. It is when we show them hope, support, and encouragement that they have a better chance of making big changes.

CHAPTER SEVEN
4P Alignment

We have talked about the complex array of tools necessary to defibrillate the arrhythmia of your health plan. In this chapter we discuss the importance of aligning your 4P alignment.

This means we will make sure all:
- Partners
- Providers
- Patients

are playing out of the same:
- Playbook

Alignment will be absolutely critical to your success. Your partners and providers were chosen because they have been successful in the past. To be successful, they had to research best practices, implement them, and dial them in so that they meshed well with everything else they were doing, so that they ultimately produced good outcomes for patients. However – now, you are asking them to be a part of your strategy, to play by a new playbook. It is ok, and encouraged to ask everyone's input about how things might be done, but at the end of the day, it is your responsibility. Often, alignment is taken for granted and assumptions of the way things should be done or will be done lead to misunderstandings. What seemed obvious to you or someone else was not obvious at all. They come out of nowhere when you least expect it. The reality is that there are many ways to succeed, which means if someone does something a different way, it doesn't mean that way is wrong or ineffective, it just means it is wrong as a part of your playbook.

Patients also need to work in alignment. They do not administer the plan or provide the care, but they need to be educated on how it works so that they can effectively utilize the plan. The first year, and especially the first few months are the most difficult. The more patients become educated on how the plan works, the easier it gets for everyone. Patient alignment is not about fire hose, one and done education in the enrollment meetings. It is more like a continuous faucet drip education, and when real-life situations come up, holding their hand. The next time they need care, they will be better equipped and it will become the new norm for how they view healthcare.

To achieve alignment with partners and providers, I do not have a special method, template email, fancy spreadsheet, or a specific meeting format to give you. Achieving alignment takes time and effort and a lot of two-way dialogue. It is achieved by involving partners and providers in important meetings to determine how things will be done, and then articulating the final playbook with everyone so that misunderstandings are prevented, and everyone works well together (as if they are one machine). Everyone must willingly and enthusiastically give the same answer to the common questions.

With Orchestral Brilliance

For each partner you have chosen as your starting lineup, I would suggest keeping a systems theory mindset. Systems theory purports that the sum, or the whole, is more important than the individual parts. Typically, improvement initiatives start out as single-point solutions, followed by more single-point solutions, and once the pieces start to tell a story and become too hard to manage independently, the puzzle pieces are formed into an articulated strategy. This was my path at Merrill Steel. Likewise, Henry Ford discovered that a team of assembly workers could produce far more automobiles and a much higher level of quality on an assembly line as compared with workers who performed the work individually. Henry Ford was a systems thinker.

By viewing your health plan through a systems theory lens, you realize that you could have the greatest healthcare partners on the planet, but if they don't mesh well and adopt a common game plan, the end result will be a disjointed mess. With this knowledge, we take the same view as did coach Herb Brooks in writing the *Miracle on Ice* story. He assembled a hockey team of college players and led them to beat the unbeatable Soviet Union team in the 1980 Olympic Games. It is an inspiring story, and it was made into an excellent movie. If you haven't seen it, I highly recommend watching it before you begin choosing and assembling your team. In the beginning, Herb was selected as the coach, and he saw that past Olympic performances were poor. Against the protocol of previous accepted selection methods, he assembled his team, made up of the right combination of strong players, but not necessarily the best players. By assembling the "best team," and by focusing on the outputs the team produces (instead of the outputs of individual partners who may or may not be acting in the best interests of the team), he was able to build a team that could beat anyone.

An orchestra is a great analogy for the synergy you should try to build. An orchestra is judged by its collective sound, not by the strength or talent of individual players. If the orchestra is striving to be great, no one should say, "The cellist was amazing, but the violinist was out of sync." Strong contributors are important, but your ability to successfully restructure your health plan will not be determined by your ability to recruit and contract with the "best of the best." It is crucial, rather, to find partners who see the world in the same ways, are flexible, and who realize that the team can only win together or lose together. You cannot afford to have a great DPC partner who doesn't play nice with the other kids, or a broker who is only interested in his or her vision. In my experience, team alignment is just as important as finding talented partners. I explain the strategy to prospective partners to get their reaction. Before I select them, I want them to know where I am going and to gauge if they are willing to go with me and live out the collective strategy. I want their input, but they cannot feel so strongly about their methods that they would conflict with mine. We may both be right, but if each partner cannot work with other partners to form a well-oiled machine, the partnership is not worth forming.

We Must Build It So They Can Go

Once your plan is operational, a key ongoing task is to build out your specialty provider network. In almost all cases, you will not need to do this from scratch. Rather, a variety of options have already been built and your role will be to find them and tap into them so they can be accessible to your members. I have mentioned a couple of the independent networks that have been built in Wisconsin and how they serve to offer competitive contracts with hospitals and independent providers alike. These independent networks exist in other states and throughout the nation. Independent networks can be structured as for-profit businesses or as nonprofit employer coops or coalitions. They are probably the easiest and best way to enable your plan to shop.

Other ways include finding an entity that has direct contracts with independent providers. In some cases, these other entities are smaller and may not have contracts with hospitals. You will need a contract or the ability to utilize at least one hospital in each of the regions you have members. Another option is to do the direct contracting yourself. This is often a last option, because most companies don't have the resources, time, or knowledge to carry this out, but some have done it successfully. If you ever feel overwhelmed by this task, remember, you don't need a hundred secondary providers. You can start with one, and build from there. For everything you interrupt, you gain. If medical tourism is an option, there are also the cash providers I mentioned. Their contracts are typically very simple—only a couple of pages long, and they will work directly with self-funded employers. My first interruptions while at Merrill Steel were with the Surgery Center of Oklahoma and the Free Market Medical Association (FMMA) network, and slowly I began to find and add other local options. With all the services the FMMA provides, they remain an option, particularly for procedures with exorbitant hospital price tags.

If you find yourself backed into a corner and are unable to obtain a hospital contract, while still retaining the freedom to shop, there are creative ways that fall out of the network realm that could be a possibility. For instance, a Sedera-like cash reimbursement model could be an option. As I discussed in previous chapters, there are new laws in place that support good-faith estimates, regardless of whether one is insured. The hospital is still legally required to give an estimate and the buyer is protected once they do.

Obedience to Authority: The Stanley Milgram Experiments

In 1963, Stanley Milgram, a psychologist at Yale University, conducted some interesting experiments on the conflict between obedience to authority and personal conscience. His interest in this topic was rooted in the Nuremburg trials after World War II: how could a person commit acts of genocide, just because they were given the orders to do so from their superiors. The experiments began in 1961, just one year after the famous Holocaust trial of Adolph Eichmann, in which his defense was that he was "just following orders." His stated defense did not hold up in a court of law and he was found responsible for his crimes.

Milgram was interested in the psychology related to how decisions are made when people are instructed to do something from someone of perceived authority. Interestingly, in the experiment, the person who represented the figure of authority wore a white coat. A solicitation for volunteer male participants was placed in a newspaper, and the experiment was constructed with a learner and a teacher. Everyone involved in the experiment was an actor, except for the volunteer subject. The teacher (the subject) was told to give the learner (the actor behind a curtain) a series of memory tests and the learner would miss them, at specific times, consistently as per the script. When the learner made a mistake, the teacher was instructed by the person in the white coat to give a shock. This was done by flipping a switch on a control panel. With each successive shock, the magnitude increased. The fictitious shocks started at 15 volts and progressed to 450 volts. The teacher could not see the learner, but he could hear him behind the curtain. The learner was given a script to emphatically act out for each level of shock. The learner's reaction started out as mildly insignificant, and progressed to what appeared to be real pain and suffering. At about the halfway point, the learner would vocalize unbearable pain and request to withdraw from the study. The authority figure would then lean in and tell the teacher to proceed, despite the person's reaction. The independent variable being measured was whether the person would follow his conscience and withdraw from the experiment or if he would follow the authority figure's instructions and continue to shock the person at increasing levels. The study ended when the participant withdrew from the study or when he flipped the final shock switch. Disturbingly, despite the learners screaming and requests to withdraw from the study, 65% of participants flipped the final switch, which was marked 450 volts! All participants were fully debriefed with details after the study and informed that no one actually suffered.

This study exemplified the power of the white coat—even over the subject's conscience. In the realm of our healthcare strategy, it is a good knowledge nugget because it helps us understand the psychology of patients in making decisions. This is why patients make decisions that they question or proceed with treatment when they know they cannot afford it. It also gives us insight as to how we can help patients traverse the healthcare landscape and make decisions that support them best, medically and financially. Simply put, we want our higher-quality DPC structure white coat guiding them and not a white coat that is rushed, motivated by RVUs, or required to refer internally to expensive specialists that may cause financial harm to the patient and the plan.

Do Americans Care About Their Own Health?

One interesting challenge you will face as you implement a consumerism model—one in which the employer takes control of the health plan and the patient takes control of his or her health—is how to inspire your members to care about their own health. By "caring about their own health," I mean adopting healthy eating habits and making other smart lifestyle choices, such as exercising regularly. It is also important we teach and inspire members to be wise financial consumers, and to choose providers that are transparent and affordable. Years ago, I was asked to take over the leadership of a wellness program for my employer. I smiled, and thought to myself, "This will be easy. All I have to do is to get people to care about their own health." And then I thought, "How in the world will I get people to care about their own health?"

There's not much dispute over the notion that the average American eats a lot more and is much less active than his or her parents or grandparents. Since the 1950s, portion sizes have increased 2x to 4x and today, it is not uncommon for us to consume the same amount of calories in one meal as would have been consumed in an entire day, two generations prior. This is clearly reflected in obesity studies. One study showed that the average male in the 1960s was 5'8" tall and weighed 166 lbs. Today, the average man is 5'9" tall and weighs 196 lbs. Women, on average, are heavier as well. The average woman in the 1960s was 5'3" tall and weighed 140 lbs. Today, the average woman is 5'4" tall and weighs 170 lbs. Considering the slight increase in average height, this means the average American is over 25 pounds heavier than those who lived just two generations ago.

Health or Wealth: Which Is More Valuable?

A colleague shared a concept with me once that really opened my eyes. He drew a chart on the whiteboard. Along the horizontal axis of the chart was the variable of time, starting at birth and ranging to age 100. The vertical axis was the variable of low to high, with 1 being low and 10 being high. The chart had two lines – one that represented health and another that represented wealth. The message was simple: as we retire and get older, we want both our financial savings and our health to be high. Typically, we envision our line for financial savings to steadily increase, with a greater sloped curve the latter half of our life. As we progress in our career, we tend to increase our income and typically pay off our home mortgage in our fifties or sixties.

The other line, which represents our overall health, starts off high and remains steady, but as we reach our fifties or sixties, it naturally declines. The eye-opening message is that the two lines will ultimately intersect. The chart makes it clear that our health should be of equal or higher concern as we live our life. Why? Because, even if we have a lot of savings going into retirement, if we are not in good health, we won't be able to enjoy it. Further, particularly with today's healthcare prices, if we have poor health, our financial savings will be gobbled up by healthcare expenses, leaving us with *no health and no wealth*.

This concept has had a profound effect on me and how I view my own health. If you know me, you know that I love deep-fried breaded cheese curds, with plenty of choices in Wisconsin. This is why I practice moderation: I only have fried cheese curds once per day (just kidding).

I have used this message to reach people to get them to care about their personal health and to participate in a wellness program. I can say from experience that it has helped reach some people to improve their lifestyle and overall health.

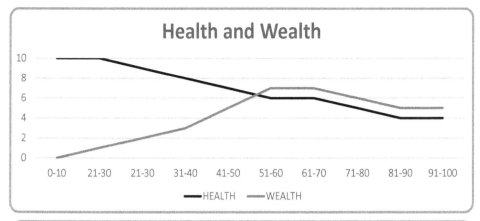

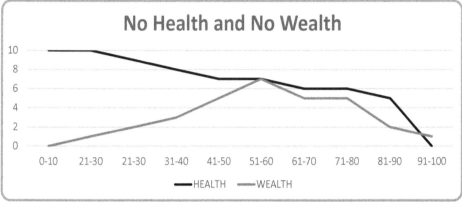

Once moving, much of your time will be spent in aligning your partners and members with your strategy. I like to view these as a three-legged stool. If one of the legs is shorter, the stool falls over. For the health plan to function optimally, all three must mesh together and be well aligned so that they work together for the common good.

Your role in this is to be the overseer, to "herd the cats," and to constantly watch and listen for how the plan is performing. Everyone must be on the same page in regard to the strategy and how it is executed.

As you are monitoring, if everything you hear reflects a well-oiled machine, smile and regularly thank all involved for executing well. If you hear of something that reflects a lack of alignment or a misunderstanding, step in and openly communicate the issue and the opportunity to improve. By viewing your model with a systems theory lens, you will quickly identify any circumstances that are out of alignment. If your car is out of alignment, it tells you, by wearing the tires unevenly or pulling you off the paved road. Continuous monitoring systems we have discussed for your health plan will tell you as well.

CHAPTER EIGHT

Win-Win Positive-Sum Outcomes

As rudimentary as it sounds, the approach to shop wisely for healthcare is considered "cutting edge" strategy for employers to fix their health plans, and collectively, our country's healthcare woes. This is not because the idea of a fully functioning free market is innovative or new. Instead, the industry has done such a fine job in designing and implementing the pseudo free market, most people no longer recognize the problem. They are unable to discern the difference between how healthcare works and the open shopping concept we take for granted in all other industries. It seems everyone spends their time "playing the game" rather than recognize that it is the wrong game altogether.

Cutting Edge

Fake hospital prices, fake insurance discounts, rushed primary care, whitecoat pinball referrals, mysterious quality, invisible prices, turning patients away with a smile if they are not "in network," a focus on symptoms instead of root causes, delay or denial of life-saving care to save money, and ultimately, a patient's inability to shop effectively have all somehow become the norm.

By recognizing these things, we can redesign and restructure employer health plans to step out of this mud onto dry ground. With clearer vision, we can break the chains and be free.

How to Get Where You Are Going

Some of the greatest achievements in world history were viewed by everyone as impossible – until someone did it. The notion that any person, regardless of creed, background, color, or gender can follow their dream is one of the things that makes America great. The Wright brothers proved the possibility of flight and Thomas Edison proved the possibility of light. One could write a whole book on this topic. America is the most innovative country on the planet. We are now faced with a problem. The wheels are falling off our healthcare system. Which American(s) will fix the problems and do something the world thought was impossible?

Visualize What Success Looks Like

In the 2023 March Madness basketball tournament, Caitlyn Clark, star player and team captain of the women's Iowa Hawkeyes basketball team, had shared her vision with the coach while she was being recruited. She visualized going to the Final Four. This year, she did better than that. She led her team to the championship game. Clark was the first women's college player to ever have a triple double, scoring over 40 points – and she did it twice! By visualizing her dream, she was able to make it a reality.

She told her fellow players before the season started that they could achieve great things by doing two things: work hard and believe. That almost sounds too simple, doesn't it? Yet it is the common people who are willing to do the uncommon things that change the world. So many, it seems, are not willing to put in the extra hard work to do great things. In athletics and in my career, I've said, "I may not be the smartest person in the room, but no one will ever out-work me." I've lived with that philosophy and hard work has become a habit for me. Mixed with persistence, it is the greatest predictor of success. Implementing what is described in this book will be hard work, but it doesn't have to feel like that. It is fun to win – much more fun than losing, or coasting through life. Jack Welch, former CEO of GE said, "Choose a job you love, and you will never have to work a day in your life."

Be Unconventional When Necessary

Dick Fosbury was a high jumper. That is, he was an athlete in the track and field event in which one jumps over a horizontal bar and lands on a soft mat. When he was 14 years old, in Medford, Oregon, he was riding his bike with his younger brother and his brother was struck by a drunk driver and killed. The loss took its toll on his parents, and they later divorced. Dick turned to athletics to find solace. He wasn't able to make the football or basketball teams, so he tried out for the track and field team. He made the team and began to learn about the high jump event.

The acceptable method at the time was known as the straddle technique. With this approach, the jumper would straddle-jump the bar, as if he was jumping over a hurdle. Dick could not clear even five feet. During a meet his sophomore year, Fosbury tried a straddle jump and knocked off the bar on his first jump. He then decided he would try something else. He had been practicing a different style—one in which he jumped so that his back was downward and he would arch his spine and legs as they travelled over the bar. This time, he cleared the bar, and over time, he perfected the technique. He was soon able to clear 5' 10". Rivals would sneer and snicker at him and said he looked like a "flopping fish." By the time he reached his senior year, he was clearing 6' 5.5". By college he was jumping over 7'. Later, he won an Olympic gold medal by clearing 7' 4.25". His style became known as the "Fosbury Flop" and it is now the accepted method for high jumpers across the globe. Dick Fosbury was willing to be unconventional. He recently passed away in March of 2023, but his legacy lives on.

Don't Listen to the Naysayers

Anyone who has been highly successful will tell you stories about their climb to the top and the droves of people who adamantly shared with them their opinion that they would never amount to anything special. It's an interesting phenomenon—one that I cannot explain. I've noticed these kinds of individuals; it's as if they're mad at you that you aspire to dream. Whenever I run into these types of people I always tell them, "If it was easy, everyone would do it."

As you might imagine, Billy Graham had this kind of fan club. He was passionate about preaching and sharing the good news of the gospel, and many folks were anxious to tell him how he would never amount to anything. A janitor at Bible school once told him, "I've seen the best come through here and I know what it takes for a preacher to make it. And let me tell you something – you ain't got it." Billy could have believed him and returned home to his family's dairy farm. But he didn't.

Perhaps the most famous story about others who didn't believe is the life of Roger Bannister. Bannister was an athlete from England who aspired to run a 4-minute mile. No one had ever run a 4-minute mile, and if you listened to the experts of the time, no one ever would. These experts included doctors, who said it was not humanly possible. They said a person's heart would explode if pushed that hard. For Bannister's own safety, they pleaded with him not to do it. Against common conception, and with many failed attempts, Bannister kept training and trying.

It was 1954 and Bannister was running for Oxford University. Bannister won the race and the announcement of his time came over the loudspeaker. The announcer teased the crowd with a delay, and then emphatically shared: 3 minutes 59.4 seconds. The crowd roared. The impossible was now possible. The psychological barrier had been broken, and his heart didn't explode. Within four years of the barrier being broken, twenty more people did it. Through Bannister's hard work and persistence, everyone could now believe it was possible.

Maybe someone has told you the same. If you go down the road described in this book, they surely will. But only one person has to believe, and as momentum is gained, more and more will.

It is my hope that the countless hours I spent writing this book will provide you with some valuable education and inspiration to write your own story and make healthcare a positive topic in your company again. Most won't believe, even fewer will try, and the only person that really needs to believe is you.

Dare to Dream

It is my hope that transformational leaders - fellow Americans, within hospital systems, insurance carriers, brokerage firms, and pharmacy benefit managers see the unsustainable path we are on and the great need for change.

I dream of a day in which hospital executives will say no to price games; a day in which hospitals will become preferred providers with clear and shared pricing, a day in which nonprofit hospitals will give more to the community than they take; a day in which providers are supported and enabled to practice medicine with a patient focus, instead of a profit focus.

I dream of a day in which insurance carriers and pharmacy benefit managers will say no to discount games; a day in which shopping is not merely allowed but encouraged, a day in which the money of hard-working Americans is not used against them in political lobbying, a day in which case management doesn't mean delaying or denying life-determining care, and a day in which medications are affordable and the prices are not manipulated for the wealth of a few.

I dream of a day in which employers take ownership of their health plan; a day in which they will realize healthcare is not just their biggest HR opportunity but their biggest business opportunity and also a great responsibility; a day in which the employer realizes that the only thing that can stop this movement is their own complacency.

I dream of a day in which the health and financial stability of communities is more important than executive bonuses; a day in which all seek positive-sum win-win outcomes and accept nothing less; a day in which American healthcare is the best in the world, both medically and financially.

I close with some visualization statements about the future of healthcare. Won't you join me in creating this reality?

The Future of American Healthcare

The future of healthcare is transparent.
The future of healthcare is affordable.
The future of healthcare is accessible.
The future of healthcare is sustainable.
The future of healthcare is understandable.
The future of healthcare is relationship-oriented.
The future of healthcare is to shop effectively.
The future of healthcare is to provide only treatment that is necessary.
The future of healthcare is to treat root causes, not just symptoms.
The future of healthcare is employers taking fiduciary ownership of their health plan.
The future of healthcare doesn't feed the beast, who is oppressive and self-serving.
The future of healthcare is a positive-sum win-win outcome for ALL.
The future of healthcare is much brighter.
The future of healthcare is in your hands.

May God bless you in your adventures.

Appendix A

Root Cause Problem-Solving Method: Quick Overview

This is a system of monitoring to identify problems quickly, and a process for solving problems and making them go away forever. The goal condition is called a *standard*. We have standards for everything. Some are written and some are not, but even when they are not in writing, generally we know if something is out of standard. Our car is supposed to start in the morning. If it doesn't, we know we have a problem. It is an out of standard condition. If a store is supposed to be staffed with 3 associates, and 2 call in, we know we have a problem. We have an out of standard condition that will cause bad outcomes for guests if we don't resolve it.

Within this monitoring system, when something is in standard, it is coded green for easy identification. No time needs to be spent on these conditions. When something is out of standard, it can be coded red to get our attention that problem solving is needed. Yellow coding can be utilized for something that is slightly out of standard. This green, yellow, red dashboard-type monitoring helps us to be efficient in identifying problems and it helps us spend our time efficiently by focusing on problems. When everything is up to standard, things operate like they should, and good outcomes follow.

Problem or Improvement? What is the difference?

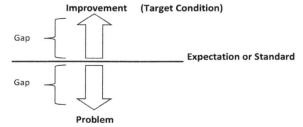

The continuous question we ask is if we have a problem, or more simply, if there is a gap between what is happening (the actual) and what should be happening (the standard). Interestingly, with both, the process thereafter is similar. Both involve closing the gap. By comparing the current situation with the standard, it tells us if there is a gap. If something is below the standard, we have a problem. If something is at or above the standard, we do not have a problem; however, there still may be a good opportunity to improve.

If the current situation is below the expected level, problem solving is necessary to understand and **eliminate** the root cause. By eliminate, we mean implementing a short- or long-term countermeasure to make it go away - FOREVER.....

It is important we view problems in the right way. Our natural inclination is to downplay problems or hope they will go away. *Problems never solve themselves.* Instead, we should be glad when we are able to identify them. The problem exists regardless of whether we know about it or choose to acknowledge it, so when we discover a problem, we can apply our problem-solving method to eliminate it, thus helping us improve.

Problem Solving Steps

1. Identify the Problem

- Conduct a Gap Analysis. A Gap Analysis is done to assess if there is a difference between what is actually happening and what should be happening. Our eyes should be trained to constantly look for gaps.

What is actually happening? _____
What should be happening? _____
Gap: Problem Statement _____

2. Assemble a Team to Solve the Problem (optional— case by case)

- Including others can bring in needed experience or it can be an opportunity for someone to develop and grow. The team should include individuals with the right experience, expertise, knowledge, and ability to effectively solve the problem.

3. Understand the Problem

- Now that you have an idea of what the problem is, "GO and SEE" it. It is important to dig deep if necessary. This may include talking with individuals, gathering data, observing, etc. Cutting this step short will result in oversights later. **If there is one step in which the most time should be spent – this is the step.** Too often this step is skipped over, resulting in the wrong problem being worked on. By understanding the problem fully, the solutions become increasingly obvious.

4. Find the Root Cause

- This step requires some patience. Several drafts may be necessary until you have listed all the causes. It is important to list each step, continuing to ask "why", even if it seems painfully detailed or slow. For cases in which there appears to be more than one root cause, a fishbone diagram can be utilized. Seek help from someone who is experienced with this.

- Sometimes this step is called "5 whys," although 5 is just an estimate. It can be 3 or 8. Keep asking why until you can't ask why anymore. Check your work by reading the problem statement, saying "why" and the next cause, then "why" and the next cause, moving downward. To check your work, start at the bottom and move upward. Read the root cause, saying "therefore," the next cause, "therefore," then the next cause, and so on. The story should make sense as you read it.

5. Develop and Implement Temporary Countermeasure(s)

- If the long-term solution can be implemented right away, this step is not necessary. The point of the short-term countermeasure is to provide a "Band-Aid"—a temporary solution, to make sure the standard can be met until the long-term countermeasure can be implemented.
- One simple test you can do to through experimentation is to "turn on" and "turn off" the countermeasure. If it causes the problem to go away and come back predictably, you know you have found the root cause and an effective countermeasure.

6. Develop and Implement Permanent Countermeasure(s)

- The key for the long-term countermeasure is to **eliminate** the problem, FOREVER…..
- The more effective we are at **eliminating** problems, the more time we have to solve other ones or to be proactive in continuous improvement (raising the standard).

7. Monitor and Confirm

- Measure and monitor the long-term countermeasure to see if the problem returns. If it does not return, it is confirmation that the root cause was found and the countermeasure has prevented recurrence. Celebrate!!
- If the problem does return, repeat the process again until it goes away permanently. This tells you the root cause was not found, there are multiple root causes, or the implemented countermeasure did not sufficiently eliminate the root cause.
- If necessary, develop a new standard or revise the current standard and train team members as needed.

Appendix B

[INSERT COMPANY LETTERHEAD]

DATE:

TO: [INSERT NAME OF BROKER FIRM]

RE: Full Compensation Request

To whom it may concern:

As you know, we are facing a long-term pattern of significant healthcare cost increases. With the longevity and viability of our benefit plan in mind, we would like to request a summary of all compensation your firm receives, as associated with our account, so that we can better understand and manage our fixed costs. This should include:

- A description of all direct compensation received;
- A description of all indirect compensation received;
- A description of the services provided to the covered plan;

We request this be in a format of line by line itemization of service, alongside compensation value. Each payer should be identified and each arrangement described. Please give me a call if you have any questions.

*This request is made per section 202 of the Consolidated Appropriations Act, 2021 (CAA). The CAA states, beginning Dec 27, 2021 brokers of group health plans will be required to disclose their compensation if they expect to receive $1,000 or more in direct or indirect compensation.

The disclosure requirement is all-encompassing and the descriptions must be clear and sufficient for us to evaluate reasonableness. This includes all forms of compensation including standard fees, ongoing compensation, bonuses, commissions, overrides, rebates, finder's fees, prepaid (advanced) commissions, payments made by third parties, incentive programs not solely related to the plan, etc.

The response must be submitted within 60 days, per liability under Section 502(i), which allows the DOL to assess penalties against service providers who do not comply.

Sincerely,

[INSERT NAME HERE]

CLIENT: _____

Compensation Disclosure

SERVICE PROVIDED	VENDOR	COST/FEE FOR SERVICE	COMP TYPE	TOTAL COMPENSATION
Core Consulting Services				
Pharmacy Consulting				
Actuarial Services				
Compliance Services				
Wellness Consulting				
Claims Audit				
Data Analytics				
Communications				
Benefits Administration				

Expected Financial Compensation From External Vendors

Categorey	EXTERNAL VENDOR	EFFECTIVE DATE	COMPENSATION TYPE	TOTAL COMPENSATION
Medical				
Pharmacy				
Dental				
Vision				
Stop Loss				
EAP				
FSA/HSA/HRA/DCA				
Group Life				
Voluntary Life				
LT Disability (Vol/Group)				
ST Disability (Vol/Group)				
Critical Illness				
Wellness				

Total Expected Compensation

Consulting Services	$	-
Compensation from Vendors	$	-
Total	$	-

Save Your Company, Don't Feed the Beast

Are any compensation multipliers or other bonuses applicable to the above categories of compensation?

☐ Yes ☐ No

If yes, are the included in the above dollar amounts?

☐ Yes ☐ No

Do you or your firm accept any non-account specific financial compensation from any products, services, or vendors you're recommending, including, but not limited to, contingent or bonus commissions, override or retention bonuses, and back-end commissions?

☐ Yes ☐ No

Do you or your firm have any other financial or nonfinancial compensation, potential conflicts of interest, or incentives replated to products, services, or vendors you're recommending, including, but not limited to, ownership, equity stakes, revenue/profit-sharing/GOP/coalition participation, preferred vendor panels, conferences or trips, or person relationships?

☐ Yes ☐ No

Please describe details related to any questions to which you answered yes above, including specific, expected, or estimated dollar value. Attached additional pages if necessary.

☐ Yes ☐ No

ADVISOR

I certify that to the best of my knowledge the above is a complete and meaningful disclosure of my firm entire compensation.

Name: _____

Entity: _____

Title: _____

Signed: _____

Date: _____

Client

Name: _____

Entity: _____

Title: _____

Signed: _____

Date: _____

If Healthcare Worked Like Construction

A summer thunderstorm rolls through and you notice that there is water dripping from your kitchen ceiling. You think to yourself; I can't really afford this. I have kids in college and tuition bills to pay, but you know it can't be ignored. You realize you need to call a contractor, and you learn from your homeowner's association that Community Care Roofing company is the only contractor approved for your neighborhood. You are concerned. How can I get a fair price if there is only one contractor? You figure, with a name of Community Care, they must be good, and you call for an estimate. You are comforted more to learn that the organization is a nonprofit entity, created to serve the public. You even take a minute to check out their website, and their stated values are integrity, transparency, community, and charity. You sleep well that night.

> You don't really understand construction, but trust that they know what they are doing.

The contractor shows up and you begin to tell him about the roof leak. He doesn't listen and only wants to confirm what insurance you have. You give him that information and he agrees to look at your roof. You may or may not need a whole new roof, but he made the trip, so he recommends one. He proceeds to measure and talk with you about shingle style, warranty, and color preference. He finishes, and before he leaves, you ask if he will be sending a quote. He smiles and responds that it is "too complicated", and he will be there in a couple weeks to begin. You think, that is frustrating and a little scary, but this is how everyone does this, so you go along with it. You see Community Care in colorful vinyl, all professional-like, on the big expensive truck and everything looks legitimate, so you brush it off and go inside.

A month and a half later, he finally shows up with his crew and they begin tearing off your roof. You don't really understand construction, but trust that they know what they are doing. You are at their mercy at this point, and you hope for the best. They perform the work and in about a week, the old roof is off, in the dumpster and the new roof is on, and looks good. You sign all the papers, and he gets in his shiny truck, smiles, and says he will send you the bill. Before leaving, he says you need some other things, and refers you to a gutter installation company and siding company. He says if you don't get those things done your house will really be at risk. For the roof bill, you're not sure what to expect, but you are guessing it will be $7,000 to $8,000, because you only have a smaller, one-story ranch home.

Over the next few weeks, you keep looking for a bill. Nothing comes, so you continue to wait. A couple months later, it arrives. It is from the delivery company for the shingles. A few days later, you get another bill from the same delivery company for felt and nails. You think, that is weird, why didn't they deliver it in one trip and why it is my cost if they didn't? No one asked me. And more concernedly, the bill for the shingles arrives and it is $12,000, and yet another one arrives for felt and nails and it is $4,500. A few days later you get a bill for the labor, and it is $22,000. You call the contractor, and he is annoyed that you are asking. He says not to worry - insurance will cover it. A few days later you get a bill for the dumpster, and it has a surcharge on it because the roads were slippery that day. And the next day, you get another bill for the removal of the roof. You call the contractor again and mention that you thought that was covered in the first labor bill, but he exclaims that is a different department. A day later you get another bill for roof sheathing repair and one sheet of plywood was used. The charge for the plywood is $1496. You call once more to ask questions. The contractor is increasingly annoyed and short tempered that you are questioning him. You explain that you can get this sheet of plywood for $42 at House Depot. He doesn't acknowledge your shopping acuity and tells you insurance will cover it. You wonder what you will do. You only have $3,500 in your savings. While you are stressing about the bills, a collection letter shows up, threatening to take you to court if you do not pay promptly. You remember a friend telling you that he had his wages garnished and a lien placed on his home for not being able to pay. Finally, the bills stop. You also learn that your insurance company is now questioning whether a second delivery for materials is covered. It was not preauthorized beforehand. After about 8 phone calls, insurance finally agrees to pay for the extra delivery. The total of the bills comes to $52,569.24 and your home deductible is $10,000. Thankfully, you have built up your 401k and decided to take a loan through your employer. You take the money out and pay your maximum out of pocket for the year. Your bank account is empty, and your retirement took a hit, but everyone got paid and you are thankful you didn't have to file bankruptcy. Hopefully, no other surprises come up.

Unfortunately, this is not an exaggerated story. This is how healthcare works every day in America.